Latina/o Studies

Short Introductions Series

Latina/o Studies

Ronald L. Mize

polity

First published in 2019 by Polity Press

Polity Press
65 Bridge Street
Cambridge CB2 1UR, UK

Polity Press
101 Station Landing
Suite 300
Medford, MA 02155, USA

ISBN-13: 978-1-5095-1256-0
ISBN-13: 978-1-5095-1257-7 (pb)

A catalogue record for this book is available from the British Library.

Library of Congress Cataloging-in-Publication Data

Names: Mize, Ronald L., 1970- author.
Title: Latina/o studies / Ronald L. Mize.
Other titles: Latina studies | Latino studies
Description: Cambridge, UK ; Medford, MA : Polity, 2018. | Series: Short introductions | Includes bibliographical references and index.
Identifiers: LCCN 2018010590 (print) | LCCN 2018028730 (ebook) | ISBN 9781509512607 (Epub) | ISBN 9781509512560 (hardback) | ISBN 9781509512577 (paperback)
Subjects: LCSH: Hispanic Americans. | BISAC: SOCIAL SCIENCE / Ethnic Studies / Hispanic American Studies.
Classification: LCC E184.S75 (ebook) | LCC E184.S75 M597 2018 (print) | DDC 973/.0468–dc23
LC record available at https://lccn.loc.gov/2018010590

Typeset in 10 on 12 pt Sabon
by Toppan Best-set Premedia Limited
Printed and bound in Great Britain by CPI Group (UK) Ltd, Croydon

For further information on Polity, visit our website: politybooks.com

Contents

Tables and Figures

Tables

Figures

Preface

The election of Donald J. Trump in 2016 did not bode well for those under consideration in this short introduction. Latinos in the United States number 54,232,205 according to the 2015 US Census estimate. They constitute the third-largest Latin American "nation" (behind Brazil and Mexico). Yet Trump secured his election by imploring White voters to expel, in his words, "the bad *hombres*," and more specifically "Mexican rapists and criminals."

Chapter 1 starts at step one: who are Latinos? This deceptively simple question is at the heart of this short introduction to *Latina/o Studies*. Beyond simple terminology and definitions, the US government construction of the Hispanic category placed disparate groups together to meet governmental needs. In response, a sense of shared, common Latino identity, or Latinidad, is in fact quite complex and contested as seen in the variations in terms: Latino, Latina, Latina/o, Latin@, Latinx. Labels and identities are consequential because names matter and they shape individual and group experiences. The chapter concludes by dispelling the commonly held myths of who Latina/os are.

Chapter 2 identifies the major historical events and trends that comprise a shared history of Spanish colonialism and US imperialism. I discuss an intellectual legacy, influencing both Latino/a history and literary studies, left by the historical events of Spanish Conquest and the settlement of the Américas, the US–Mexico War, the Spanish–American War, US military invasions of Cuba, and puppet governments installed to serve US interests (e.g., the Trujillo dictatorship in the Dominican Republic and the CIA-sponsored overthrow of Árbenz in Guatemala). The response was an emergent counter-imperialist impulse by Latin American *revolucionarios* and *independentistas* (e.g., Martí, Bolívar, Albizu Campos, Juárez, Villa, Zapata, the Flores Magón brothers). Within the United States, Latina/o leaders emerged during the Chicano and Boricua civil rights and power movements of the 1960s and 1970s, followed by the sanctuary movements of the 1980s, and most recently embedded in the immigrant rights movement of the 2000s. The purpose of this chapter is not to be exhaustive but to be illustrative, looking at the various intellectuals, periods, and patterns so that the selection reflects contemporary scholarship on the historical origins of US Latina/o communities in terms of US government relations, impetuses for migration, and residential settlement patterns.

In chapter 3, I discuss the origins of Latina/o Studies through Puerto Rican and Chicano studies. I first discuss the aligned civil rights and power movements, as undergirding forces opening higher education to Puerto Rican Studies, particularly in the Northeast. This is the period during which most Puerto Rican Studies and Chicano Studies programs began, paralleling or reflecting similar developments in other area studies, e.g., Black Studies, Women's Studies, Native American Studies, Asian American Studies, and Peace Studies.

In the Southwest, the origins of Latina/o Studies can be clearly traced within the rise of Chicano Studies programs. I discuss how Chicano Studies arose both in response to Oscar Lewis' "culture of poverty" characterization of Mexicanos and as part and parcel of the civil rights and power movements. A pre-Chicano Studies, pre-"culture of poverty" era can certainly be identified through the work of Paul Schuster Taylor, Carey McWilliams, and Manuel Gamio. I discuss the originators (Julian Samora, Americo Paredes, and others) as well as the cultural nationalist, machismo, and heteronormative impulses in early Chicano Studies scholarship. The early interventions of Gloria Anzaldúa will be highlighted to identify how Chicana Studies arose to challenge restrictive early masculinist iterations.

On the East Coast, Puerto Rican studies similarly arose to challenge the "culture of poverty" characterization embodied in Lewis' *La Vida: A Puerto Rican Family in the Culture of Poverty – San Juan and New York*. The pioneers of Puerto Rican studies also drew insights and energies from the civil rights and power movements in addition to political work on the island calling for independence from US colonialism, and even earlier in the prescient example of Elena Padilla (1958, 2011). I discuss developments in the rise of Chicano/a Studies and Puerto Rican Studies as autonomous fields as well as early attempts to connect struggles and scholarly analyses, as evidenced by the short-lived *Revista Chicano-Riqueña*.

One narrative strain I explore in chapter 4 is how within Puerto Rican Studies units and scholarship we see the arrival of Dominican Studies, as well as how within Chicano Studies we see the arrival of Central American Studies. Jorge Duany (2008 [1994]) in Puerto Rican Studies and Rodolfo Acuña (1998) in Chicano Studies are among the first to introduce the experiences of Dominicans, Guatemalans, and Salvadorans into their respective fields' discussions. Another strain I discuss is how the full-fledged arrival of Latina/o Studies developed from experiences not traditionally addressed in Chicano and Puerto Rican Studies. The early work of Felix Padilla (1985), studying Chicano and Puerto Rican synergies in Chicago, began discussions of a truly Latino political consciousness. Current analyses of Latinidad, as mentioned earlier, provide a strong basis for Latina/o Studies as a full-fledged field both distinct from and an integral part of Puerto Rican and Chicana/o Studies.

Chapter 5 discusses women of color feminism that expounds upon intersectional analyses and lived experiences to show the interconnections of lives in struggle. The chapter begins with the key formative collections in women of color feminism by highlighting the full range of their literary forms (poetry, playwriting, short stories, novels, and social criticism). The themes of multi-identities, standpoint, situated and subjugated knowledges, and gender relations are highlighted in literary and theoretical contributions. Then I discuss how gender studies worked its way into the focus of Latina social scientists and humanists. The chapter finishes with the interrogations of sexuality in the work of queer studies. The focus is on prominent themes in gender, queer, and intersectional analyses.

Chapter 6 identifies a major development in the transdisciplinary field of Latina/o Studies: a resurgent focus on popular culture and Latina/o representations in all forms of media (news, popular culture, music, art, theater, new social media, Spanish-language media) through a variety of fields, including visual studies and performance studies. The first part of the chapter addresses hegemonic representations of Latina/os in popular culture, particularly mainstream mass media that rely on stereotypes, hypersexualized objectifications, hyperviolent male criminalizations, and all too often invisibilizing forms of background or non-representation. The homogenization of Latina/o representations is juxtaposed with the heterogeneous responses on the part of Latina/o creators and artists. The second part of the chapter discusses Latina/o-originated forms of new media, *musica*, *teatro*, *arte*, and corporate Spanish-language media studies.

Chapter 7 takes on the emerging methodological approaches that are reshaping how Latina/o Studies operates in more comparative, intersectional, and engaged forms. No longer is it assumed that a particular

Latino community operates in a bubble; each is in fact in connection with other communities (both in solidarity and in conflict) that shape the community as much as the community itself. I identify examples of Latina/o alliances and struggles with other racialized communities. I also discuss the participatory action research model that arose concomitant with the rise of ethnic studies (particularly Chicano and Puerto Rican Studies) and how the contemporary discussion of engaged scholarship is embedded within this long and oft-ignored history. Finally, I discuss the rise in border studies and how both socially constructed physical and mental borders are shaping Latina/o identities. The aim of this chapter is to highlight new methodologies and analytical approaches, such as the importance of *testimonios* to Latina *feministas* and the rise of LatCrit in legal and education studies.

Chapter 8 discusses the emerging theoretical developments designed to understand contemporary Latina/o lived experiences. I discuss two theoretical trends: colonization (from coloniality of power, settler colonialism, and decolonization, to postcolonialism) and Latina/o racializations. These illustrate issues not addressed in Latina/o Studies heretofore, as well as the cutting-edge theories that impel the field into long-term divides among Latin American and Latina/o Studies, intra-Latino divisions, citizens and immigrants. I also discuss the shared colonial histories that shape contemporary lived experiences, bridges among Latina/o communities, and current manifestations of Latinidades, as well as intra-Latino racializations, interracial relations, and emerging Latinidades defying the imposition of post-9-11 terrorist–immigrant linkages.

In the conclusion, the future of Latina/o Studies is considered in relation to the external and internal threats to its health and longevity. Potential future areas of inquiry are also detailed.

Acknowledgments

The author dedicates this book to the thousands of former students at the ten colleges and universities where I have taught. In particular, Latinx students often come to sociology and ethnic studies with a thirst for knowledge as well as for a validation of their place in the panoply of Latin-o/a/@/x identities. There's nothing more disappointing for a professor than when students don't see themselves reflected in their course material. This short introduction on Latina/o Studies was written specifically to ameliorate those letdowns. It's a wholly impossible task to fully and accurately represent the range of Latina/o experiences, viewpoints, and perspectives, and if at any point you the reader see yourself reflected in this critical survey of the field, please note that was my intent.

I am deeply grateful to the editorial team at Polity, who committed to this project prior to my coming to the book as its author. In particular, Jonathan Skerrett has always demonstrated not only a strong commitment to cutting-edge fields such as Latina/o Studies, but also an abiding professionalism that always makes me most willing to write with Polity. A very early version of this book (as a prospectus) was conceived with the esteemed scholar Clara Rodríguez, and I am deeply grateful for those early conversations. Versions of chapter 2 were presented at the Sixth Biennial Siglo XXI Inter-University Program for Latino Research Conference: Mapping of Latino Research, University of Texas San Antonio, San Antonio, Texas, on May 19, 2017, and at the Forum for China-LAC Relations: Globalization, Anti-Globalization and Alternative Globalizations, Anhui University, Hefei, China, on September 24, 2017. I'm grateful to my colleagues in Women, Gender, and Sexuality Studies and in Ethnic Studies, who daily make me a better and more informed scholar. In particular, Qwo-Li Driskill and H. Rakes provided most helpful commentary and suggestions on chapter 5. As always, any remaining errors or oversights remain the responsibility of the author.

The field of Latina/o Studies, much like the presence of Latina/o folks in the United States, all too often is slighted, overlooked, or downright attacked. Given the longstanding use of Latino immigrants as the foil in political debates, the rise of Donald Trump and his ilk sadly came as no surprise to Latina/o Studies scholars. We already knew about Jeff Sessions, Kris Kobach, James Sensenbrenner, Lou Barletta, Rick Santorum, John Tanton, Peter Brimelow, Richard Lamm, Russell Pearce, Mark Krikorian, Nathan Deal, Steve King, and Joe Arpaio. To think of this (mostly far right) fringe, xenophobic movement as occupying the White House, the Justice Department, the Department of Homeland Security, and both chambers of Congress seemed not only unfathomable but a true travesty of the progress fought for since the civil rights era. Whether it be "We shall overcome" or "Si, se puede," the rallying cry of prior generations is the gift an older generation gives to the new: that out of adversity we triumph together, and, in the words of Emiliano Zapata, "Si no hay justicia para el pueblo, que no haya paz para el gobierno/If there is no justice for the people, there will be no peace for the government."

Abbreviations

AWOC	Agricultural Workers Organizing Committee
CCCHE	Chicano Coordinating Council on Higher Education
CIW	Coalition of Immokalee Workers
CLS	Critical Legal Studies
CRT	critical race theory
CUNY DSI	Dominican Studies Institute of the City University of New York
DACA	Deferred Action for Childhood Arrivals
EEOC	Equal Employment Opportunity Commission
HB	House Bill
ICCAS	Institute for Cuban and Cuban American Studies
IIRIRA	Illegal Immigrant Reform and Immigrant Responsibility Act
IUPLR	Inter-University Program for Latino Research
LatCrit	Latina/Latino Critical Legal Theory
LFG	Latina Feminist Group
NFWA	National Farm Workers Association
MALCS	Mujeres Activas en Letras y Cambio Social
MeCHA	Movimiento Estudiantil Chicano de Aztlán
NACCS	National Association for Chicana and Chicano Studies
OMB	Office of Management and Budget
PAR	participatory action research
PRSA	Puerto Rican Studies Association for Research Advocacy and Education
QTPOC	queer, trans, people of color
SB	State Bill
UFW	United Farm Workers

1

What's in a Name?
Hispanic, Latino:
Labels, Identities

"What's in a name?" The eternal question, asked by Juliet Capulet, was first penned by William Shakespeare and makes a link among naming, nature, and human sensation, by describing a rose that "by any other name would smell as sweet." Quite ironically, Juliet's and Romeo Montague's deaths are testaments to the importance of naming, as the significance of their feuding last names sets into motion a whole series of mishaps and misunderstandings leading to their untimely deaths.

For scholars in Latina/o Studies,[1] "what's in a name" is a longstanding question in the field (see Gutiérrez 2016, Mora 2014, Oboler 1995, Rodríguez 2000, Rumbaut 2009). In their[2] classic on "ethnic labels," Suzanne Oboler (1995: 166) notes "the names adopted by different groups or imposed on them by others emerge as a result of particular historical and political contexts." Ramón Gutiérrez (2016) asks the question explicitly to begin *The New Latino Studies Reader*.

To whom are we referring when we speak of Latinos? Currently, the US government defines Hispanics or Latinos as an ethnic group, "who trace their origins to Spain … Hispanic origin can be viewed as the heritage, nationality, lineage, or country of birth of the person or the person's parents or ancestors before arriving in the United States. People who identify as Hispanic, Latino, or Spanish may be any race."[3]

The US government created the term "Hispanic" to group together Puerto Ricans, Mexicans, and to a certain extent Cubans in their enumeration. For Puerto Ricans and Mexicans, the accounting related to civil rights legislation that provided protections for those subject to racial discrimination in housing, education, voting rights, and public accommodations. Fleeing Castro's communist regime, Cubans were enumerated for the purposes of extending refugee status and state subsidies to help exiles regain their economic footing in South Florida. Those included in the Hispanic category grew over time to also encompass Central Americans, South Americans, and Caribbeans whose national origin could be traced to Spanish colonization.

The purpose of chapter 1 is to provide clarity to the labeling and identity processes that inform Latino/a Studies. Partially an explication of keywords, partially a map of the field, this chapter explores the labels deployed (Hispanic, Latino, Puerto Rican, Mexican American, Chicano, etc.) alongside the identities they represent. I will discuss not only definitions imposed by the US Census but also emerging identities explored by Latina/o Studies scholars, including Latinidades, transnational, Indigenous, Afro-Latino, Asian Latino, Latino/a, Latin@, and Latinx identities.

Constructing Hispanics

In Latina/o Studies, the construction of the Hispanic category has been traced both in the context of how the US Census measures race in historically variant ways to serve larger political ends and also in terms of how the 1980s was deemed the "Hispanic decade," by viewing Census constructions in relation to Spanish-language media and Hispanic advocacy organizations. Clara Rodríguez (2000) traces the history of how race was historically defined by the US government within the Black/White binary to explain why the recent construction of the Hispanic category is defined by the Census as an ethnic, not racial, distinction. More recent analyses look beyond the Census to identify how "the Hispanic category became institutionalized as bureaucrats, activists, and media executives forged networks and worked together to build panethnic organizations that popularized the notion of a Hispanic identity" (Mora 2014: xiii).

The creation of the Hispanic label is a US government invention for the purposes of enumerating a specific subgroup of the US population. Officially designated in the Office of Management and Budget's (OMB) Directive 15, the 1977 directive has a longer history – in particular, the US Census' role in naming Hispanics. In the pursuit of equal rights, the collection of racial statistics after 1960 was designed to determine status eligibility for civil rights protections and affirmative action participation. "Drawing on the categories employed in a 1950 government form, the Equal Employment Opportunity Commission (EEOC) in 1964 identified four minority groups: Negro, Spanish-American, American-Indian, and Asian" (Prewitt 2005: 8). Yet in the same decade, the US Census categorized all Latinos as White. "In the 1960 census, enumerators were instructed to record: Puerto Ricans, Mexicans, or other persons of Latin American descent as 'White' unless they were definitely of Negro, Indian, or other non-white race" (Bennett 2000: 172).

The discrepancy between being categorized as simultaneously a minority and part of the majority was not fixed in the decade between 1960 and 1970, even though there was a shift from imputation to self-identification. This was not done for noble reasons of racial accuracy and self-clarification; in reality there were many more mail-surveys distributed in the 1970 Census (approximately 70 percent of households received mail-in questionnaires), and thus, direct enumeration was next to impossible. The history, from 1790 to 1960, of enumerators determining the race of respondents was officially over.

In 1970, the questionnaires remained essentially the same as in 1960 but respondents were asked to choose their race. Only one circle could be filled in. For Latinos, the only applicable bubble was "other" unless they self-identified as Black, White, American Indian, of certain Asian national origins, or Hawaiian. It was not until the passage of Public Law 94-311 in 1976 that US Congress specified rules "relating to the publication of economic and social statistics for Americans of Spanish origin or descent."

Signed by President Gerald Ford in June 1976, it remains the only law in the country's history that mandates the collection, analysis, and publication of data for a specific ethnic group, and goes on to define the population to be enumerated. The law, building on information gathered from the 1970 census, asserted that "more than twelve million Americans identify themselves as being of Spanish-speaking background and trace their origin or descent from Mexico, Puerto Rico, Cuba, Central and South America, and other Spanish-speaking countries"; that a "large number" of them "suffer from racial, social, economic, and political discrimination and are denied the basic opportunities that they deserve as American citizens"; and that an "accurate determination of the urgent and special needs of Americans of Spanish origin and descent" was needed to improve their economic and social status. (Rumbaut 2009: 23)

The resulting operationalization of this law was issued in May 1977 in OMB Statistical Policy Directive Number 15 related to "Race and Ethnic Standards for Federal Statistics and Administrative Reporting." The directive defined a Hispanic as: "A person of Mexican, Puerto Rican, Cuban, Central or South American or other Spanish culture or origin, regardless of race." Hispanic was thus defined as an ethnic group that derives its ancestry from Spanish-speaking nations. Though Rumbaut is technically correct in stating that Public Law 94-311 was the first to mandate the collection of data for an *ethnic* group, requirements for measuring racial groups are as old as the Census itself.

The term "Hispanic" was coined by the US government, but has no organic resonance with the manner in which Latino communities actually identify themselves. For both Latino immigrants and US-born Latinos, the Census categories simply do not coincide with identities based on conceptualizations of race in Latin America or identities constructed via national origins. The imposed term brought together disparate groups that often lived in completely different regions and embodied distinct migration and reception histories. It also imputed specific racialized notions that Latinos defy to this day.

> For the past three decades, Hispanics have been able to check Hispanic ethnicity along with "some other race" on the census. (An unprecedented 42.2 percent of Hispanics checked "some other race" on the 2000 census. Moreover, 97 percent of those checking "some other race" were Hispanics.) Put differently, the "some other race" option has served as a political safety valve for the Census Bureau by masking the stark opposition that the official U.S. taxonomy mandates between ethnicity and race, and the rather inadequate race options available to Hispanics. (Hattam 2005: 66)

The Census defines race not as a scientific or anthropological categorization, but as one that categorizes people by tracing "origins" to Europe/North Africa/Middle East (White), Africa (Black), Asia, the Americas, or the Pacific Islands. In 2000, the US Census dropped the requirement that people self-identify as solely one race, harkening back to longstanding essentialisms about race and the "one-drop" rule that claimed one drop of Black blood confirmed a person's racial status as Black. The multiracial option (checking off more than one race) ended the one-race rule. In the 2010 Census, only about 2.9 percent of the US population self-identified as more than one race. For Latino immigrants, who more often explicitly trace their origins in mixed race terms (specifically through *mestizaje* or mixtures of Spanish, African, and Indigenous heritage), the Census-imposed US racial categories simply do not make sense as viable options, when "Hispanic" was imputed as an ethnic category, separate from one's race.

A primary complication in ascertaining the Latino population is the United States' inconsistency in the application of its labels. Depending on the agency and the "long" or "short" protocols of OMB Directive 15, one finds Latinos are sometimes defined as a race. At other times, only Puerto Rican and Mexican American citizens comprise the Latino minority category for purposes of program eligibility. Directive 15, under the auspices of the OMB, gives the option to respondents of collapsing race and ethnicity questions to make Latinos one of the five options and not a separate ethnicity question. By contrast, other divisions such as the EEOC, the Office of Civil Rights, and other programs that implement the Civil Rights Acts of 1964, 1965, and 1968, define Latinos as racialized groups to be protected from discrimination. In defining who Latinos are, the US Census' variable patterns of inclusion and exclusion point to a distinct lack of historical congruence between contemporary and past categorizations. Current inconsistencies obscure accurate representations of the largest minority group in the nation.

For instance, the US Census does not define Brazilians (the fourth-largest immigrant group from South America, behind Columbians, Ecuadorians, and Peruvians) as Hispanic due to their former status as a Portuguese colony. Their situation fully epitomizes the arbitrary imposed label of "Hispanic." Similarly, French-speaking Haiti is a nation that shares the island of Hispaniola (as Columbus dubbed it in the name of the Spanish Crown in 1492) with the Dominican Republic. Haitians are not categorized as Latinos; Dominicans are. The Bureau's criteria for inclusion versus exclusion as "Hispanic" (geographic origin, language, prior Spanish colonial status, ethnicity but not race) make it difficult to understand how Argentineans are considered Latino but Filipinos are not; why Costa Ricans are Latino but Belizeans are not; why Spaniards are Latino but Cape Verdeans are not; why Cubans and Puerto Ricans are Latino but peoples of the Caribbean islands of the West Indies are not; why Dominicans from the Dominican Republic are Latino but Dominicans from Dominica are not. This imposed ethnic category and its numerous limitations cut to the heart of identity formation: are identities imposed from outside agents or constructed by individuals themselves? Are they essentialist and unchanging, or additive and developmental; unitary or multiple; mutually exclusive or intersecting and overlapping? For Latinos, these questions become the basis for shared conversations about how the category of Latino is embodied in daily lived experiences. For Latino immigrants, understanding what it means to be Latino is informed both by their nation of origin and by the communities they migrate to in the United States.

Embodying Latinidad: Latino, Latina, Latina/o, Latin@, and Latinx

If we, more often than not, are not talking about "Hispanics," then how do folks with Latin American origins refer to themselves? In Spanish, the term *latinoamericanos* is often used to refer to folks who trace their origins to Latin America, and specifically for those residing in the United States, the nomenclature is often shortened to Latino. Since the early 1990s, changes in self-identification have all sought to challenge the masculinist aspects of the Spanish language: hence one sees a shift over that time from Latino to Latina to Latino/a to Latina/o to Latin@ to Latinx.

Latina/os in the United States, recognizing the problematic gendered nature of Spanish-language rules and practices, have sought since 1977 to shed both the US-government-imposed definition of "Hispanic" and the flawed assumption that masculine forms of names are stand-ins or universal designators. Quite simply, Latino either subsumes or negates the experiences of Latinas. As a result, the slash designator "Latina/o" was first used to respect the unique experiences and identities of Latinas. It reordered the importance of women distantly from that expressed in the short-lived masculine-first "Latino/a." Beginning in the early 2000s, Latina/o scholars attempted to shorten the designation by using Latin@ (Cantú and Fránquiz 2010, Grosfoguel, Maldonado-Torres, and Salvidar 2006, Valdés 1996).[4] How to pronounce @ was clearly an issue (as Chican@/Latin@ studies scholar Karma Chavez noted in a National Public Radio article; quoted in Demby 2013).

Most recently, a similar criticism from queer and trans folks notes that feminine/masculine forms negate gender non-conformance, trans, and queer identities and have called for the use of Latinx to provide a more inclusive category not reliant upon gender binaries (see de Onís 2017). The earliest scholarly mention of Latinx is in a 2014 Master's thesis from Emory's Women, Gender, and Sexuality Studies department:

> I choose to use the word "Latinx" instead of "Latina/o" or "Latina" or "Latin@" to symbolize and include gender nonconforming Latinxs, to challenge gender binaries, and to queer myths about a unified homogenous Latinidad and challenge conventional identity politics. The term "Latinx" is used as a linguistic political intervention to create space for nonbinary, gender queer, gender nonconforming Latinxs. (Alvarado 2014: 4)

Alvarado notes they first located the Latinx term on online organizing spaces and blogs. It is unclear if Latinx will go the same way of obsolescence as Latin@ but the term is not without controversy. As detailed by de Onís (2017: 79), "this signifier [Latin-a/o, @, x] invite[s] reflection on the evolution, fluidity, and slipperiness of language. Engaging questions about the 'x' signifier and the extent to which the symbol advances intersectional social justice efforts is both urgent and vital."

When we use the term Latino, who is left out? ... women. When we use the term Latina/o or Latin@, who is not being included? ... gender non-conforming Latinxs. This is not a case of gender neutrality (as often claimed in online forums and blogs), this is about (non-conforming) gender inclusivity in the face of gender-restrictive language practices. What is clear is that the challenges of imposed definitions (from either government or linguistic conventions) will continue to be opposed and new terms will always be introduced to better align experiences with language and identities with names.

Eschewing government-imposed definitions of identity, definitions of what it means to be Latino are embedded in the understanding that identities are a result of social relations, not merely labels or categories. Identities are the social locations that individuals, groups, or communities inhabit within larger systems of oppression and privilege. Scholars write about Latinidad to describe the shared social locations that Latina/os inhabit, regardless of their unique national origins.[5] It holds great promise as an incredibly helpful concept for those studying Latina/o politics (see Barreto and Segura 2014, Beltrán 2010, Garcia 2016, García Bedolla 2005, 2014). Cristina Beltrán (2010: 4) offers the most succinct defense of applying Latinidad as "the sociohistorical process whereby various Latin American national-origin groups are understood as sharing a sense of collective identity and cultural consciousness." But the majority of scholars deploying Latinidad are in the humanities: primarily literature and history (Caminero-Santangelo 2009, Irizarry 2016, Rivera-Servera 2012, Rodríguez 2003; see also the "Latinidad: Transnational Cultures in the United States" series from Rutgers University Press and the "Writing in Latinidad: Autographical Voices of U.S. Latinos/as" series from University of Wisconsin Press). In daily lived experiences, Latino communities embodying Latinidad – what Milagros Ricourt and Ruby Danta (2002) refer to as *convivencia diaria* in their study of Latinos[6] living together in Corona, Queens – are actually quite difficult alliances to maintain, as Diana Garbow (2016) confirms in their study of how Colombianidad in Philadelphia most often takes the form of intra-Latino distinctions.

Miami is a global, majority-minority, multiethnic city that serves as the transnational hub for commerce, people, and Latina/o culture in the Caribbean region. Much of the research has been on the Cuban exile presence but increasingly migrants from Puerto Rico, Mexico, the Dominican Republic, Colombia, Peru, and Nicaragua constitute Miami's "subgroups of Latinos [that] feel like members of a pan-Latino majority group in Miami [that] occurred both because they found and connected with culturally similar others, and because the worldviews, beliefs, and behaviors of many subgroups were not marginalized in Miami's mainstream cultural landscape" (Aranda, Hughes, and Sabogal 2014: 295). Latinos are central to Miami's status as a global city and the authors' respondents often note how it "feels like home," regardless of one's Caribbean nation of origin. Focusing on language usage among Puerto Rican, Mexican, and MexiRican (members of both communities) Spanish speakers in Chicago, the linguistic aspects of intra-Latinidades demonstrate how language ideologies separate groups and distinguish generations according to language usage, and how even the use of English "so" and Spanish "*entonces*" is a key discourse marker of bi-/monolingual proficiencies (Potowski 2015, Rosa 2015, Torres and Potowski 2008).

A Latino by any other name ...

What has remained consistent, though, is that the majority of Latina/os tend to eschew the panethnic label and identify more in terms of their national origin.[7] Mexicans, Puerto Ricans, Cubans, Salvadorans, Dominicans, Guatemalans tend to self-identify as such (or their Spanish equivalent). In the contemporary era of post-1965 immigration, this tendency has only heightened due to transnational ties that make it easier to remain intimately connected to one's nation of origin. At its most basic level, transnationalism connotes "making parts of one's life simultaneously in more than one country" (Smith 2006: 210). Changes synonymous with globalization – travel, technology, communications, international division of labor, and citizenship rules – activate the ability to converse instantly with relatives in home countries or to maintain dual citizenship and travel easily and comparatively cheaply between two nations, all making transnationalism possible. The question is now less of becoming American and much more of what *América* is becoming. In a call for transnational Latina/o studies, María Josefina Saldaña-Portillo (2007: 506) sees four analytical components that proceed from the panethnic approach, which:

- foregrounds United States nation-formation as an expansionist project in the Americas, with neocolonial interventions in the nineteenth and twentieth centuries that have generated wave after wave of "Latina/o" immigration;
- demonstrates the continued dependence of the US economy on Latin American markets, natural resources, *and* undocumented immigrants whose racially marked bodies are easily subjected to extra-economic forms of exploitation;

- compares the distinct racial legacies of the Anglo-American and Spanish colonial governmentality, and analyzes how Latina/o subjectivity is forged between these competing racial ideologies;
- analyzes the improvisation of resistive identity and cultural production in the wake of this history of racial migration.

This approach rejects the European-centered ethnic understanding of immigration as a uni-directional process of assimilation, pluralism, or melting pots. Transnationalism posits that identities in a globalized world must navigate other poles such as cosmopolitanism or parochial nationalism, polyvocality or univocality, and the continuum of incorporation beyond identity to more substantive economic, political, and social forms.

The various ways in which what it means to be Latina/o can then be more fully conceptualized than a monolithic definition. Scholars have approached Afro-Latin@ histories and cultures to account for "people of African descent in Latin America and the Caribbean as a whole"; also, "in the United States, the term 'Afro-Latin@' has surfaced as a way to signal racial, cultural, and socioeconomic contradictions within the overly vague idea of 'Latin@'" (Jiménez Román and Flores 2010: 2). The authors then proceed to organize their edited collection along four thematics: the aforementioned group history, transnational discourses, Black–Latina/o relations, and Afro-Latin@ lived experiences.

Relations between Asian Americans and Latinos have a long history in Latina/o Studies. Tomás Almaguer (1984) was the first to discuss the Oxnard sugar beet strike of 1903 in terms of the Japanese-Mexican Labor Association. Subsequent scholars of the United Farm Workers (UFW) union make reference, however brief, to the origins of labor strikes in Delano, California, that were mounted by the Filipino-led (chiefly Larry Itliong and Philip Vera Cruz) Agricultural Workers Organizing Committee (AWOC) (Ferriss and Sandoval 1998, Galarza 1970, Garcia 2014).[8] More recent research conducted by Rudy Guevarra (2012) and Anthony Ocampo (2016) identifies the complicated relationship among Latinos, Asians, and Filipinos in southern California. It is a legacy of Spanish colonialism, US imperialism, and longstanding labor migration to the service industries of urban California and the agricultural fields of rural California. The reason Ocampo (2016: 11) refers to Filipinos – often Spanish-surnamed and adherents of Catholicism – as the "Latinos of Asia" is captured best by one of their respondents: "'It's hard because we're the only Asian country that has been colonized by Spain for three hundred years,' Lia said. 'It really changed us because we're more Latin. We have more similarities with Latin culture than other Asians. Filipinos are the Mexicans of Asia.'" Barring an extended discussion of the conflation of Latin, Latino, and Mexican, the takeaway from Lia's insight is that from the perspective of Filipinos, US constructions of Asian and Latino ethnicities, races, or panethnicities simply do not fit. The Mexipinos of San Diego that Guevarra identifies represent a longstanding connection between the two communities that resulted in many intermarriages and offers insights into Filipino and Mexican experiences as neither separate nor distinct. An emerging literature on mixed race studies often centers on Latinos vis-à-vis Asian Americans, Anglo Americans, African Americans, Pacific Islanders, and Native Americans (Delgado 2013, Johnson 2003a, 2003b, O'Brien 2008, Romero 2012, Rondilla, Guevarra, and Spickard 2017).

The final insight that has emerged from thinking about the complexities of identity and contemporary migration patterns is the literature on indigeneity that recognizes the increasing number of Indigenous migrants from Mexico and Guatemala. An edited collection resulted from a conference sponsored by the University of California Santa Cruz that convened "eighteen indigenous migrant leaders of Mixtec, Zapotec, Triqui, Purépecha, Chatina, and Mayan origin, as well as academics, applied researchers, journalists, trade unionists, local civic leaders, lawyers, and foundation representatives" to discuss the organizing successes and challenges of transnational civil society organizations among Mexican Indigenous migrants (Fox and Rivera-Salgado 2004: 29–30).

Who Latinos are, who Latinos are not

The myths that have been constructed about who Latinos are and who they are not make it very difficult to separate fact from fiction, lived experience from stereotype. The current political landscape (i.e., the rise of Donald Trump) has yielded characterizations of Latinos as "bad hombres" as well as rapists and criminals. Some actual facts would be helpful here to correct the political hyperbole.

- Latinos are the largest minority of the US population (17.1 percent).
- Most Latinos are US citizens (64.8 percent).
- Most Latinos are English-proficient (69 percent).
- Even though the vast majority of Latinos are of Mexican origin (64 percent), Latinos represent almost thirty national origins and Census-designated categories such as "Spanish American" and "Central American" (see table 1.1).
- Most Latino immigrants are *not* undocumented (only a quarter of all immigrants are undocumented) (Lopez and Bialik 2017).
- Latinos reside in every US state but nearly two-thirds (65 percent) are concentrated in the five states of California, Texas, Illinois, New York, and Florida.
- Additional states with more than 1 million Latinos include Arizona, Colorado, New Mexico, and New Jersey.

Table 1.1 Census counts of Latinos by national origin (2015)

	United States	
	Estimate	Margin of error
Total US population:	316,515,021	*****
Not Hispanic or Latino	262,282,816	+/–2,053
Hispanic or Latino:	54,232,205	+/–2,036
Mexican	34,640,287	+/–52,590
Puerto Rican	5,174,554	+/–27,796
Cuban	2,014,010	+/–15,603
Dominican (Dominican Republic)	1,719,678	+/–15,955
Central American:	4,886,930	+/–30,182
Costa Rican	144,258	+/–5,308
Guatemalan	1,296,634	+/–17,381
Honduran	785,332	+/–12,849
Nicaraguan	407,288	+/–9,941
Panamanian	190,557	+/–5,477
Salvadoran	2,022,687	+/–21,353
Other Central American	40,174	+/–3,363
South American:	3,274,416	+/–23,232
Argentinean	262,841	+/–6,683
Bolivian	112,953	+/–3,721
Chilean	149,472	+/–3,939
Colombian	1,060,519	+/–13,614
Ecuadorian	677,183	+/–13,167
Paraguayan	22,767	+/–1,877
Peruvian	620,074	+/–10,958
Uruguayan	62,902	+/–3,088
Venezuelan	273,343	+/–6,390
Other South American	32,362	+/–2,558
Other Hispanic or Latino:	2,522,330	+/–28,605
Spaniard	756,552	+/–11,955
Spanish	511,369	+/–9,078
Spanish American	26,038	+/–1,727
All other Hispanic or Latino	1,228,371	+/–19,162

Source: US Census Bureau, 2011–15, American Community Survey 5-year estimates

- Latinos, on average, are much younger than White Americans (median age 28.7 as compared to 43.3 non-Hispanic White population).
- Mexican immigration is neither a horde nor an invasion; in fact, "Net migration from Mexico fell to zero in 2011, with return migration to Mexico equaling new arrivals to the United States" (Malavé and Giordani 2015: 10).
- Immigrants (undocumented and legal) are much less likely to commit crimes or become incarcerated than US citizens (Nowrasteh 2017, Rumbaut 2008, Sampson 2008).
- Immigrants are not taking jobs from US citizens; the Pew Hispanic Foundation found that "no consistent pattern emerges to show that native-born workers suffered or benefited from increased numbers of foreign-born workers" (cited in Chomsky 2007: 8).
- Immigrants are not a drain on social services and in fact do pay taxes, as Chomsky (2007: 39) summarizes: "the majority of immigrants, being of prime working age and ineligible for many public services, tend to contribute more to the public sector than they actually use."

Following the largest Mexican-origin population, Puerto Ricans are the second-largest group, representing 9.5 percent of all Latinos. Depending on the accuracy of the data and the margin of error in the estimates, Salvadorans, Cubans, Dominicans, Guatemalans, and Colombians are the remaining Latino populations with more than a million residents each in the United States. Even though we refer to Latinos in terms of their national origins, the vast majority (64.8 percent) were born in the United States or are US citizens born outside the United States (see table 1.2).

Table 1.2 Latinos categorized by citizenship (2015)

	United States		
	Estimate	Margin of error	Percent of share
Total Hispanic or Latino population:	54,232,205	+/–2,036	100
Born in state of residence	26,746,921	+/–41,994	49.3
Born in other state in the United States	6,227,502	+/–30,291	11.5
Native; born outside the United States	2,150,985	+/–14,105	4.0
Foreign born	19,106,797	+/–60,551	35.2

Source: US Census Bureau, 2011–15 American Community Survey 5-year estimates

The history of Latina/o Studies is intricately connected to the need to dispel myths of who Latina/os are and more accurately represent how Latina/os think about themselves and experience the United States. In the next chapter, I will trace the origins of Latin American thought in the independence and revolutionary movements of the 1800s that would later influence Latina/os in the development of the civil rights and power movements of the 1960s. In chapter 3, I will discuss how the rise of Boricua (Puerto Rican) and Chicano (Mexican American) Studies was connected to dispelling the "culture of poverty" myth that had been applied to both communities by White male scholars.

2

Historical Groundings: The Origins of Latina/o Thought

The European conquest of the Americas begins in 1492 when Cristoforo Colombo/Christopher Columbus, under the aegis of the Spanish crown, lands on the island he christens Hispaniola. A return trip the following year unleashes the unabashed desire to claim riches, land, and Indigenous labor and souls as justification for the Spanish government's financing of transatlantic voyages. In fact, the Spanish government finances well over twenty missions between 1492 and 1521.[1] From a European standpoint, it was promoted as the Age of Discovery. For Indigenous peoples of the Americas, it was an Age of Conquest and Resistance.

In clear relief, the invasion of Mexico and Hernan Cortes' (1521) march on Tenochtitlan, the capital of the far-reaching Mexica empire, illustrated the violent brutality of conquest, the avarice of extracting riches from Indigenous populations, and the ensuing conflict between Catholic redemption and genocidal impulses that shaped European–Native American relations for all subsequent centuries.

> They came in battle array, as conquerors, and the dust rose in whirl-winds on the roads. Their spears glinted in the sun, and their pennons fluttered like bats. They made a loud clamor as they marched, for their coats of mail and their weapons clashed and rattled. Some of them were dressed in glistening iron from head to foot; they terrified everyone who saw them. Their dogs came with them, running ahead of the column. They raised their muzzles high; they lifted their muzzles to the wind. They raced on before with saliva dripping from their jaws. (León-Portilla 2006: 41)

The 1494 Treaty of Tordesillas divided the Américas between Portugal and Spain. The early focus of Spanish conquistadors was the settlement of Hispaniola (present-day Dominican Republic and Haiti) and nearby Cuba, while Portuguese efforts concentrated more on present-day Brazil. As the nations of Europe envisioned their competing colonial projects as a matter of divvying up the rest of the world under their purview, in the Américas that most often implicated the Portuguese in Brazil, Spain in the rest of South America as well as Central and North America (including Florida and the US Southwest), and England, France, and at times Russia and the Netherlands vying for the rest of North America. For Indigenous communities, that meant the wreaking of a destruction that displaced or destroyed settled ways of life by the millions, attested to by figure 2.1, which gives an idea of the number of distinct documented tribes established in the Américas before the arrival of the Europeans.

The Spanish conquest of the Américas held dominion until the early 1800s when a nascent sense of revolution and independence spread throughout the Américas (partially inspired by the American and French Revolutions but also related to the Napoleonic wars that destabilized Spanish control over the colonies). Key figures are important in exploring the history of anti-colonial thought (independence) and nation-building (revolution) in Latin American politics and philosophy.

Known as "El Libertador/The Liberator," Simón José Antonio de la Santísima Trinidad Bolívar Palacios Ponte y Blanco was the most visible leader who liberated New Granada (Venezuela, Colombia, Panamá) and Perú (Peru, Bolivia, and Ecuador) from the shackles of Spanish colonialism. As stated in his "Oath Taken in Rome" (1805), "I swear by my Country that I will not rest body or soul until I have broken the chains binding us to the will of Spanish might!" The nations of Bolivia and the Bolívarian Republic of Venezuela are named after him, as are their national currencies and innumerable town squares, statues, and busts throughout the Americas. As well as being the subject of renowned novelist Gabriel García Márquez' *The General in His Labyrinth*, Simón Bolívar's legacy cannot be overstated.

> Loving what is most useful, inspired by what is most just, and aspiring to perfection as she breaks free of the Spanish nation, Venezuela has regained her independence, her freedom, her equality, and her national sovereignty. Constituting herself as a democratic republic, she has outlawed monarchy, distinctions, nobility, and special rights and privileges. She has established the rights of man, the freedom to work, think, speak, and write. (Bolívar 2003 [1819]: 36)

Beyond the hyperbole above, the political impetus and accompanying political philosophy that Bolívar represents are a bit more complicated.

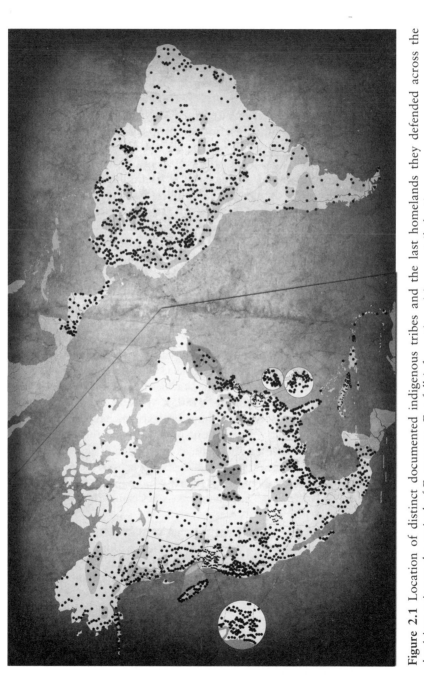

Figure 2.1 Location of distinct documented indigenous tribes and the last homelands they defended across the Américas prior to the arrival of Europeans. For full information visit www.tribalnationsmaps.com.
Source: based on Tribal Nations of the Western Hemisphere by Aaron Carapella 2018

Most certainly, a disdain for colonization and the Spanish-imposed systems of slavery and Indigenous oppression was a major driving force in his military and political roles. "Considering that justice, policy, and the country imperiously demand the inalienable rights of nature, I have decided to formally decree absolute freedom for the slaves who have groaned under the Spanish yoke during the three previous centuries" (Bolívar 2003 [1816]: 177). The articles of justification following the decree make it clear the purpose was to have a full citizenry, workforce, and military (see "Letter to General Francisco de Paula Santander: On Slave Recruitment" [2003/1820: 182–3] for further confirmation of his military service intent). His "Decree on Indian Rights, Lands, and Tribute" (1820) defends civil and economic rights, communal lands, religious tolerance, and ending the practice of tributes (or obligatory payments to the church). Bolívar's rationale is that Indians deserve "the most paternal attention" due to their status as the "most aggrieved, oppressed, and humiliated" (2003 [1820]: 184), yet he still required Indigenous peoples to pay an annual Indian tax or "personal tribute," and appointed *fiscales* (court prosecutors) to serve as guardians or protectors to cement the paternalist relationship of those he deemed unable to self-govern.

Citing Montesquieu's (1748) *Spirit of Laws* to the effect that state rules should be suitable to each nation's unique circumstances, Bolívar (2003 [1819]: 37) sees Latin American independence as regionally, geographically, and historically unique: "This then is the code we should consult, not the one written for Washington!" Bolívar's views on revolution have clear roots in the European Enlightenment and the French and, to a lesser extent, American Revolutions, but his bourgeois origins – born into one of the most affluent families of *criollos* (the name for the Spanish-heritage elite born in the colonies) in New Granada – subjected his philosophy of revolution and independence to criticisms ranging from those of philosopher Karl Marx to those of novelists García Márquez and Manrique. Marx (1858) characterized Bolívar as a Napoleonic dictator, specifically "the president and liberator of Colombia, the protector and dictator of Peru, and the godfather of Bolivia." Always referring to his character as "the General," García Márquez (1990) begins and ends his story not with the heroic rise of Bolívar, but with his tragic fall from power. Manrique (2007) recounts events not from Bolívar's perspective, but from those of his lover and fellow revolutionary Manuela Sáenz and her two slaves, Jonatás and Natán, to demonstrate the continued marginalization of women's rights and African slaves' human rights in Bolívar's vision.[2]

The Bolívarian Revolution, as it came to be known, was Bolívar's proposed unification of the former Spanish colonies of the Américas, as expressed in the Congress of Panama (1826), where Bolívar envisioned a confederation in which "[t]he interests and ties that already unite the

American republics that were formerly Spanish colonies should be given a fundamental basis that will perpetuate, if possible, the duration of these governments" (Bolívar 2009 [1824]: 165). Bolívar's influence is present throughout Latin America to this day, with everyone claiming they carry on the legacy of their progenitor, from former Venezuelan socialist president Hugo Chávez (1999–2013) to the ultraconservative, nationalist dictatorship of former president Marcos Pérez Jiménez (1952–8). There is an uncritical, yet warranted, celebration of Bolívar as the father of both Latin American independence in individual nation-states and a larger vision of pan-Americanism that unites the region.

Bolívar's relationship to the United States was quite limited and his sole trip solidified his belief that the United States was not a model for Latin American independence due to its reliance on slavery and inability to emulate European advances in democracy. Bolívar's uncle provided fiscal support for his back-up option, the University of Virginia, but like most American intellectuals of his time with the means, he traveled to Europe to continue his studies. On his 1805 return from Europe, he visited the United States for about five months and though he did not write about his visit during the time, his travels took him to Charleston, South Carolina, and Philadelphia, Pennsylvania, where he saw a slave-holding, leisurely, segregated South and an industrial, commercial, consumerist North (Arana 2013). Both felt completely, yet distinctly, separate from South America. He would go on to state later that the United States "appears destined by Providence to plague América with miseries in the name of Freedom" (Bolívar 2008: 135).

José Julián Martí Pérez enters the public stage roughly forty years after Bolívar but most certainly inspired by his predecessor's vision. Martí engineered a revolt against Spanish colonialism in Cuba that would again inspire Latino/as and Latin Americans in the Américas to this day. In contrast to Bolívar's decorated military history, Martí was very much an intellectual and political philosopher who, when entering armed combat for the first time, met his untimely death by charging Spanish lines with his lone accompanying soldier ... the two-man charge was not effective.[3]

After his passing, Martí's poem "Guantanamera," originally published in their Versos Sencillos ("Simple Verses"), was adapted into the song that is perennially associated with Cuba. Born in Havana, Cuba, on January 28, 1853, Martí heeded the call of Cuban liberation as a schoolboy and was imprisoned by the Spanish authorities by age 16. A gifted writer and thinker, Martí would eventually become the authoritative voice on matters of Cuban independence, abolition of slavery, and the threat of US imperialism. He spent much of his adult life in exile that took him to Madrid, Mexico City, Guatemala City, Caracas, and New York City.

"Nuestra América," published in 1891, is Martí's most recognized polemic, where he distinguishes "our" America – Latin America – from its North American neighbor – the United States. "The disdain of the formidable neighbor who does not know her is our America's greatest danger, and it is urgent – for the day of the visit is near – that her neighbor come to know her, and quickly, so that he will not disdain her" (Martí 2002 [1891]: 295). These words were written seven years before the Spanish–American War that led to the United States usurping the Spanish colonial holdings of Guam, the Philippines, and Puerto Rico, and temporary control of Cuba.

But during the time of Martí's writing, his immediate concern was removing the shackles of Spanish colonialism and identifying sustainable forms of governance for nascent nation-states. "America began enduring and still endures the weary task of reconciling the discordant and hostile elements it inherited from its perverse, despotic colonizer with the imported forms and ideas that have, in their lack of local reality, delayed the advent of a logical form of government" (Martí 2002 [1891]: 292). One of the central means of constructing this new, logical, albeit regionally specific (à la Bolívar's call for independence) form of government was through a process of self-education. "To know the country and govern it in accordance with that knowledge is the only way of freeing it from tyranny. The European university must yield to the American university. The history of America from the Incas to the present must be taught in its smallest detail, even if the Greek Archons go untaught" (Martí 2002 [1891]: 291). Knowledge, education, learning, and history would be the guideposts for newly independent nations, and the subject matter would pre-date European contact to inspire local, regionally relevant forms of governance. Martí's untimely death in 1895 did not squelch his intellectual legacy, and his modernist writings would inspire future generations to commemorate their fierce independence in statues that can be found around the world, from Havana, Cuba, to Miami, Florida, and Central Park, New York City, to *Secretaría de Educación Pública*, Mexico City, Sofia, Bulgaria, and Delhi, India. As Laura Lomas (2008: 282) concludes, "that Martí divides colonial society into a pretentious oligarchy and a multiracial mass of producers reflects a sense of the social content that he would infuse into the revolution and into his Latino modernism."

In many ways, Martí prefigures the challenges Latin American nations faced once they secured their independence. Between 1810 and 1826, all Spanish colonies in Latin America, except Cuba and Puerto Rico, secured their independence from Spain. Aspiring nation-states struggled to maintain national sovereignty as European nations sought to re-colonize the Américas, but it was their neighbor to the north that wreaked the most havoc on new Latin American nation-states.

As soon as Mexico established its independence from Spain in 1821, the United States, espousing two seemingly disparate philosophies (Monroe Doctrine and Manifest Destiny), eyed Mexico's northern territories from Tejas to Alta California. The Monroe Doctrine was issued in his annual statement to Congress in 1823 by then president James Monroe when he declared that the Western hemisphere was off limits to future European colonization, as this would represent an act of aggression "dangerous to our [US] peace and safety." The United States established itself as the protector of the Américas with the doctrine and often intervened in Latin American internal affairs under its auspices. Manifest Destiny was an ideology, popularized in newspapers and by prominent historians, that by the divine will of God, the United States was destined to occupy the hemisphere from sea to shining sea. Westward expansion would justify not only the forcible taking of the northern half of Mexico, with the annexation of Texas and the US–Mexico War of 1846–8, but also claiming the Oregon territories and, later, former Spanish colonies as spoils of the Spanish–American War of 1898.

Mexico's road to independence was initially hard fought and under constant threat. On September 16, 1810, a priest named Miguel Hidalgo y Costilla began, albeit unwittingly, an eleven-year conflict to secure independence from Spain with what is commonly referred to as *El Grito de Dolores*. Leading troops of mestizos and Indigenous soldiers, the struggle for independence would galvanize the most oppressed under the banner of *Nuestra Virgén de Guadalupe* and cast the *peninsulares* (Spanish-born elite) as the targets of 300 years of oppression, placing *criollos* in a contradictory class location of either choosing to side with their *peninsulares* oppressors to re-establish Spanish royal rule (Conservatives), or try to negotiate an armistice to reject Bourbon reforms in favor of home rule, if not fully advocate for independence (Liberals). Independence was not secured until 1821 and only two decades passed before the United States invaded first Texas and then Mexico City.

In the interim, France attempted to colonize Mexico. Benito Juárez, the first Indigenous Mexican president (1861–72), hailing from a rural, poor, Zapotec community in Oaxaca, expressed the sentiments of the burgeoning nation in the following terms: "The government of the republic will fulfill its duty to defend its independence, to repel foreign aggression, and accept the struggle to which it has been provoked, counting on the unanimous spirit of the Mexicans and on the fact that sooner or later the cause of rights and justice will triumph."[4] His Proclamation to the Mexican people, shortly before the May 5, 1862, Battle of Puebla (recognized today as "Cinco de Mayo"), made liberal reforms and ending foreign intrusion hallmarks of the nation-state.[5] On the other hand, in the name of modernizing Mexico, his eventual successor Porfirio Díaz enacted a series of land reforms and eased direct foreign investment barriers that resulted in a twenty-seven-year period, known as the Porfiriato, characterized by authoritarian dictatorship, widespread poverty, and US robber barons extracting Mexican wealth.

Around the same time, rumblings and discontent about Spanish colonialism in Puerto Rico began to find a united, public voice. On the island, there have always been, even if not regularly acknowledged, challenges to Spanish colonialism from the time of the original Indigenous inhabitants of Puerto Rico, from the Taino Rebellion of 1511 onward. The public outcry was subsequently quashed until *El Grito de Lares* was proclaimed on September 23, 1868, to end Spanish colonial rule. This rebellion was quickly put down and the next day the Revolutionary Committee and insurgents were jailed, tortured, killed, or exiled. Yet this did not quell the steadfast belief in independence, and those who escaped prosecution still articulated their opposition to Spanish colonial rule. Eugenio María de Hostos supported an Antillean Confederation – the idea that the Spanish colonies in the Caribbean should unite into one nation to thwart not only Spanish colonialism but also the Monroe Doctrine's self-appointed declaration of the United States as protector of the Américas. The Puerto Rican Nationalist Party, under the leadership of Dr. Pedro Albizu Campos, recognized that US (*Yanqui*) imperialism would be no better than Spanish colonialism. "Let Puerto Rico become a factory ... A factory needs no legislators nor political power ... Puerto Rico will be another Hawaii. We Puerto Ricans will be day-laborers, foremen, and policemen to guarantee to investors, against any opposition on our part that may arise, the enjoyment of our wealth" (Albizu Campos 1980 [1930]: 179). More prescient words have rarely been uttered.

The shift in focus from independence to anti-US imperialism, after the Spanish–American War of 1898, spread across all of Latin America as the United States sought to extend its reach and power throughout the Western hemisphere. The United States, for its part, never settled for anything less than military, economic, political, and social hegemony. Agricultural firms like the United Fruit Company established Honduran, Guatemalan, and Cuban governance regimes as banana republics where monocultural export agriculture dominated the national economy. Often military dictatorships, bolstered by the US government, were installed to ensure US corporate and anti-communist interests were prioritized. These dictatorships included Bonilla in Honduras (1912–13), Trujillo in the Dominican Republic (1930–61), post-Árbenz installed presidents in Guatemala (1954–86), Somozas in Nicaragua (1936–79), and military dictatorships in Argentina, Bolivia, Brazil, Chile, Colombia, Cuba, Ecuador, El Salvador, Panamá, Paraguay, Peru, Uruguay, and Venezuela.

Much is known about these dictatorships; little is known of the resistance movements that challenged US hegemony in Latin American affairs. We are just beginning to see Latina/o Studies scholars make the connections from independence and revolutionary movements in their nations of origins to contemporary social and political thought among immigrants and their second generation. Ginetta Candelario's long-term project of uncovering nineteenth- and early twentieth-century feminist voices and movements in the Dominican Republic is a great example of such work (see Candelario, Manley, and Mayes 2016).

The most widely recognized opposition to US imperialism is clearly found in the events and actors associated with the Cuban Revolution. Cuba was nominally a free nation after the Spanish–American War, but the Platt Amendment of 1901 gave the United States rights to directly intervene in Cuban affairs and required Cuba to lease lands for US military bases. After a series of US-sponsored and puppet dictatorships led by Fulgencio Batista (1940–4, 1952–9), Batista was overthrown by Fidel Castro's 26th of July Movement, and as a result, the Cold War found a singular focus in US–Latin American affairs. Fidel Castro is ever present on the island to this day, even after his death in 2016, and quotes are to be found on billboards and posters throughout Cuba. One poster located in the Plaza Carlos III shopping mall can be translated as follows:

> Particularly, to the youngest revolutionaries, I recommend the highest standards and iron discipline, without ambition for power, arrogance, or vanity. Beware of bureaucratic methods and mechanisms … In the new era that we live in, capitalism neither works nor is it an instrument, it is like a tree with rotten roots from which spring only the worst forms of individualism, corruption, and inequality.[6]

His criticisms of totalitarian bureaucracy and corruption are quite applicable to Cuban state socialism under his rule, even though his criticism of capitalism's excesses, materialism, and inequality articulate with Latina/o criticisms of a US-dominated world and worldview. Guerra (2016: 140) identifies how the US fixation on Castro impacts "other refugees from Central America and the Caribbean [who] often feel frustrated by the invisibility of their culture and the Castro-centrism that tends to pervade public representations of the Cold War."

The development of Latino/a critical social thought has tended to bypass Castro due to his controversial, and indefensible, authoritarian tactics, but his co-conspirator, similarly controversial, Ernesto "Che" Guevara has often, not always, bypassed criticism to serve as an icon for resistance, a symbol of opposition to US imperialism. An embodiment of the Bolívarian Revolution, his early travels took him from his home in Argentina across Latin America to witness poverty and starvation firsthand (see *The Motorcycle Diaries*, Guevara 2003). He also participated in Árbenz' land redistribution in Guatemala (reforms opposed by the United Fruit Company, who conspired with the US government to depose Árbenz) and the overthrow of Batista in Cuba. In his 1964 address to the United Nations general assembly, Che chastised the UN for not holding the United States accountable for its domestic apartheid state and imperialist ambitions.

> The time will come when this Assembly will acquire greater maturity and demand of the U.S. Government guarantees for the life of the blacks and Latin Americans who live in that country, most of them U.S. citizens by origin or adoption ... It must be clearly established, however, that the government of the United States is not the champion of freedom, but rather the perpetrator of exploitation and oppression against the peoples of the world and against a large part of its own population. (Guevara 1964; see also Anderson 1997: 617)

Over the next three years, Guevara transformed from spokesperson and vanguard leader of the Cuban socialist state, lambasting racism and imperialism on a global stage, to guerrilla fighter attempting to recreate the battles fashioned after South American independence from Spanish colonialism campaigns (led by Bolívar and San Martín), to involvement in socialist revolutions that would culminate in Bolivia, where Che met his demise with CIA assistance.

Conclusion

The long history of revolutionary and anti-colonial thought is always already present in Latino/a political consciousness. It's the ground we walk on, the water we drink and swim in, the air we breathe. This legacy of revolutionary and independence thought provides the cultural repertoire that subsequent generations draw upon, particularly as these progenies inhabit the belly of the beast. Even Porfirio Díaz once quipped, "Poor Mexico, so far from God, so close to the United States."

As much as consciousness is bequeathed via politics, cultural representations such as art, music, literature, and theater are often more effective in conveying memories that transcend space, time, and generations. The Mexican Revolution was fought over the future of a nation not bound by either Spanish colonialism or US imperialism. "The Mexican Revolution remains one of a kind in a century of social upheaval and anticolonial struggle perhaps because the monumental Mexican struggle contained elements such as local grievances and antiforeign campaigns against political and economic subjugation that appeared in all the other great social revolutions" (Meyer and Beezley 2000: 433). The political ideas that swirled around the revolution deeply challenged the previously settled Liberal–Conservative lines and introduced new forms of political thought, from social liberalism, anarchism, Trotskyism, Stalinism, and socialism to communism.

Interestingly, the expansion of political choices was certainly articulated by Francisco "Pancho" Villa, Emiliano Zapata, and the Flores Magón brothers, but it was the global impact of the artwork of the great Mexican muralists (José Clemente Orozco, David Alfaro Siqueiros, and Diego Rivera), the architecture and art of Juan O'Gorman, and the art of Frida Kahlo, to name some of the most prominently recognized, that has transcended time and space. One does not have to look closely at the artwork of the time to recognize the trenchant criticisms of colonization, imperialism, capitalism, class exploitation, racism, and patriarchy. Revolutionary politics inspired revolutionary art and culture. A contemporary example was on display in a 2016 *día de los muertos* exhibit in Mexico City's Benito Juárez International Airport. It offered an extensive linkage of past to present, how revolutionary-era ideas still resonate to this day. The *calaveras* (skulls) and *catrinas* on display were fashioned after the illustrations and print work of José Guadalupe Posada. *La Catrina* served as indictment of Mexican society emulating European standards and ways of living (lavish dress and hats), even while the people are so impoverished that they starve to death (figure 2.2).

Figure 2.2 *La Calavera Catrina*
Source: Zinc etching by José Guadalupe Posada (c.1910–13)

Before the Mexican Revolution, the newspapers carrying Posada's *La Catrina* provided the social commentary and criticism to envision massive social change and dislodge the emulation of European high fashion when basic living standards were not attainable. The interesting thing about the 2016 *catrinas* is they are fashioned as two Chicana/o icons: a zoot suiter and a female UFW protestor (figure 2.3). The politics of both icons will become readily apparent in the next chapter's focus on the origins of Chicano Studies in the United States.

Figure 2.3 *Día de los muertos* display at Benito Juárez International Airport
Source: Author's photographs, Mexico City (2016)

3

Origins of Latina/o Studies: Puerto Rican and Chicano Studies

In Mexico, *Catrinas*, which have come to symbolize *día de los muertos*, serve as year-round reminders of the unholy trinity of individualism, materialism, and inequality. Yet according to Regina Marchi (2009: 25), the linkage between *calaveras* (in particular, sugar skulls) and *día de los muertos* is a relatively new and European Catholic phenomenon that dates back to the 1920s, just following the era when Posada first introduced *La Catrina* (see chapter 2). This claim of recent appearance is certainly disputed within Mexico where pre-Columbian ceremonies honoring the dead were inextricably linked to skulls and skeletons. Celebrations of *día de los muertos* in Mexico are most often family- and friend-based, yet more public displays in Mexico City's el Zócalo and in state-run museums throughout the nation are more visible today (see figure 3.1). Marchi in *Day of the Dead in the USA* (2009: 70–82) notes that the use of *ofrendas* (altars) during Day of the Dead celebrations in the United States are more often for explicitly political purposes, such as to mark the deaths and struggles associated with Mexican American and immigrant experiences: immigrant deaths as a result of the militarization of the US–Mexico border, longstanding abuses of farmworkers, Indigenous genocide, and US military intervention.

The historical landscape initially established by Latin American thinkers has a direct influence on the ideas developed by Latinos in the United States from the period of social unrest to today's politicized *ofrendas*. The 1960s and 1970s set in motion Puerto Rican and Chicano civil rights and power movements that fundamentally changed the way we talk about and study Latino (dis)settlement in the United States. This chapter will

Figure 3.1 Zócalo celebration
Source: Día de Muertos 2010 © nmarritz_flickr

talk about how the protest movements informed and in fact gave birth
to Puerto Rican and Chicano Studies. First, precursors of the 1960s will
connect the thinkers of the last chapter with twentieth-century Puerto
Rican *independentistas* and Chicano *insurgentes*. Then, the linkages will
be explored between Latin American political philosophy and the ideas
informing founding documents such as the thirteen-point program of
the Young Lords, the epic poem *Yo Soy Joaquin, El Plan Espiritual de
Aztlán*, and *El Plan de Santa Barbara*. Finally, both Puerto Rican and
Chicano Studies arose to combat characterizations of Latinos as stuck
in a "culture of poverty." How a politics of negation became a politics
of affirmation defines how higher education came to know the earliest
incarnations of Latina/o Studies.

Latina/o protest movements

Precursors of the Chicano and Puerto Rican Movements were certainly
prevalent prior to the turbulent 1960s. *Mutualistas* or mutual aid

societies sprung up as soon as Mexican American and Puerto Rican communities established themselves in major US cities (see Hernández 1983, Sánchez Korrol 1983). The earliest documented attempts at bringing groups together were separately commissioned *congresos* or issue-focused conventions (in 1911 Texas and 1938 California). *El Primer Congreso Mexicanista de 1911* was held in Laredo and was informed by eight themes: Mexican nationalism or patriotism, uniting against US oppressors, radical working-class ideology, culture and language maintenance (including bilingual schools), lynchings and the criminal justice system, social problems impacting women, "social" or racial discrimination (including integrating schools), and economic development (Limón 2003: 229–30). *El Congreso de Pueblos de Hablan Española* was first held in Los Angeles, California, in 1938 and focused on radical labor organizing, combating racial discrimination, immigrant rights and relief agency calls for deportations, "civil rights, health and housing, and youth" (García 1989: 151). The short-lived *congreso* convened throughout the Southwest until it was disbanded in 1942. Leaders did not disappear but moved into community service organizing (like Bert Corona), labor union organizing (like Luisa Moreno), and specific issues such as the Sleepy Lagoon Defense Committee (like Josefina Fierro de Bright) in defense of Mexican American youth.

A sensationalized murder trial began in 1942 after a young Chicano, José Díaz, was murdered on August 1 at Williams Ranch neighborhood (rural Los Angeles), often frequented as a swimming hole. "Sleepy Lagoon was a popular Eastside reservoir used by young Mexican Americans who were barred because of race from using the city's public pools" (Vargas 2010: 250). The trial accused a large group of youths, identified them as a gang, and eventually convicted twenty-four young men of murder or conspiracy. On appeal, the Sleepy Lagoon Defense Committee (including *Congreso* organizer Josefina Fierro de Bright, lawyer and public intellectual Carey McWilliams, community organizer Bert Corona, and executive secretary Alice McGrath) defended the legal rights of these twenty-four Mexican American youth who were framed on murder charges. As Michael Denning (1998: 18) notes: "the two years of the defense campaign coincided with a moral panic about 'Mexican crime' that swept Southern California, culminating in the 'zoot suit' race riots of June 1943." The wartime racialization of Mexican youth allowed a murder trial to take place where stereotypes of pack-animal-like Chicano street gangs were entered as evidence while Navy servicemen, with impunity only months later, summarily beat and harassed Chicano street youth who wore the fashionable zoot suits. As Eduardo Obregón Pagán (2003: 202) claims, "the work of the Sleepy Lagoon

Defense Committee represented a working experiment in interracial cooperation in the defense of cherished liberties."

In the case of Puerto Rico, the call for independence was the over-riding organizing force both on the Island and among Puerto Ricans residing in the United States. New York City became the epicenter for Puerto Rican migrants and El Barrio, or Spanish Harlem, became the neighborhood synonymous with Nuyoricans. From the outside, the com-munity was characterized as poverty-stricken, gang-infested, and crime-ridden, whereas from within, the community was much more variegated and connected with surrounding neighborhoods from the Upper East Side to Harlem.

The full-fledged movement to secure civil rights and power arose in the late 1960s as a wave of social change found expression in the net-works of organizations pre-dating the civil rights movement, and among youth who were fed up with the status quo and incremental change promised by mainstream organizations. In New York City, the Young Lords became the expression of disaffected youth seeking revolutionary change. In their "Young Lords Party 13 Point Program and Platform," they articulate the power movement that found affinities with the Black Panther Party and the Chicano-centered Brown Berets. Their platform called for an independent Puerto Rico and liberation for US-based Puerto Ricans, but it also called for global revolution.

The Young Lords Party is a Revolutionary Political Party Fighting for the Liberation of All Oppressed People

1. We want self-determination for Puerto Ricans – Liberation of the Island and inside the United States. ... Que Viva Puerto Rico Libre!
2. We want self-determination for all Latinos.... Que Viva La Raza!
3. We want liberation of all third world people. ... No Puerto Rican Is Free Until All People Are Free!
4. We are revolutionary nationalists and oppose racism. ... Power To All Oppressed People!
5. We want community control of our institutions and land. ... Land Belongs To All The People!
6. We want a true education of our Creole culture and Spanish language.
7. We oppose capitalists and alliances with traitors. ... Venceremos!
8. We oppose the Amerikkkan military. ... U.S. Out Of Vietnam, Free Puerto Rico!
9. We want freedom for all political prisoners. ... Free All Political Prisoners!
10. We want equality for women. Machismo must be revolutionary ... not oppressive. ... Forward, Sisters, In The Struggle![1]

11. We fight anti-communism with international unity. –… Viva Che!
12. We believe armed self-defense and armed struggle are the only means to liberation. …Boricua Is Awake! All Pigs Beware!
13. We want a socialist society. … Hasta La Victoria Siempre!

Point (11) identifies Che Guevara by name and point (13) gives his most famously attributed quote, which translates roughly as "until victory, always.." Point (6) is reminiscent of Martí's model of self-education that truly reflects Puerto Rican history, language, and culture. Points (1)–(3), (5), and (12) express the need for local control and self-determination for Puerto Ricans (island and mainland located), Latinos, and all oppressed peoples, even if armed struggle is necessary to achieve liberation. The racism that shaped the contours of Puerto Rican oppression are opposed in points (4) and (8). Point (4) invokes a nationalism that within the Puerto Rican context can range from an independent nation of Puerto Rico to cultural nationalism that politicizes what it means to be Puerto Rican, that is, Boricua. The Young Lords were not the only organization advocating for Puerto Rican rights; other Puerto Rican associations in the Northeast (primarily New York but also New Jersey, Connecticut, and Pennsylvania) include Fuerzas Armadas de Liberación Nacional, Puerto Rican Forum, ASPIRA, Taller Puertorriqueño, Puerto Rican Legal Defense and Education Fund (now LatinoJustice-PRLDEF), El Museo del Barrio, Nuyorican Poets Café, Hope Community, Inc., and labor union locals such as the Service Employees International Union 32BJ (property services) and 1199 (health care).

On the other side of the nation, the Southwest was experiencing an uprising of "the forgotten people" (Sanchez 1940) and the 1960s and 1970s bore witness to the rise of the Chicano Movement. Rather than one single movement, it was comprised of multiple efforts dispersed geographically. In Texas, the focus was on electoral politics and the formation of a third political party to represent the interests of Tejanos – La Raza Unida Party. The Mexican American Youth Organization organized a national convention to form the party, which was successful in local elections – first in Crystal City – and ran two Texas gubernatorial candidates throughout the 1970s (see Gutiérrez 1999, Montejano 2010). In New Mexico, the issue was restoring Spanish and Mexican land grants, which resulted in the incarceration of Reies López Tijerina, the leader of La Alianza de las Mercedes, and the ensuing armed raid on the Tierra Amarilla courthouse (Tijerina 2000). In Colorado, the Crusade for Justice, led by Rodolfo "Corky" Gonzales, partnered with La Raza Unida Party, fought for civil rights, school desegregation, housing, and community-organized self-help (Vigil 1999). In rural California, the rise of the UFW was the most publicly visible sign, as union leaders Dolores Huerta and César Chávez led strikes, pilgrimages, and boycotts to improve the lives of farmworkers (Mize and Swords 2010). In urban California, particularly East Los Angeles, the focus was on the schools and the high rates of Chicano "push-outs," which led to mass walkouts known as the L.A. Blowouts (see Muñoz 2007). Mariscal (1999) contends that if there was a unifying force that made the movement, it was anti-Vietnam War protests, under the guise of the Chicano Moratorium, which organized the largest numbers but also prompted a police backlash that resulted in the use of lethal force leading to the death of Chicano journalist Ruben Salazar (see also Oropeza 2005, Salazar 1995). The winds of change were swirling in a Mexican American context.

Even cultural expressions, which drew upon the Mexican revolution-ary art tradition, were grounded specifically in Chicano-centered issues. The art of the Chicano Movement drew upon the great mural traditions of Mexico: as the Royal Chicano Air Force artists used Aztec imagery and symbolism to represent real struggles of Chicanos in Sacramento, the Bay Area, and Oregon (Diaz 2017), the artists of San Diego's Chicano Park used similar leitmotifs to protest California Department of Trans-portation's dismantling of Barrio Logan by running Interstate 5 through the heart of the neighborhood, spoken-word artists Taco Shop Poets used the medium to address Chicano struggles, and later on the work of Judy Baca and SPARC in Los Angeles highlighted the lost histories of Mexican and Chicano presences, in relation to the city's interracial and gendered histories.

The aforementioned are just a small sample of the forms of cultural expression developed during the Chicano Movement. One of the best examples is the epic poem, entitled *Yo Soy Joaquin*, written by Rodolfo "Corky" Gonzales and eventually turned into a short movie by the UFW's Teatro Campesino director Luis Valdez. The poem begins:

Yo soy Joaquín,
perdido en un mundo de confusión:
I am Joaquín, lost in a world of confusion,
caught up in the whirl of a gringo society,
confused by the rules, scorned by attitudes,
suppressed by manipulation, and destroyed by modern society.
My fathers have lost the economic battle
and won the struggle of cultural survival. (Gonzales 2003 [1967]: 76)

It then goes on to identify the colonizer/colonized status of Chicanos by identifying with a series of historical figures: Cuauhtémoc, Nezahualcóy-otl, Moctezuma, Hernan Cortes, Miguel Hidalgo, "Morelos! Matamoros!

Guerrero!," Benito Juárez, Pancho Villa, Emiliano Zapata, Porfirio Díaz, Victoriano Huerta, Francisco Madero, Juan Diego, The Virgin of Guadalupe, Tonantzín, Diego Rivera, David Alfaro Siqueiros, José Clemente Orozco, and four Mexican American figures characterized by Anglos as bandits or murderers but recognized as Chicano tragic heroes, namely Joaquín Murrieta, Elfego Baca, and the Espinosa brothers of Colorado's San Luis Valley. "Aztlán" was reincorporated from pre-Columbian Indigenous mythology to represent the homeland of the Mexicas, the wandering tribe from the seven caves of the north, who would eventually come to settle in Tenochtitlan and rule the "Aztec" empire. Chicano claims to their Mexican homeland redefined the US Southwest as Aztlán.

For Gonzales, Chicano identity is squarely rooted in the Mexican male heroes that preceded him. It's a convoluted identity of Indigenous colonized, European colonizer, and mixed or mestizo lineages.

> The Indian has endured and still
> Emerged the winner,
> The Mestizo must yet overcome,
> And the gachupín will just ignore.
> I look at myself
> And see part of me
> Who rejects my father and my mother
> And dissolves into the melting pot
> To disappear in shame.
> ... I was both tyrant and slave. (Gonzales 2003 [1967]: 82)

Noteworthy is that this poem serves as a full-scale rejection of the assimilation paradigm. In the Southwest, all too often what it means to be "American" is to be not Mexican. Before the Chicano civil rights movement, being Mexican meant being subject to racism, violence, derogatory epithets, and segregation. Through the 1970s, often being called "Mexican" was a term of derision used by Anglos. So, to claim pride in Mexico was a call to reject the melting pot, to reject the forced assimilation many Chicanos faced in public schools where they were physically punished if they did not adhere to speaking English-only, and to reject the idea that American and Mexican were incompatible.

Politically, Gonzales' ideas in *Yo Soy Joaquin* found expression and application in the Denver Youth Conference, held in 1969, resulting in one of the founding documents of the movement: *El Plan Espiritual de Aztlán*. The seven-point plan called for unity, community control of the economy, culturally and linguistically relevant education, institutional power, self-defense, cultural identity, and political liberation.

1. UNITY in the thinking of our people concerning the barrios, the pueblo, the campo, the land, the poor, the middle class, the professional – all committed to the liberation of La Raza.
2. ECONOMY: economic control of our lives and our communities can only come about by driving the exploiter out of our communities, our pueblos, and our lands and by controlling and developing our own talents, sweat, and resources ...
3. EDUCATION must be relative to our people, i.e., history, culture, bilingual education, contributions, etc. Community control of our schools, our teachers, our administrators, our counselors, and our programs.
4. INSTITUTIONS shall serve our people by providing the service necessary for a full life and their welfare on the basis of restitution, not handouts or beggar's crumbs ...
5. SELF-DEFENSE of the community must rely on the combined strength of the people. The front line defense will come from the barrios, the campos, the pueblos, and the ranchitos ...
6. CULTURAL values of our people strengthen our identity and the moral backbone of the movement ...
7. POLITICAL LIBERATION can only come through independent action on our part, since the two-party system is the same animal with two heads that feed from the same trough.[2]

Officially anonymously authored but often credited to Chicano poet Alurista, the plan was designed to create a model of community solidarity and autonomy. It was a Chicano-centered vision in the face of an Anglo establishment that relegated Chicanos to perennial second-class citizenship. What became the most contentious outcome of the conference was the stated role of Chicanas in the movement. Maylei Blackwell, in their gender-based critique of the Chicano Movement, notes that a women's caucus was formed to discuss "the issue of the traditional role of the Chicana in the movement, and how it limited her capabilities and her development," yet when the caucus representative reported back to the full conference, they stated "It was the consensus of the group that the Chicana woman does not want to be liberated" (Blackwell 2011: 139). On the one hand, the "masculinist nationalism" of the movement precluded many options for women's participation, but on the other hand, the caucus found White feminism offered very little in terms of addressing the lived experiences and life chances of Chicanas.[3]

Yet the focus on education would find further expression in 1969 at the Chicano Coordinating Council on Higher Education (CCCHE) conference that resulted in the formation of the student organization Movimiento Estudiantil Chicano de Aztlán (MeCHA) and the manifesto

El Plan de Santa Barbara. In *El Plan*, the following preconditions were established for Chicano Studies to thrive in higher education settings:

1) admission and recruitment of Chicano students, faculty, administrators and staff,
2) a curriculum program and an academic major relevant to the Chicano cultural and historical experience,
3) support and tutorial programs,
4) research programs,
5) publications programs,
6) community cultural and social action centers. (CCCHE 1969: 10)

The lack of access to higher education for Chicanos would only be remedied by building sufficient infrastructure for full inclusion. Every conceivable aspect of higher education institutions (from admissions to curricula, student services to research and publication, and community engagement) would require fundamental transformations to address the needs of a community that had little to no presence in the nation's colleges and universities. Again, as much as inclusion of Chicanos was fought for, the status of Chicanas in *El Plan* is shockingly missing. The Plan has been criticized for leaving women out altogether. "A lack of consciousness about sexism and gender can be inferred. Sociologist Mary Pardo's analysis of 'El Plan' shows that not once did it make reference to women, female liberation, or Chicana studies. Indeed, 'El Plan' was a 'man'-ifesto" (Orozco 1997: 266).[4] The shortcomings of a male-centered Chicano Movement will be discussed in more detail in chapter 5, but to understand the masculinist and nationalist elements, it helps to know the historical context in which these ideas were constructed, often in opposition to how Anglo social science portrayed Latinos in conformance with the negative stereotypes of the times.

Culture of poverty

The scholar most responsible for solidifying the negative characterizations of Latinos is most certainly the anthropologist Oscar Lewis. Lewis first focused on Tepoztlán, a village near Mexico City that had been previously investigated by Robert Redfield. Tepoztlán began sending migrants to the low-income neighborhoods of Mexico City and Lewis saw the opportunity to extend the gemeinschaft/gesellschaft (rural/urban, community/society) thesis of Redfield by showing how urbanism and capitalism impacted the daily lives of former peasants (*campesinos*) turned slum dwellers. In their first book on their fieldwork, *Five Families*,

Lewis proposes that a culture of poverty is how peasants-turned-proletarians respond to their new surroundings. The culture of poverty exhibits forms of machismo and "lower-class values" that can be summarized as "the culture of the poor, for it has its own modalities and distinctive social and psychological consequences for its members," with "remarkable similarities in family structure, the nature of kinship ties, the quality of husband–wife and parent–child relations, time orientation, spending patterns, value systems, and the sense of community" (Lewis 1959: 16). A separate culture, often exhibiting pathological tendencies, perpetuates poverty from generation to generation. "The Mexican cultural emphasis upon male dominance and the culture of *machismo* or masculinity is reflected … in which the husband is clearly the dominant and authoritarian figure" (Lewis 1959: 29). As much as Lewis saw this as a quintessentially urban poor Mexican trait, he sought to extend his claims to other locales to demonstrate the culture of poverty was a response to economic changes.

Lewis moved his studies of Tepoztlán and Mexico City to San Juan, Puerto Rico, and New York City to make the claim that the culture of poverty transcended rural and urban, colonial satellite and industrialized metropole, Mexican and Puerto Rican, island and mainland. It was the beliefs, traditions, values, and behaviors that led to multi-generational poverty among Latinos. It wasn't capitalist inequality, colonialism, or racism that structure oppression, it was always a matter of cultural maladaptations. A distinct, separate culture was the cause and effect of poverty. This work influenced most scholars interested in Latin American and Latino affairs, and was extended to African Americans by Daniel Patrick Moynihan in his infamous report on the "Negro Family" (1965) that informed President Johnson's War on Poverty programs. Overall, the culture of poverty can be summarized as exhibiting the following seven traits:

1. feelings of hopelessness and despair that arise from success not being a reality;
2. ignorance, suspiciousness, and illiteracy;
3. generational poverty due to psychological socialization into trait (1) (basic values and attitudes);
4. psychological alienation and lack of group ties/solidarity;
5. informal organization – gangs at best;
6. no adherence to middle-class values, marriage not emphasized;
7. marginality, hopelessness, dependence, and inferiority.

Lewis' most widely read book is *La Vida* (1968), which focused on five members of the Ríos family who lived in San Juan and New York City. The family was selected not only because of the seven traits but because they were engaged in prostitution. Criticisms abound but a summary of problems with Lewis' very small, highly selective sample and his "day in the life" methodology reads as follows. "The book had an exclusive focus, obfuscated the colonial relationship, conveyed a strong sense of 'otherness,' used a deficit model, applied inappropriate contexts for analysis, generalized from extreme cases to the whole group, and depreciated the indigenous view of political events" (Rodríguez, Olmedo, and Reyes-Cruz 2003: 298). In many ways, the first scholars of Puerto Rican and Chicano Studies arose to explicitly challenge and criticize the imposition of culture of poverty stereotypes onto dynamic, complicated Latino communities.

Puerto Rican Studies

Quite contrary to the culture of poverty assertions, the first scholars in Puerto Rican studies were focused on the history of how both the island and mainland supported vibrant, even at times militant, organizations to advocate for the well-being of *puertorriquenos*. Unquestionably, the first scholar to challenge the culture of poverty thesis was University of Chicago-trained anthropologist and Puerto Rican Elena Padilla. Their *Up From Puerto Rico* and recently re-released Master's thesis on comparative migration from Puerto Rico to New York City and Chicago always carried a subtle challenge to Lewis' characterization of Puerto Ricans as stuck in a culture of poverty (Padilla 1958, 2011). Since Padilla, the subsequent focus was on how the Nuyorican community thrived in terms of cultural maintenance, well before the New York City Puerto Rican Day Parade that until recently marked the pride in and cohesion of Puerto Rican identity. Since the early part of the twentieth century, formal organizations such as voluntary associations, bodegas, and sports clubs fostered a strong sense of *comunidad* (community solidarity) and belonging. Duany (2002: 187–91) identifies the formation of the *Alianza Obrera Puertorriqueña* (1923), Porto Rican League (1923), *Liga Puertorriqueña e Hispana* (1926), *Los Jíbaros* (1928), and Porto Rican Democratic Club (1922) pre-dating the postwar Migration Division of the Department of Labor and the Department of Puerto Rican Community Affairs, which were both charged with establishing voluntary associations to facilitate the assimilation of Puerto Ricans living in the northeastern United States.

> Puerto Ricans organized themselves well before the first government agencies attempted to supervise their adjustment to mainland life. These associations reflected the migrants' diverse interests and social composition, from trade unions and Masonic lodges to baseball leagues and voting clubs. They suggest the rich texture of social life among

Puerto Ricans in the United States during the first half of the twentieth century. (Duany 2002: 191)

Often, *mutualistas* (mutual aid societies) developed along lines of solidarity to provide the social safety net not being provided by the US government. Other voluntary associations, such as local hometown associations, developed footholds in New York City to ease the transition from the island. Sánchez Korrol, in their pioneering account of Nuyorican history, identifies that after the "Great Migration" of Puerto Ricans following the interwar and postwar periods, organizations abounded to meet the needs of both island and mainland communities.

El Congreso del Pueblo, led by community activist Gilberto Gerena Valentín, represented some eighty clubs in 1956, the year of its incorporation. The hometown clubs, maintaining the same active level of sophistication prevalent in the period between the world wars, provided shelter, jobs, emergency financial help, and other social benefits. But under the umbrella of *El Congreso*, the clubs took on a broader, more militant stance and led mass demonstrations against injustice, racism, police brutality, and discrimination. (Sánchez Korrol 1983: 226).

Though most organizations sponsored by the colonial government were designed specifically to facilitate assimilation in the postwar period, many of those organizations became more militant and less accommodationist during the civil rights era. This occurred at a time when Puerto Ricans were well organized in group associations and in community celebrations via festivals and parades, and were increasingly challenging their imposed characterization as trapped in a culture of poverty, or in the new vernacular of the "underclass."

Gina Pérez' study of Chicago's Puerto Rican community demonstrates how residential mobility was based on always trying to improve living conditions while challenging the forces of displacement, underinvestment, and gentrification.

Grassroots efforts to resist these changes are constructed transnationally, as community organizers strategically deploy cultural symbols to construct a "Puerto Rican space" that preserves neighborhood use values. These efforts to deter displacement through resistance, political mobilization, and coalition-building challenge an image of the underclass that emphasizes pathological behavior, presenting instead a portrait of agency and collective action among poor and working-class Puerto Ricans whose lives are circumscribed by the politics of uneven development that increasingly define the "global city" of Chicago. (Pérez 2004: 130)

These findings of a well-organized community often exhibiting forms of agency and collective action ran contrary to the established scholarly accounts of Puerto Ricans, by mostly non-Puerto Ricans. "Between 1938 and 1972, there were a total of 20 major social science works written on Puerto Ricans [– only one written by a Puerto Rican] … The methodologies and approaches common in much of the early literature contributed to the exclusive focus on Puerto Rico and the tendency to obfuscate the colonial relationship" (Rodríguez et al. 2003: 294). The self-contained island was often defined as the source of its own problems, but when Puerto Rico was discussed as a "miracle" or "crown jewel" of the Caribbean, it was always the result of the United States' influence, and never was the Puerto Rican presence on the mainland recognized or discussed.

This "miracle" narrative culminated in Operation Bootstrap, which was designed to modernize the Puerto Rican economy by claiming the island's unique colonial status with the United States would translate into unrivaled prosperity. "Its viability rested on two inducements: industrialization by invitation or the relocation of U.S. corporate and manufacturing interests to the island in exchange for lucrative tax incentives, and a cheap Puerto Rican labor pool that was educated and Americanized" (Sánchez Korrol 1983: 215–16). Multi-year tax breaks and free land and factory buildings brought US pharmaceutical and other businesses to the island in droves. The Puerto Rican industrial economy boomed in the 1950s and 1960s.

> But in the early seventies it became clear that the Bootstrap industrialization plan also had its darker side: It never fully incorporated the island's growing population into the workforce; it displaced thousands from agrarian production and reinforced the island's dependency on the United States; and the radical decline of the island's agrarian sector had caused higher unemployment and an escalation in the importation of basic food staples. (Sánchez Korrol 1983: 217)

The unintended result was a massive migration of Puerto Ricans to the United States.

It is not coincidental that in the midst of Operation Bootstrap, there arrived on the scene a young man whose novel would come to define the dilemmas that Puerto Ricans faced navigating poverty, race, and choices in El Barrio at a time that severely constricted the range of opportunities. Piri Thomas' *Down These Mean Streets* (1997 [1967]) has become a classic: a coming-of-age memoir of the son of a Puerto Rican mother and Cuban American father who struggles to locate his Puerto Rican identity in the United States, a country that doesn't recognize him as *morenita* or as Puerto Rican but as Black. Navigating a state of constant migration (mostly within El Barrio but also to Long Island and "Down South"), survival for Thomas descends into drug addiction and eventually jail time.

> The struggle that ensues for the protagonist regards his ethnic-racialized identity in the most general way. He initially identifies as Puerto Rican but is in his immediate social environment racialized as an African American because of the color of his skin. For the better part of the text, these two ethnic-racialized identities sit in tremendous tension. Piri himself does not know what he "is," since he is constantly dispossessed of the agency that might allow him to name himself. Can he, the text repeatedly asks, reasonably claim an African American *and* a Puerto Rican identity in the United States of the 1950s? (Viego 2007: 2)

The roots of Boricua Studies can be found in a group of scholars who analyzed Puerto Rican communities that settled in New York City (Sánchez Korrol 1983), Chicago (Padilla 1985), Hartford, Connecticut (Cruz 1998), and Philadelphia (Whalen 2001). Over time, there was a focus on Puerto Rican popular culture (Aparicio 1998, Flores 2000, Negrón-Muntaner 2004) and colonial citizenship (Cabán 2001, Dávila 1997, Denis 2016, Duany 2002, Meléndez 2017, Ramos Zayas 2003). One center, beyond all others, established research programs on Nuyorican and mainland identities and experiences. Better known simply as El Centro, the Center for Puerto Rican Studies/Centro de Estudios Puertorriqueños was formed in 1973 to bring together community activists, faculty, and students in New York City to foster research on the Puerto Rican experience in the United States. El Centro's first director, Frank Bonilla, would later co-establish the first consortium of Latino research centers (more in chapter 4) but they also maintained active research agendas in Brazil, Latin America, Puerto Rico, the Caribbean, and the United States focusing on Latinos. The focus of El Centro varied but its centerpiece contributions, due to its original director and current director Edwin Meléndez, have been in the areas of political economy and development theories, poverty and well-being, the effects of colonization, migration, and struggles for independence and political incorporation. In 1992, the Puerto Rican Studies Association for Research Advocacy and Education (PRSA) was founded and their symposia and conferences continue the legacy of Bonilla by focusing on lingering central issues since El Centro's founding and new areas of interdisciplinary inquiry.

Bonilla always asked big questions and one of their major themes can be found in a title of an Inter-University Program for Latino Research (IUPLR) working paper they frequently presented, "Brother, Can You Paradigm?" (1997). They saw Puerto Rican and Latino Studies as offering completely new paradigms to the way we think about nations, citizenship, and belonging. "Events of the 60s and 70s shook the prevailing assimilationist orthodoxy, leading its principal exponent to propose adjustments in the 'paradigm' to take into account types and degrees of assimilation along with continuing conflict and class inequality as lasting features of interethnic relations" (Bonilla 1985: 148). Well before the field shifted away from primarily historical analyses of Puerto Rico's Great Migration, from the end of World War I to the post-World War II waves, Bonilla had the prescience to foresee the nascent civil rights and power movements as key topics of analysis for Puerto Rican Studies' policy implications and community relevance.

Memoirs and scholarly accounts of the Young Lords Party have been recently published. For about a decade, Miguel "Mickey" Melendez' *We Took the Streets* served as the sole first-person account of the Young Lords Party in New York. More recently, Enck-Wanzer (2010), Young Lords Party and Abramson (2011, updated from the original 1971 account), and Morales (2016) have further expanded our knowledge base about women's roles in the Young Lords Party, differences between Chicago and New York chapters, and the social support services they provided to their communities. "[T]he Lords significantly disrupted a symbolic economy founded on the stigmatization of Puerto Ricans as both criminally inclined and politically docile. In the process, the Young Lords transformed not only how the world saw Puerto Ricans but also how they saw themselves" (Negrón-Muntaner 2015: 6).

Chicano Studies

Similarly, the Chicano Movement fundamentally transformed how Chicanos saw themselves: no longer as "foreigners on their own land" but as reclaimers of Aztlán, the mythical homeland of the Mexica that would come to be known as Chicano country – but with the twist that US institutions would need to be reconfigured and reimagined to house this emerging political force. *El Plan de Santa Barbara*, with its blueprint for Chicano inclusion in higher education, operated with pride in an identity all too often maligned by Anglos.

Chicanismo draws its faith and strength from two main sources: from the just struggle of our people and from an objective analysis of our community's strategic needs. We recognize that without a strategic use of education, an education that places value on what we value, we will not realize our destiny. Chicanos recognize the central importance of institutions of higher learning to modern progress, in this case, to the development of our community. But we go further: we believe that higher education must contribute to the formation of a complete man who truly values life and freedom. (CCCHE 1969: 9–10)

Chicanismo was extended into the formation of the first Chicano Studies programs, whose faculty met in subsequent years to develop a *concilio* and expand the field. "These institutes [at California State University Long Beach, Arizona State University, and University of Colorado Boulder] led to the formation of El Concilio Nacional de Estudios Chicanos, which provided a response to the practical problems that had resulted from the growth of Chicano Studies programs and the limitation with *El Plan*" (Soldatenko 2009: 43). Limitations centered on a fairly undeveloped curriculum plan and an incipient understanding of what made Chicano Studies an interdisciplinary, if not transdisciplinary, approach rather than simply Chicano History or Chicano Literature or Chicano Sociology. As Acuña (2011: 95) notes, one of the largest Chicano Studies Departments – California State University, Northridge (CSUN, known then as San Fernando Valley State) – rejected the model imposed by the CCCHE, as this Valley State curriculum was deemed "too nationalistic and directed them to abolish their mariachi classes and other Mexican cultural classes."

The conjoined criticisms of cultural nationalism and sexism would plague the field for decades. As late as the 1980s, Chicano Studies was a predominantly male-dominated field and women's issues were relegated to a single chapter or section that read and felt like afterthoughts. A premier collection of literary essays edited by Anaya and Lomeli, entitled *Aztlán: Essays on the Chicano Homeland*, included Alurista, Rudolfo Anaya, Luis Leal, J. Jorge Klor de Alva, and Ramón Gutiérrez to cover a wide swath of topics: myth, identity, Aztlán as homeland, relations with Puerto Rican nationalism, and Indigenous mythology.[5] Only one woman is included in the collection, Gloria Anzaldúa, and their essay is heavily based on their *Borderlands/La Frontera: The New Mestiza* (1987). Their conclusion is very much a rupture with the rest of the collection, an intervention to call out Chicano history and literature depicted as de-gendered or male-centered.

La mojada, la mujer indocumentada, is doubly threatened in this country. Not only does she have to contend with sexual violence, but like all women, she is prey to a sense of physical helplessness. As a refugee, she leaves the familiar and safe homeground to venture into unknown and possibly dangerous terrain.

> This is her home
>   this thin edge of
>   barbwire. (Anzaldúa in Anaya and Lomeli 1989: 203)

More about Anzaldúa's influence in chapter 5, but at this stage it is key to point out that Chicanas' experiences simply could not be reduced to Chicano nationalism due to the double threat of sexism and racism. Myth, identity, and homeland are recognized as sites of both resistance and oppression.

Acuña's *Occupied America: A History of Chicanos* (2014) is the touchstone for Chicano Studies textbooks on how Chicano Studies was formed, taught, and understood. The core content of the book, now in its eighth edition, remains essentially unchanged: the state geography chapters (on Texas, New Mexico, Arizona, and California) in part I are nineteenth-century history, while what changes is the substantive twentieth-century chapters, sometimes arranged by periodization (Depression, World War II) or by decade, on the topics of immigration, labor, community and resistance, politics, and recent developments. What is interesting is how the architecture and theoretical apparatus of each edition change with the times, and how a textbook initially charged with applying internal colonialism to the Chicano experience morphed into using the Mexican underclass approach in the third edition (1988) and, more recently, early world systems theory in the twenty-first-century editions. *Occupied America* has changed with the times to reflect the shifting underpinnings of Chicano Studies.[6] The textbook can be read as a rejection of how American History was taught to exclude Chicanos as well as direct criticism of how higher education viewed Chicanos from the early 1970s to today.

The internal colony thesis stems from Robert Blauner's (1972) *Racial Oppression in America*. Mario Barrera, Rudy Acuña, and Tomás Almaguer picked up on the concept and applied it to Chicano communities. The internal colony distinguishes White European immigrants from racialized minorities and the social processes that similarly situate the Third World internationally colonized from the internally colonized. The United States "owes its very existence to colonialism, and ... along with settlers and immigrants there have always been conquered Indians and black slaves, and later defeated Mexicans – that is, colonial subjects – on the national soil" (Blauner 1972: 52). In their criticism of the internal colony model, Cervantes notes the logical response to international colonialism is anti-colonial, nationalist liberation movements. "Consistent with this application, those who subscribe to the internal colonial model have examined the Chicano Movement with a view toward demonstrating the bases of contemporary Chicano nationalism" (Cervantes 2003: 334). An actual Chicano nation certainly never came to fruition and rarely was nation-building a Chicano Movement goal. Adherents of internal colonialism have waned and each of the previously mentioned authors no longer see the internal colony analogy as a particularly useful analytic, but it clearly provided a great improvement over how Mexican Americans were viewed in pre-Chicano Movement scholarship.

Nick Vaca (1970a, 1970b) surveyed the literature from 1912 to 1970 and found scholars consistently defined Anglo–Chicano and US–Mexico relations, and the resultant inequality, in terms of cultural differences, psychological predispositions, biological inferiorities, the Spanish language as a handicap, and stereotypes (such as laziness, drunkenness, low intelligence, and proneness to criminal activity). They summarize that

> cultural determinism again afforded the scientific evidence to place blame for poor academic achievement upon the shoulders of the Mexican-American. With biological determinism the source of the ill was as being "in the blood"; with cultural determinism it was seen as part of the *internalized* cultural heritage. In either case the generating source was seen as internal to an individual, and thus the individual's own fault. (Vaca 1970b: 21)

Importantly, during this time a lone voice, according to Vaca (several voices in actuality), was challenging these stereotypes and forms of determinism – longtime University of Texas Professor George I. Sanchez. I have argued elsewhere that Sanchez held his own cultural determinist views of Mexican immigrants (see Mize 2016b: 35–7), but he nevertheless was a fierce advocate for Mexican Americans and his work in concert with other, earlier progenitors of Chicano Studies, including Cary McWilliams (public intellectual and advocate), Paul S. Taylor (labor economist of Mexican migration), Manuel Gamio (originator of the life story method), Americo Paredes (Tejano borderland folklorist), Ernesto Galarza (public intellectual and labor organizer), and Julian Samora (first Chicano sociologist), represents voices opposing the racism endemic to the mainstream social science scholarship of the times.

Chicano Studies developed in response to this scientific racism by focusing first on community formation and strength in California and Texas, and to a much lesser extent Arizona and New Mexico, with the remainder of Aztlán ignored. Barrera (1989) analyzed the Southwest as a whole whereas Almaguer (1994) focused on the state of California. These place-based histories often began after the Treaty of Guadalupe-Hidalgo and ended at the very latest with World War II. In California, East Los Angeles (Griswold del Castillo 1980, Romo 1983, Sánchez 1995), Corona (Alamillo 2006), and Santa Barbara (Camarillo 1979) received early and important treatments. In Texas, state-level analyses abounded (see de León 1983, Foley 1999, Montejano 1987), but local histories of El Paso (García 1981, Perales 2010), San Antonio (Montejano 2010), and South Texas (Foley et al. 1988) were also important.

Beyond the two states, historians have explored Chicano history of the border (Martínez 2006), early Indigenous/–Spanish colonial relations in New Mexico (Gutiérrez 1991), and rural areas of mining and agricultural communities on the Front Range of Colorado (Deutsch 1989). Key contributions that take a less place-based approach but rather focus on labor segments where Chicana/os predominate include histories of cannery work and labor organizing (Ruiz 1987, Zavella 1987), domestic service or maid industry (Romero 1992), and factory production (Vargas 1999). One rationale for why the early histories all stopped at World War II is provided by Balderrama and Rodríguez (2006), who identify events of the Great Depression – what they refer to as the Great Repatriation – that serve as a natural stopping point. In their *Decade of Betrayal*, they trace the events that led to Mexicans being identified as the cause of the Great Depression and the resultant government-backed mass repatriation program that resulted in millions of Mexican immigrants and US citizens of Mexican ancestry being indiscriminately deported.

From its origins, Chicano Studies deeply interrogated the relationship between race and class (see Almaguer 1994, Barrera 1989, Foley 1999, Montejano 1987) and early Chicana studies pioneers also introduced gender analyses (see Baca Zinn 1993, Romero 1992, Ruiz 1987, Segura 1993, Zavella 1987). The professional association representing Chicano Studies was initially formed in 1972. "The association's most recent organizational name change took place in 1995 during the NACS annual conference held in Spokane, Washington. The membership voted to rename the association the National Association for Chicana and Chicano Studies, in recognition of the critical contribution and role of Chicanas in the association" (NACCS n.d.). Part of this recognition was also based on longstanding, and often ignored, demands by Chicanas who challenged the sexism and cultural nationalism of the professionalization of early Chicano Studies. MALCS (Mujeres Activas en Letras y Cambio Social) was founded in 1983 to center Chicana feminist experiences within Chicana/o Studies.

Much like the developments in Puerto Rican Studies, a renewed focus on the Chicano Movement as a site of inquiry can be found in more recent books by movement leaders turned scholars. Carlos

Muñoz' (2007) *Youth, Identity, Power* was one of the first to analyze the Chicano Movement through the lens of education in California, where the demonstrations analyzed by Muñoz included ones he himself participated in or led. Similarly, Ernie Vigil was a veteran leader of the Crusade for Justice in Denver, Colorado, and has written the definitive history of the organization (Vigil 1999). Autobiographies, or *testimonios*, by Reies Tijerina (2000), Bert Corona (García 1995), Cesar Chavez (2008), Dolores Huerta (García 2008), and José Angel Gutiérrez (1999) give readers a front-row seat on how events unfolded. Finally, analyses by Montejano (2010) and the many collected works edited by Mario T. García, including that of fallen journalist Ruben Salazar (1995), retain a prime focus on the movement through male eyes.

Conclusion

Puerto Rican and Chicano Studies arose out of the civil rights and power movements to challenge the culture of poverty lens and stereotypes that predominated in how both communities were portrayed in the scholarly literature. While their cultural nationalisms and machismo proved difficult to dislodge, an early experiment in what would eventually become Latina/o Studies can be found in a short-lived academic/creative arts journal. *Revista Chicano-Riqueña* was an interesting venture in bringing together Chicana/o and Boricua Studies. The special issue on *La Mujer* (1978, 6 (2)) features poems by María Herrera Sobek and twelve other *poesias*, followed by *prosias* (prose essays) by Sylvia Lizárraga and Norma Alarcon in Spanish, English, and Spanglish. Those are accompanied by a photo essay, book reviews (*reseñas*), and a *critica*. The dynamic range of creative output, coupled with the coming together thematically on *la mujer*, prefigures the "Telling to Live" collaborative to be discussed in chapter 5, and clearly identifies the long history of bringing women's issues into the fields since nearly their origins.

According to the National Association for Chicana and Chicano Studies (NACCS), there were 45 Chicano Studies programs,[7] 3 Puerto Rican Studies,[8] 1 Central American Studies, and 28 Latino Studies[9] offering at least an undergraduate major as of 2007 (the latest update) in higher education institutions in the United States. Though under constant threat, the institutionalization of Chicano, Puerto Rican, and Latino Studies represents a huge victory that can be traced all the way from the self-education appeals of Jose Martí to the "13-Point Program and Platform" of the Young Lords and *El Plan de Santa Barbara*.

4

The Arrival of Latina/o Studies: Bringing in Central American, Cuban, and Dominican Studies

Though it is important to note that the two precursors to Latina/o Studies are Puerto Rican and Chicano Studies, the question quickly becomes: what about the other seventeen nations of Spanish Latin America that send immigrants to the United States? Aren't they Latino too? The answer is obviously yes, though the scholarly literatures to answer this question are still very much in development. In this chapter, we will see that within Puerto Rican Studies units and scholarship there was the arrival of Dominican Studies, and within Chicano Studies there was the arrival of Central American Studies. Jorge Duany (2008 [1994]) in Puerto Rican Studies and Rodolfo Acuña (1998) in Chicano Studies are among the first to introduce the experiences of Dominicans, Guatemalans, and Salvadorans into their respective fields' discussions. Another strain to be considered is how the full-fledged arrival of Latina/o Studies developed from experiences not traditionally addressed in Chicano and Puerto Rican Studies. The early work of Felix Padilla (1985), studying Chicano and Puerto Rican synergies in Chicago, began discussions of a truly Latino political consciousness. Current analyses of Latinidad, as mentioned earlier, provide a strong basis for Latina/o Studies as a full-fledged field both distinct from and an integral part of Puerto Rican and Chicana/o Studies. Yet none of these developments would have occurred if it had not been for the efforts of Frank Bonilla and the institutionalization of Latina/o Studies efforts he led.

As mentioned previously, Bonilla was the original director of El Centro, the Center for Puerto Rican Studies at the City University of New

York. El Centro developed a research team system with Bonilla creating and often leading task forces, such as those focused on "History" and "Prison." Bonilla and his colleagues' efforts led to both academic and community-based outcomes. The History Task Force eventually released the full-length analysis of Puerto Rican migration and development in *Labor Migration under Capitalism* (1979). The Prison Task Force developed and implemented a prison college-level study program in New York State. One of Bonilla's tasks was to work with other Latino research center directors to create the Inter-University Program (IUP) with Albert Camarillo at Stanford University, Gilberto Cárdenas at the University of Texas at Austin, and Juan Gomez-Quinones at the University of California, Los Angeles (UCLA). The IUP added "Latino Research" to its name to become IUPLR.

> As Director of IUPLR, Bonilla was the principal coordinator of the project entitled, "Latinos in a Changing U.S. Economy." The multinational team he assembled tracked the impact of international, national, and regional forces in shaping labor force participation and earnings of Latinos in the U.S.[1]

That task force resulted in the publication of *Latinos in a Changing U.S. Economy* (Morales and Bonilla 1993). The focus on political economy can very much be credited to Frank Bonilla. The IUPLR, currently directed by Maria de los Angeles Torres, is housed at the University of Illinois at Chicago and is constituted by twenty-three research centers, academic departments, and the Smithsonian Latino Center.

Bridges to Latina/o Studies

Originally published in 1994, Jorge Duany's *Quisqueya on the Hudson: The Transnational Identity of Dominicans in Washington Heights* (2008) coincided with the inauguration of the Dominican Studies Institute of the City University of New York (CUNY DSI), founded and originally directed by Silvio Torres-Saillant. The analysis of transnational Dominican immigrants residing in the Washington Heights neighborhood of New York City (north of the upper West Side of Manhattan) was a first of many firsts: the first study of Dominicans from a scholar best known for their contributions to Puerto Rican studies, the first publication from the CUNY DSI, and certainly the first study of transnationalism linking the Dominican Republic to New York City.[2] The following five findings summarize the ethnographic study:

1. The cultural values and practices of Dominican immigrants in Washington Heights are primarily oriented toward the Dominican Republic.
2. The Dominican community of Washington Heights has created a transnational identity as a result of migration and resettlement in a new environment.
3. Dominican popular culture expresses a vibrant ethnic identity, through everyday language, music, religion, and foodways.
4. Dominican immigrants have reshaped the symbols of their nationality into an ethnic culture on the margins of mainstream U.S. culture.
5. Most Dominican immigrants in Washington Heights resist assimilating into mainstream U.S. culture, and remain attached to their home language and culture. (Duany 2008 [1994]: 31).

The formative monograph on Dominican transnationalism both helped to create the field of Latino Studies, with a specialization in Dominicans, and identified what would become the neighborhood with the largest concentration of Dominicans outside the Dominican Republic.

On the West Coast, Chicano historian Rudy Acuña identified changes to historically Chicano communities of Los Angeles in work that would eventually lead to Central American Studies. In their fourth edition of *Occupied America*, Acuña notes how Central Americans fleeing civil war and violence were rarely extended refugee status if the party in charge was defined by the 1980s Reagan administration as US allies. For Salvadorans and Guatemalans, war did not translate into permanent residency status, so much of the impetus for legalization from the Central American immigrant population arose out of these particular circumstances. Acuña estimates that 300,000 Salvadorans and 50,000 Guatemalans had settled in Los Angeles by the mid-1980s.

> The area where Salvadorans live in LA is one of the city's most crime-ridden areas and one of the nation's most densely populated. Near MacArthur Park, there are as many as 147 people per acre – or four times the average density of Manhattan and ten times that of Los Angeles as a whole. Many families are crammed into ramshackle apartment buildings and residential hotels. However, about 70 percent of the 15,000 Salvadorans polled said they are not going back. (Acuña 2014: 429)

As Guatemalans and Salvadorans received refugee status at a rate of only 2–3 percent, whereas Nicaraguans received refugee status at a rate of about 80 percent, the crowding that this former Chicano neighborhood experienced with the Salvadoran influx put the marginalized experiences of Central Americans on the Chicano Studies map, thus leading to Latina/o Studies.

Central American Studies

The first studies of Central Americans (almost always Salvadorans and Guatemalans) were rooted in the context of migrants fleeing violence and civil war. Hamilton and Stoltz Chinchilla, in their pioneering studies, note Central Americans "differ from many other immigrant groups in that they are neither strictly economic migrants nor accepted as refugees, but have the characteristics of both" (2001: 2). Many years after their initial study (Hamilton and Stoltz Chinchilla 1991), the debate over who is an economic migrant and who is a political refugee basically locked Central Americans into this perennial question. Most of these ensuing questions revolve around conditions of migration, though very few are about conditions of settlement. And all too often, when comparisons are invoked, it is most often vis-à-vis Mexican immigrants.

Subsequent work by Cecilia Menjívar notes:

> The discrepancy between the conditions of war and violence that many Salvadorans left in their homeland and their official reception as economic migrants [not political refugees] by the U.S. government shaped the questions in early studies of Salvadoran migration ... Thus scholars of Central American migration in general, and of the Salvadoran case in particular, focused on the root causes of these flows and the political forces that shaped them. (Menjívar 2000: 6)

Menjívar goes on to discuss the eligibility for benefits, size of population, sanctuary movement, and incorporation as areas of inquiry once the field took settlement seriously. "Thus, Central Americans' labor force participation became an important emphasis, as did issues of settlement, community formation and intraethnic conflict, acculturation, and adaptation" (2000: 7).

Interestingly, the reigning debate at the time on the relevance of social networks in relation to upward mobility was seriously upended by these scholars' research. In many ways, the case of Salvadoran immigrant settlement demonstrates just how badly networks operate in the process of settlement, even when they are the major impetus for migration. "This study examines the effects of the receiving context on the dynamics of informal networks, taking into account internal social differentiation such as gender and generation to present a more nuanced account of the inner workings of the [Salvadoran] immigrants' social worlds" (Menjí-var 2000: 9). The expansion of focus to take into consideration gender, citizenship, and generation is a key indicator of what the field currently encompasses.

As a result of the difficulties of settlement as either undocumented or recipients of temporary protected status, another related push for legalization came from the situation faced by many Central American immigrants (predominantly from El Salvador and Guatemala but also from Nicaragua and Honduras) during the Reagan administration. Reagan's foreign policy was based on the "domino" theory, which posited that communist movements in particular nations of the Third World would have the effect of pushing other nations along the same path of communist revolutionary movements, rejecting capitalism as the mode of development. The Reagan administration went to great pains, covert and overt, to fund and arm political regimes supportive of US corporate interests and capitalist ideologies by quashing radical insurgent movements in Central America.

> Today, it is clear that the consistency of U.S. support for military regimes and dictatorships across the region of Central America and the Caribbean played a major role in the creation of diaspora communities across the U.S. that can trace their origins to the Cold War, a period that spanned the end of World War II through the collapse of the Soviet Union in the early 1990s. (Guerra 2016: 128)

As people fled the civil wars and violence, only those who supported capitalism and US aims but were living in socialist nations were given refugee status. Those attempting to escape state-sponsored death squads and violence in El Salvador and Guatemala were deemed economic migrants due to their governments' favorable status with the Reagan administration.

The result was a sizable group of US citizens who challenged foreign policy and the selective application of immigration and refugee laws by providing sanctuary for those fleeing the violence of US-sponsored military regimes. The sanctuary movement was an organization of approximately 200 churches, often supported by Latino-serving organizations similar to the community service organization (CSO) developed by Bert Corona (mentioned in chapter 3), some universities and university towns, and eventually the state of New Mexico when then-Governor Toney Anaya declared it a sanctuary. The idea was based upon the biblical scripture of using the church to provide safe passage for those persecuted under unjust and oppressive laws. The leaders of the movement contended that the Reagan administration was defying not only the 1951

United Nations Convention and Protocol on Refugees but also the 1980 US Refugee Act, which committed the United States to provide refugee status for those with a "well-founded fear of persecution" or whose "life and liberty would be threatened." The selective application of this refugee status determination was based almost wholly on nation of origin and whether the current administration of that nation was on good terms with the current US administration or not. In addition, refugee status did not translate into permanent residency status, so much of the impetus for legalization from the Central American immigrant population arose out of these particular circumstances.

Very much in its incipient phase, the institutionalization of Central American Studies has been recently inaugurated at CSUN with the very first Central American Studies department offering an undergraduate major. In some ways, the department was spun-off from Chicano/a Studies at CSUN, which is likely the largest department in the United States.

> The Central American studies program was established in 2000 to recognize the large and growing Central American community in the United States ... CSUN has one of the largest populations of Central American students in the country, with nearly 4,000 students born in Central America or with immigrant parents. Most of the students are Salvadoran or Guatemalan ... Douglas Carranza, chair of the department, ... said the department has a trifold mission: to empower the large and growing Central American community in the U.S. by promoting academic excellence, community involvement and cultural diversity; to open spaces of global citizenship and dialogue between academia and society that contribute to the construction of a Central American identity; and to promote an understanding and appreciation of the diverse Central American cultures, ethnicities, experiences and worldviews from an interdisciplinary, global perspective. (Morgan 2015)

Arias (2003) notes the difficulty of conceptualizing Central American studies or a hyphenated identity of Central American-American when not only national origin but also internal differentiation (based on politics, race, colonial history, etc.) make it so very hard to conceptualize who fits under the Central American umbrella, unless it is simply a shorthand for Guatemalan or Salvadoran.

> We cannot even speak of "Central America" without running the risk of a greater homogenization of national identities than is truly the case in the region. Central American migration to the United States

includes, after all, a heterogeneous array of social groups, among which we can name anti-Sandinista Nicaraguans, small groups of Hondurans and Costa Ricans, as well as Indigenous, Afro-Caribbean and "Ladino" (mestizo) sectors from each of these nations. This does not take into account Belizeans and Panamanians, who have a greater degree of integration with African-American and Afro-Caribbean US populations as opposed to Latinos. (Arias 2003: 172)

Recent issues of the journal *Latino Studies* feature sections on Central Americans' centrality to the field in terms of bringing unique insights to immigration studies, social networks, US immigration enforcement and foreign policies, trauma, Indigenous and Afro-Latino studies, US anxiety, cultural productions, lived experience, and political participation (Arias and Milian 2013, Baker and Hernandez 2017, Menjívar 2017). As we will discuss later, how Latina/o Studies is conceptualized informs debates about Central American, South American, and other regional markers of identity that only make sense in a US reception context, if they make any sense at all.

Cuban American Studies

Cubana/os: always characterized as the exception to the rule, the quintessential political migrants – deemed refugees or exiles, rarely immigrants. Fitting the Cuban American experience into Latina/o Studies is only difficult if one assumes there is one, unitary Cuban experience. As scholars from historian Maria Cristina García to political scientist María de los Angeles Torres attest, those assumptions could not be more misplaced. In *Havana USA*, García (1996) offers a nuanced, historically informed analysis of three waves of Cuban refugees and notes, at the time of their writing, a subsequent, fourth wave of working-class Afro-Cubans who collectively questioned the automatic social mobility of the enclave. "Emigrés of the first wave (1959–1962), disproportionately White and middle class, will find it difficult to relate to the new immigrants, whom they consider rough, poor and uneducated. The fact that many of the new immigrants are black or of mixed racial heritage, and were once the faithful revolutionary proletariat, widens the cultural chasm" (García 1996: xi). They observe that third wave Marielitos (referring to the Mariel Boatlift) and an emerging fourth wave of *balseros* (a derisive term used to often refer to Afro-Latino Cubans) found a very different reception upon arrival than the first-generation Cubans, who were welcomed with open arms and pocketbooks by the US government. The larger migration patterns followed four very discernible stages where race relations in Cuba became mapped onto the US color line. The first to leave during the Revolution were the big business owners, hotel and tourism managers, government leaders, wealthy landowners, and other elite that were not sympathetic to communism, and were direct targets of Castro's military forces. Miami became the major recipient but other cities played host to this group with high levels of economic and social capital. Following the White elite, the middle class (teachers, professionals, managers) who did not want to live under Castro also left and settled in the Miami neighborhoods of Little Havana and Hialeah.

The promise of return, of toppling the Castro regime with US assistance and returning the Cuba-of-old to its former glory, held sway for so long in so much of the exile community that permanent US settlement politics were always eclipsed by events on the island. The Cuban Adjustment Act of 1966 and the Refugee Act of 1980 gave Cubans fleeing the Castro state-socialist regime comparatively easy entry to and refugee status in the United States. In response to the fourth wave – what until recently was the policy known as wet foot/dry foot – Cubans interdicted in the waterways of the Florida straits would be returned to Cuba, whereas those who made it to US soil would be eligible for refugee status. The uniqueness of US policies favoring Cuban exiles compared to other Latinos, with the exception of Nicaraguan refugees who also settled in Miami after fleeing the socialist Sandinistas, often translates into either a foil for comparison (to blame other Latinos for their poverty or settlement problems) or difficulties fitting Cubans' different political orientations, US reception contexts, and worldviews with other Latino groups.

Exile politics have transformed over the decades, particularly with the role of a second generation who only know Miami as their home and who have pursued a very difficult politics of settlement compared to their parents, who more often pursued exile politics of return. As early as the 1970s, de los Angeles Torres (2001) notes, a pluralization of exile politics, in relation to Cuba, began to surface with some exiles openly advocating for lifting the trade embargo, normalizing relations with Cuba, and visiting the island.

More complicated and nuanced histories of arrival, settlement, and internal differentiation are building on earlier studies to define Cuban American Studies today. An interest in the resettlement of unaccompanied children, prompted by the 2000 case of Elián González, has resulted in a focus on the events of Operation Pedro Pan (Peter Pan) and the clandestine transportation of thousands of Cuban children to the United States during the early part of the Revolution. The children were consistently used as pawns in the geopolitical Cold War battle between the United States and Cuba.

The U.S. origins of the children's exodus were part of a massive covert program aimed at overthrowing the Cuban revolution. This program included provisions for immigration and evacuation of agents. The U.S. government, mainly through the CIA, ran visa waiver programs. These programs relied on historically unprecedented relationships with private and religious refugee relief organizations; one Catholic priest was given the power to issue blanket visa waivers to any Cuban children under sixteen. All this was to be temporary until Castro's government was overthrown and the children returned to their parents, many of whom were underground fighters. The invasion failed, but the secret immigration mechanisms were left intact until 1962, when the United States ordered a quarantine of the island and halted all flights. By that time, over 14,000 unaccompanied refugee minors had entered the United States. (de los Angeles Torres 2004: 250–1)

When the children grew up and years later temporarily returned to Cuba to improve relations, they found themselves used by the Cuban government to demonstrate the depths of US imperialism and Cuban exile complicity.

Never able to escape anti-Castro politics, the attempts to institutionalize Cuban American Studies has struggled in places such as the University of Miami. There, exile community members called out the supposed ouster of the director of the Institute for Cuban and Cuban American Studies (ICCAS) when the university purportedly attempted to bypass the Institute to initiate scholarly exchanges with universities in Cuba. In 1991 Florida International University (FIU) founded the Cuban Research Institute, currently directed by Jorge Duany, who was born in Cuba but raised in Puerto Rico and Panamá, and is "dedicated to creating and disseminating knowledge about Cuba and its diaspora."[3] FIU states that it has the largest number of undergraduate students of Cuban origin of any university outside Cuba.

Negotiations with members of the exile community and the scholarly demands of transnational inquiry are often at odds. Does one conduct research in Cuba? Does one take a political stance on Castro or the CIA? The difficulties of reconciling generation, politics, class distinctions, location, history, and even family place many Cuban American scholars in positions that other Latina/o Studies scholars may not have to reconcile.

Dominican Studies

Due to the early focus on transnationalism, the study of emigrants from the Dominican Republic, who are as a whole fairly recent migrants, continues to develop the various facets of transnational ties. In addition to those who move fairly often and regularly between two nations (transmigrants), in-depth analyses of dual citizenship and of core and expanded forms of transnationalism include studies of entrepreneurship/ institutions, political activity (e.g., with candidates running for office in the Dominican Republic campaigning in Washington Heights), remittances (social and economic), and religious practices. The first studies of Dominican immigrants to Boston or New York all recognized that return migration, continued ties between nations, and the forces of globalization are making the immigrant experience markedly distinct from that of prior generations. Based on the cities under investigation, all too often in these early studies the reference points are earlier waves of European immigrants (Duany 2008 [1994], Grasmuck and Pessar 1991, Levitt 2001, Pessar 1996). It really is not until the work of second-generation Dominican scholars that we begin to see questions of central relevance to Latina/o Studies being asked.

The key book to asking new questions is *Black Behind the Ears* by Ginetta Candelario. As Candelario notes of the Duany study (see p. 47), their research team imputed race by classifying respondents as White, Black, or Mulatto based on "the researchers' own observations of their phenotypes. A footnote to this single reference to racial identity called for further investigation of how racial terminology and perception change on migration" (Candelario 2007a: 11). This set the stage for an analysis of the racialization of Dominican immigrants.

"For much of Dominican history, the national body has been defined as not-black, even as black ancestry has been grudgingly acknowledged. In the place of blackness, officially identity discourses and displays have held that Dominicans are racially Indian and culturally Hispanic" (Candelario 2007a: 2). Anti-Haitian sentiment is key to this characterization as often what it means to be Dominican is not to be Haitian. From the Dominican dictator Rafael Trujillo's *blanqueamiento* (the campaign, beginning in 1937 with the Haitian border massacre, to "Whiten" the island by forcing Haitians out of the nation by deportation and violence) to more recent border battles and the rescission of Haitian descendants' citizenship (as late as 2014), anti-Blackness very much informs Dominican identity. How ironic, given the large portion of the population that have direct African slave ancestors, a rate that has been estimated at over 90 percent. One of the most interesting elements of Candelario's work is the distributed field sites where they trace discussions of racial identity. "This book is about Dominican identity discourses that negotiate blackness and Hispanicity in four related and mutually referential cultural sites of identity display – travel narratives, the museum, the beauty shop, and the female body – in three historically connected geographic locations (Santo Domingo, New York City, and Washington, D.C.)" (Candelario 2007a: 6). Race is not only commemorated and politicized but also experienced in daily living and emplotted onto bodies.

The institutionalization of Dominican Studies, like that of Central American Studies, is very much a singular story from an institutionalization perspective. The CUNY DSI, currently directed by Ramona Hernández, was founded in 1992 after pressure from the Council of Dominican Educators. Frank Bonilla, then director of El Centro, was one of the key actors who pressed for the Institute. A prolific center, it has become the hub for Dominican Studies (within both the United States and the Dominican Republic but also encompassing the worldwide diaspora of Dominicans).

South American Studies

There are no institutional centers, institutes, or departments dedicated exclusively to the experiences of emigrants from South America. Often housed in Latina/o Studies departments, South American Studies lacks specific institutional recognition. In one of the first chapter-length reviews of the "other other Hispanics," Marilyn Espitia (2004: 259) offers this characterization: "South American Latinos originate from a total of nine distinct countries: Argentina, Bolivia, Chile, Colombia, Ecuador, Paraguay, Peru, Uruguay, and Venezuela." The US Census refers to all non-Mexican, non-Puerto Rican, and non-Cuban Latinos as "other Hispanics." A 2007 book, with basically the same title, devotes its last section to an extended discussion of Brazilian immigration (Falconi and Mazzotti 2007).

South Americans in the United States on average have the highest levels of education among Latino groups, are often middle-class or wealthy, are recent immigrants, and are not geographically concentrated into specific neighborhoods, cities, or states to the same degree as, say, Cubans in South Florida or Dominicans in Washington Heights, Manhattan. As Michael Jones-Correa (2007: 28) notes: "Not only are most of the Other Latinos still first-generation immigrants, but most are also quite recent arrivals." As a result, the focus on South Americans within Latina/o Studies is still very much in its incipient phase and will only increase in prominence as South American communities coalesce around transnational community formation (given the high rates of dual citizenship), political incorporation (given the high rates of voter turnout among those who qualify to vote), and embodying Latinidades in daily experiences.

The Arrival of Latina/o Studies

From the story of the founding of Central American, Cuban, and Dominican Studies, it should be clear that many actors from Chicano and Puerto Rican Studies assisted in their development to culminate in a full-fledged Latina/o Studies experiment. Latino Studies, in its thinnest definition, incorporates national-origin specialists to offer a variegated picture of who Latinos are, including their transnational, mixed race, and comparative contexts. Folks like Acuña, Bonilla, and Duany are central to adding new Latino communities into the established fields. Recent institutionalizations by the Latina/o Studies Association have led to national conferences beginning in 2014. The IUPLR hosts biannual scholarly conferences, in addition to events such as the Latino Art Now! Conference in 2016, to establish a Latina/o presence in both scholarly and art worlds.

Recent contributions to Latina/o Studies are best encapsulated in encyclopedia projects edited by (1) Vicki Ruiz and Virginia Sánchez Korrol (2006), *Latinas in the United States: A Historical Encyclopedia*; (2) Suzanne Oboler and Deena González (2005), *The Oxford Encyclopedia of Latinos and Latinas in the United States*; and (3) Oboler and González (2015), *The Oxford Encyclopedia of Latinos and Latinas in Contemporary Politics, Law, and Social Movements*. The first included 580 entries on Latina history, the second contained 900 entries, and the third included 450 entries. These encyclopedias set the terrain for the field, identify established and emerging topics and themes, and are key to establishing the field of Latino Studies for future scholars. The scholarly journal *Latino Studies* was edited by Suzanne Oboler for years and is now edited by Lourdes Torres at DePaul University, which also hosts the *Diálogo* journal edited by Elizabeth Martinez' Center for Latino Studies. Cabán (2003: 6) in *Latino Studies* asserts:

> Latino Studies has evolved from its insurrectionary and somewhat turbulent origins as Chicano and Puerto Rican Studies into its current incarnation as a multidisciplinary academic field that explores the diversity of localized and transnational experiences of Latin American and Caribbean national origin populations in the United States ... I draw a distinction between Latino Studies as a field of study and Latino Studies as an academic unit of instruction and research in the university.

All too often, "Latino" Studies stands in for one national-origin group as if the experiences of Colombians, Mexicans, Ecuadorians, Salvadorans, or Guatemalans stand in for all Latino groups. Frankly, this tends to happen most often when Anglo social scientists study "new" destinations. Or, it comes from often Latino social scientists who are from a minority Latino community within a larger, more prevalent community (say, Cubans or Salvadorans studying a predominantly Mexican destination or Dominicans studying a predominantly Puerto Rican destination).

The list of titles specific to Latinos in the United States is not expansive but recently is growing. Currently, the major introduction into Latino Studies is *The Latino/a Condition*, co-edited by Richard Delgado and Jean Stefancic (2010). Touted as the definitive introduction to Latinos, the book is unfortunately very specific to the Mexican American experience and there are only a handful of examples from other Latino groups. Similarly, the collection edited by Daniel Arreola (2004), entitled *Hispanic Spaces, Latino Places*, is touted as a definitive introduction to Latino communities yet is too heavily Mexican-centric to be broadly construed as Latino. A dearth of actual plurality in deploying Latino Studies is often in evidence in the burgeoning literature introducing Latinos and their relation to relevant topics such as identity, social movements, education, and popular culture. Puerto Rican and Chicano Studies tend to predominate in the major texts purporting to be Latino Studies.

Vázquez and Torres (2003), in *Latino/a Thought*, expand their focus to the largest three Latino groups – Mexicans, Puerto Ricans, and Cubans – and note: "The need remains for chronological-thematic texts that adequately and specifically address the political thought of many other Latino/as who are also in the United States as a result of geopolitical-economic forces that have affected their countries and who are also in a quest for public citizenship: Dominicans, Ecuadorians, Salvadorians, Colombians, Nicaraguans, Panamanians, Chileans, and many others from the Americas" (2003: 2). Sáenz and Morales (2015) expand their histories from three to the seven largest Latino populations in the United States (adding the Dominican Republic, El Salvador, Guatemala, and Colombia to the largest three).

Many of the edited collections designed to introduce Latina/o Studies concur with two major figures in the field: "Latina/o Studies emerged from social movements and political struggles rather than from a purely cerebral rumination about what was needed in the academy … And this tie to Latina/o communities with accountability to their social needs and struggles has remained a central philosophical tenet of the field to the present day" (Flores and Rosaldo 2007: xxi). Their *Companion* to the field is broken down into: *Vidas*, centered on the telling of life stories; *Actos*, advocating certain critical practices or methods; and *En La Lucha*, addressing institutional struggles in the production of knowledge (Flores and Rosaldo 2007: xxvi). Juan Gonzalez (2011), in their best-selling history of Latinos, breaks their book down into three parts: Roots (*Las Raíces*), Branches (*Las Ramas*), and Harvest (*La Cosecha*). From historical to contemporary, all authors note the complexity of telling the full plurality of Latina/o and Latin American experiences. Key topics have begun to emerge in the telling of these stories: Latinos' "divergent backgrounds, modes of integration, and their experiences in this country" with the issues of "migration; demographic patterns and processes; education; labor force participation; income and poverty; housing; health; religion and religiosity; political participation and activism; the politics of identity; gender, sex roles, and feminism; sexuality; Latina/os in the media; and cultural production" (Rodríguez, Sáenz, and Menjívar 2007 xxi).

When Latina/o Studies is more than simply an amalgamation of disparate national-origin groups, Latinidades identify the places where Latina/os come together in their daily lived experiences. This does not occur everywhere, due to the US penchant for segregation, even within the Latino category, but in specific spaces where disparate Latina/o groups come together, scholars have come to understand those daily relations as embodying Latinidades. The first to point this out is Felix Padilla (1985) in their pioneering research on Puerto Ricans and Mexicans in Chicago who together developed a Latino political consciousness.

Some of the most interesting manifestations of Latinidad or panethnic Latino identities are formed when different national-origin communities find themselves experiencing the United States together. Mize and Peña Delgado (2012: ch. 2) situate Latinidades in a framework to understand: (1) the shared legacy of Spanish colonialism and US imperialism, (2) imposed definitions of Hispanic or Latino labels, (3) traditional and new Latino destinations, (4) Latino politics, and (5) intra-Latina/o relations in daily lived experiences. Alvarez (2013), a Dominican immigrant from New York City, details the affinities constructed between them and the Mexican custodians working at the University of Colorado while they were a graduate student. In this case, they offer this definition: "Latinidad: people of Latin American descent 'coalesce' into a unified 'place' in which we feel connected to each other across time, geography, and language" (Alvarez 2013: 51).[4] Ethnographic research by Ricourt and Danta (2002: xi) documents "*convivencia diaria*, or 'daily-life interaction', in apartments and houses, on the streets, in stores, in workplaces, and in churches ... creating a unique Latino panethnic community." The shared public spaces of streets, schools, social service organizations, and parks are connected to the private spheres of residences, workplaces, churches, bodegas, and other ethnic shopping strips in shaping how these daily interactions develop a strong grassroots sense of Latinidad among Columbians, Ecuadorans, Chileans, Salvadorans, Venezuelans,

Argentineans, Bolivians, Uruguayans, Cubans, Dominicans, Puerto Ricans, and Mexicans living together in the Corona neighborhood of the borough of Queens. "As a multi- and interdisciplinary site of academic inquiry, Latina/o Studies examines the multiple factors that affect the everyday lives of US Latina/os. Such heterogeneity challenges scholars to find new, interdisciplinary approaches that can address our multiple and shifting realities" (Aparicio in Flores and Rosaldo 2007: 39). The contributions of Latina/o Studies were greatly expanded by the focus on gender and sexuality, which is the center of attention in the next chapter.

5

Latina Feminism, Intersectionalities, and Queer Latinidades

When Latinas claimed their rightful place within Latina/o Studies and, in response, organizations such as NACCS explicitly recognized the contributions of Chicanas, the field fundamentally changed. The shift was marked by an acknowledgment of the field's origins but always with an eye to ending the repetition of committing the sins of old and to leaving past mistakes behind, often through a thorough analysis of what went wrong. The designation "Chicano" quite effectively summarizes the earlier divides between cultural nationalists who saw their vision of Chicanismo as the pathway to enlightenment and revolution and those whose experiences (based on gender, sexuality, citizenship status, etc.) were left out from this unitary signification. The origins of the term "Chicano" are unknown but the connotation of the term prior to its invocation during the Chicano Movement was derogatory, as a signifier of poor, working-class Mexicans. It was a term internal to the Mexican community that still carries this negative connotation among some older Mexican Americans and throughout Mexico. What it meant to members of the Chicano Movement was a reclamation of a term that identified and affiliated with Mexicans living in poverty. The struggle waged by predominantly university student activists was to be one with *la comunidad pobre*. Some of this identification was organic in that a significant portion of the participants in El Movimiento were former farmworkers or first-generation college students with families squarely rooted in other working-class occupations. But for others who were cemented in the Hispanic middle class and "found" their Chicano roots during their college years, the term was intended as a means of crossing class divides in mutual opposition to Anglo racial oppression (however, not necessarily in opposition to Anglo capitalism). An early criticism was voiced by two leading Chicana studies scholars, Angie Chabram and Rosa Linda Fregoso.

> The shortsightedness of Chicano studies intellectuals was that they assumed that the construction of their own self-representations as subjects was equivalent to that of the totality of the Chicano experience, and that this shared representation could be generalized in the interests of the entire group. This myopia did not permit them to see that this new representation would be alien to other Chicana/os who had their own self-representations, their own forms of practices and resistances. (Chabram and Fregoso 1990: 206)

In particular, representations of "the Chicano" tended to be highly restrictive by excluding Chicana women and queer folks, recent Mexican immigrants, and Mexican Americans who did not agree with the Movement's ideals. As Maylei Blackwell (2011: 93–4) notes: "Ultimately, we can understand nationalism as a signifying practice of political meaning-making rather than strictly as a narrowly defined ideology. Thus, the Chicana feminist critique of nationalism should be understood as a critique both of the ideology and of the way the cultural logic of nationalism was used to legitimate the patriarchal abuse of power and authoritarianism." In this chapter, we discuss the reclamation of lost voices who define Latina Studies. From there, we identify advances in theorizing gender and sexuality from Latina subject positions. The social locations of Latinas are the foci of Latina social scientists and historians who analyze women's roles and gender relations. Finally, we see how queer Latinidades are reconfiguring discussions of gender and sexuality in Latina/o communities.

Reclamations/*Recuperaciónes*

One of the untruths that defines colonized history is the claim that Latinas did not contribute to the development of Latin American or Latino literary thought. If a lineage is identified, it is either that of great political theorists such as Martí or Bolívar (see chapter 2) or that of distinguished authors such as Octavio Paz, Carlos Fuentes, and Gabriel García Márquez. History and literature are not simply the sole voices of men, no matter how much those great men may protest. Part of the work undertaken by Latina Studies contributors is that of feminist reclamation: reclaiming the lost voices of Latinas, writings that were driven into obscurity. These voices include, in terms of Mexico's history, the overlooked contributions of Doña Maria/La Malintzin/La Malinche as an active agent in Spaniard–Indigenous first contact, Jovita Gonzalez as Tejana border folklorist, María Cristina Mena as the first Chicana author, María Amparo Ruiz de Burton as the first Latina author writing books in English, Sor Juana Inés de la Cruz as colonial-era feminist philosopher, and Juana Belen Gutiérrez de Mendoza as feminist journalist during the Mexican Revolution (Cotera 1997: 41). Collectively, they testify to the lost history and voices of Mexican women from the Spanish colonial to the US imperialist eras. In Puerto Rico, Lola Rodríguez de Tió (first female poet of Puerto Rico), María Bibiana Benítez (author of *La Ninfa de Puerto Rico* [The Nymph of Puerto Rico]), Alejandrina Benitez de Gautier (author of *Aguinaldo Puertorriqueño* [Ode to Puerto Rico]), Luisa Capetillo (feminist author and labor activist), Ana Roque de Duprey (founder of *La Mujer* magazine), and Julia de Burgos (nationalist poet) also point to the need to reclaim women's voices lost in the history of Puerto Rican independence movements. It is all the more important to note that early women writers in Latin America persisted despite the lack of access to formal education for most women and the resultant low literacy rates among Latin American women.

The revived, exalted status of La Malinche (the Indigenous woman, alternatively referred to as Doña Maria and La Malintzin, who served as informant and forced lover to the leader of Spanish conquistador Hernán Cortés) by Chicana scholars is one example of elevating mestiza formations. It runs completely counter to how male intellectuals in Mexico (in particular, Octavio Paz) have portrayed La Malinche as the traitor responsible for the downfall of the Indigenous population of Mexico, or as the Indigenous woman responsible for the "death of the Indigenous race." For instance, Chicana feminists have identified how La Malinche was abandoned by her family, developed multilingual proficiencies to serve as translator, and navigated complex social relations by strategically developing a close relationship with Cortés (a good brief summary can be found in Ramírez 2009: 38–9). From these reclamations, we can see how Latinas have been at the forefront of generative women of color feminist interventions.

New directions/*Direcciones nuevas*

Though some Latina feminist work looks back in history to reclaim lost voices, other authors write to stake claims to their place in the present and prefigure future directions in Latina and Chicana feminist thought. Key literary contributions include Gloria Anzaldúa's *Borderlands/La*

Frontera, Cherríe Moraga's *Loving in the War Years*, Sandra Cisneros' *The House on Mango Street*, *Woman Hollering Creek*, and *Caramelo*, Ana Castillo's *So Far from God* and *Massacre of the Dreamers*, Lorna Dee Cervantes' *Emplumada*, Julia Alvarez's *How the Garcia Girls Lost Their Accents*, C. Cristina Garcia's *Dreaming in Cuban*, Esmeralda Santiago's *When I Was Puerto Rican*, and Helena Viramontes' *Under the Feet of Jesus* and *Their Dogs Came with Them*. Each of these books develops themes that inform our understanding of life filtered through Latina eyes, with frankly too many themes for this short introduction. In their stead, we will focus on themes developed in an influential trilogy of edited collections that are also central to understanding Latina contributions to and shaping of women of color feminism: *This Bridge Called My Back* (Moraga and Anzaldúa 1981), *Making Face, Making Soul: Haciendo Caras* (Anzaldúa 1990), and *This Bridge We Call Home* (Anzaldúa and Keating 2002).

One angle on the unifying thread of these collections is referred to by editor Cherríe Moraga as a "theory in the flesh" (Moraga and Anzaldúa 1981). The idea succinctly summarizes that philosophical concepts, ways of thinking, worldviews, and theories are based first and foremost on daily living and our full sensual responses to the systems of oppression that govern daily lives and have a direct and physical impact on our bodies.

> A theory in the flesh means one where the physical realities of our lives – our skin color, the land or concrete we grew up on, our sexual longings – all fuse to create a politic born out of necessity. Here we attempt to bridge the contradictions in our experience:
> We are colored in a white feminist movement.
> We are the feminists among the people of our culture.
> We are often lesbians among the straight.
> We do this bridging by naming our selves and by telling our stories in our own words. (Moraga and Anzaldúa 1981: 23)

This Bridge Called My Back brought together what we refer to today as women of color feminism in one collection that featured poets, scholars, and essayists that questioned both White-woman-centered feminism and the patriarchal, heterosexist, heteronormative practices within racialized groups. Edited by Cherríe Moraga and Gloria Anzaldúa, the collection recognized many of the women of color writers who were ignored by White feminist and ethnic nationalist publication outlets. As Aurora Levins Morales notes in conclusion to their essay pondering internationalism: "*A revolution capable of healing our wounds. If we're the ones who can imagine it, if we're the ones who can dream about it,* if we're the ones who need it most, then no one else can do it. *We're the ones*" (in Moraga and Anzaldúa 1981: 56).

The collection is not content to simply identify Latinas or women of color in the here and now; there is a distinct call for future envisionings and possibilities. The vision for the future is identified as "*El Mundo Zurdo*, the left-handed world; the colored, the queer, the poor, the female, the physically challenged. From our blood and spirit connections with these groups, we women on the bottom throughout the world can form an international feminism" (Moraga and Anzaldúa 1981: 196). Although the language used to include people with disabilities is dated, there is a distinct call here by US-based feminists of color to reach out to those similarly situated in the Global South and seek forms of global solidarities from the bottom.

The characterization of the Third World, often using phrases such as "Third World feminism," is incredibly dated and shockingly uniform in its depiction by First World writers. Regardless of their intent to seek solidarity, they have not taken on Trin T. Minh-ha's (1989) challenge to seriously consider that "there is a Third World in every First World, and vice versa." What Chela Sandoval (2000) refers to as "U.S. Third World feminism" is much more aptly named "postcolonial or transnational feminism" in its global context and "women of color feminism" in the US context. Building solidarities is still very much a work in progress.

Making Face, Making Soul/Haciendo Caras, edited by Gloria Anzaldúa, was released in 1990 as the follow-up to *This Bridge* with the wistful admonition to the publishing industry that nothing further had been published in the interim. The organization of the essays was in seven parts: (1) the wounds and scars of racism; (2) combating racism, sexism, and internalized violence; (3) love, humor, and optimism; (4) singing our songs in the face of silencing and repressing; (5) women of color as artists, writers, and intellectuals; (6) alliances; and (7) critical theories of consciousness and occupying spaces. The tone in 1990 was an explicit critique of the massive denial of racism in what was often defined in the United States as a "color-blind" society. This is best captured by poet Lorna Dee Cervantes (Anzaldúa 1990: 4) in "Poem for the young white man who asked me how I, an intelligent, well-read person, could believe in the war between races."

> I believe in revolution
> because everywhere the crosses are burning,
> sharp-shooting goose-steppers round every corner,
> there are snipers in the schools ...
> (I know you don't believe this.)

You think this is nothing
but faddish exaggeration. But they
are not shooting at you.)

It might seem odd in the era of President Trump that folks in the 1980s and 1990s were claiming that we had reached a post-racial society, that the words of Martin Luther King – to explicitly reject and challenge racism based on color – would be defined as the main mode to deny the existence of races and therefore racism (the twisted logic that provides the basis for color-blind racism). Cervantes' poem pierces through the veneer that we have solved our racial dilemmas and moved past race. The images of White supremacists burning crosses, neo-Nazi marching "goose-steppers," and snipers in schools reflect not only an African American experience but also Latino lived realities.

This Bridge We Call Home, edited by Gloria Anzaldúa and AnaLouise Keating, was published in 2002. What can be considered the third in a trilogy, the essays in *Home* take a decidedly different tack.

> In these pages we move from focusing on what has been done to us (victimhood) to a more extensive level of agency, one that questions what we're doing to each other, to those in distant countries, and to the earth's environment ... Twenty-one years ago we struggled with the recognition of difference within the context of commonality. Today we grapple with the recognition of commonality within the context of difference. (Anzaldúa and Keating 2002: 2)

Making connections, finding common cause, within an intersectional framework, the most recent collection identifies the interconnectedness of the world through global ecological degradation and the forces of globalization, but also on a much more transcendental level. There is certainly a spiritual turn that marks the third anthology: whether it be a spiritual envisioning of future possibilities or a spiritual linkage to the past, often in the form of revisionist mythologies of Mexica goddesses Coatlicue, Coyolxauhqui, and Xochiquetzal.[1]

> Like Coyolxauhqui, let's put our dismembered psyches and patrias (homelands) together in new constructions. It is precisely during these in-between times that we must create the dream (el sueño) of the sixth world. May we allow the interweaving of all the minds and hearts and life forces to create the collective dream of the world and teach us how to live out ese sueño. May we allow spirit to sustain and guide us from the path of dissolution. May we do work that matters. Vale la pena, it's worth the pain. (Anzaldúa 2015: 22)

In Mexica and Mayan cosmologies, there is not one world but five marked by the passing of five suns; the present moment, *el quinto sol*, will require transcendence to a "sixth world" that is comprised of new imaginings, new ways of living, new *sueños* (dreams). The difficulties that lie ahead in forging *el mundo zurdo* invoke the pain and suffering referred to in the former collections.

Yet Anzaldúa always looks forward and throughout the corpus of their writings, from two children's books to their posthumously published dissertation (Anzaldúa 2015), consistently roots future possibilities in what flowered most fully in *Borderlands/La Frontera*, articulated as mestiza consciousness. The new mestiza consciousness is *"una conciencia de mujer*. It is a consciousness of the Borderlands" (Anzaldúa 1999: 99). Those borderlands are physical and place-bound but they are also internalized and imaginary in the consciousness of Latinas. Whether internal or physical, borders are horribly devious in their consequences.

> *Una lucha de fronteras/*A Struggle of Borders
> Because I, a *mestiza*,
> continually walk out of one culture
> and into another,
> because I am in all cultures at the same time,
> *alma entre dos mundos, tres, cuatro,*
> *me zumba la cabeza con lo contradictorio.*
> *Estoy norteada por todas las voces que me hablan*
> *Simultáneamente.* (Anzaldúa 1999: 99)

Entering multiple worlds, head spinning in the confusion of contradictions and the simultaneous voices to be spoken, Anzaldúa recognizes the conflict and struggle of borders that inflict damage but also result in forms of polyvocality. Negotiating multiple cultures and often serving as the bridge among them, Latinas are traversing multiple intersectionalities that likely result in simultaneously navigating multiple identities and boundaries.

Central to Anzaldúa's traversing of borders and negotiating identities is their sexuality.

> When a "lesbian" names me the same as her, she subsumes me under her category. I am of her group but not as an equal, not as whole person – my color erased, my class ignored ... Call me de las otras. Call me loquita, jotita, marimacha, pajuelona, lambiscona, culera – these are words I grew up hearing. I can identify with being "una de las otras" or a "marimacha," or even a jota or a loca porque – these

are the terms my home community uses. I identify most closely with the Náhuatl term patlache. (Anzaldúa 2009: 163)

The difficulties of conceptualizing identity in its intersectional forms is in no way comparable to the difficulties of living multiple, intersecting identities of marginalization. Anzaldúa notes that the name "lesbian" is not only based in English but also rooted in White, economically privileged lesbian life experiences. She identifies more with many terms used in a derogatory manner in Spanish, yet self-defines with the non-derogatory, non-judgmental Náhuatl term "patlache" to invoke connections with a spiritual past and to reflect new future possibilities.

Analyses/*Análisis*

Theorizations from Latina perspectives certainly reflect the valuable contributions of the collections trilogy and of literary works, but additionally, a body of research and analysis has been developed by Latina social scientists and historians to capture the contemporary lived experiences of Latinas and their historical contributions. Many of these latter contributions have been summarized in *Latinas in the United States: A Historical Encyclopedia*, which "focuses on how Latinas have shaped their own lives, cultures, and communities through mutual assistance and collective action and how our understanding of pivotal events ... becomes transformed when they are viewed through women's eyes" (Ruiz and Sánchez Korrol 2006: xv). Building the field of Latina history relies initially on encyclopedias such as this one because there are simply not enough scholarly outlets to capture the diversity of historical experiences and historiographical approaches that have emerged since the 1980s. The very first monograph in Chicana history was published by them in 1987.

The origins of the field can be traced to the first book by Vicki Ruiz, really an innovator in Latina history, and their co-edited women of color anthology *Unequal Sisters*, now in its fourth edition, prefaced as a "multicultural women's history text." The most recent edition (Ruiz and DuBois 2007) includes key contributions in Latina history from Devra Weber, Miroslava Chávez-García, Virginia Sánchez Korrol, Alicia Schmidt Camacho, James Brooks, and Vicki Ruiz. Together, they collectively place the variegated histories of Latinas into a larger re-telling of US history. "Sexuality and power drive much of recent Chicana historiography and yes, there exists a significant body of critical scholarship that can, indeed, be characterized as distinctly Chican*a*, emphasis on the feminine *a*" (Ruiz in Flores and Rosaldo 2007: 173).

The result is a revisiting of conventional stories told in Chicano history and a completely new set of understandings when women are centered in the analysis. A great example is Catherine Ramírez' *The Woman in the Zoot Suit* (2009). Writing on what has been one of the quintessentially male topics in the literature, Ramírez' inventive work problematizes the "forgotten gender" in World War II-era zoot suit or *pachuca* culture. They note the reason for the exclusion is that "while the el *pachuco* could be and was incorporated into cultural nationalist ideology as a father, son, or brother, la *pachuca* was excluded because of the ways she articulated a dissident femininity, female masculinity, and, in some instances, lesbian sexuality, consequently threatening the heteropatriarchal family" (Ramírez 2009: 110–11).

In sociology, two collections interrogate contemporary Latina lived experiences: *Challenging Fronteras* (Romero, Hondagneu-Sotelo, and Ortiz 1997) and *Women and Migration in the U.S.–Mexico Borderlands* (Segura and Zavella 2007). As the editors of the earlier book note, "The intersectionality of race, ethnicity, class, and citizenship affects individual consciousness, intra- and inter-group interaction, and each group's access to institutional power and privileges" (Romero et al. 1997: x). Though gender and sexuality do not enter into the intersectional frame in the editors' description of the anthology, gender figures prominently in each of their own work (Romero's *Maid in the U.S.A.* [1992], Hondagneu-Sotelo's *Gendered Transitions* [1994], and Ortiz's coauthored *Generations of Exclusion* [Telles and Ortiz 2009]), and part four of the collection, "Paid and Unpaid Work: Negotiating Gender Relations," highlights several key contributions on gender roles, work–life balance in dual earners' families, and the politics of work and family for garment workers. The latter volume presents "a binational approach that would include structural forces and women's agency as well as incorporate U.S. and Mexican perspectives on women on either side of the U.S.–Mexico border" (Segura and Zavella 2007: 2). The development of Latina history and social sciences deepens the analytical contributions of academic disciplines to Latina/o Studies while keeping the focus on gender relations and the better understanding of not only Latinas but also the social relations they occupy.

Institutionally, the national organization MALCS provides a venue for the field to continue to progress and evolve over time.

This organization of Chicana/Latina women in higher education was founded in 1983 at the University of California, Berkeley. MALCS's charter and activities demonstrate familiarity with Chicana concerns, a feminist orientation, and sensitivity to cultural concerns. Each year MALCS organizes a four-day summer institute which includes panels on Chicana research and workshops on Chicana empowerment. (Pesquera and Segura 1997: 299)

Queer Latino Studies and QTPOC critique

From the previous section, it is clear that both gender and sexuality play major roles in reshaping the field of Latina/o Studies. From the perspectives of gay, lesbian, queer, and trans Latina/o subject positions, revisiting the notion of Latinidad is one of the driving theoretical contributions in the elaboration of queer Latindades. Queer, trans, people of color (QTPOC) studies are forthcoming in book projects and dissertations in process that will reshape the field in the coming years. José Esteban Muñoz (1999: 7–8) draws a clear line of inspiration for their work on emergence and disidentifications from Moraga and Anzaldúa's *This Bridge Called My Back* as well as Chicana "identity-in-difference" proponents Chela Sandoval and Norma Alarcón. Queer theory posits that identity is not fixed but rather a set of performances cohering around differences that either conform to heteronormative standards for subjects or constitute emergent disidentifications, "survival strategies the minority subject practices in order to negotiate a phobic majoritarian public sphere that continuously elides or punishes the existence of subjects who do not conform to the phantasm of normative citizenship" (Muñoz 1999: 4). Whereas Muñoz (1999, 2009) roots queer Latinidad in utopian visions, identifying a politics of envisioning possibilities, Juana María Rodríguez (2014) roots their analysis of sexual futures in sovereignty debates and plebiscite votes (for statehood, continuing commonwealth status, or independent nation-state) in Puerto Rico, sex and mambo dance, and sexual fantasy (pornographic representations, performance art, other porn archive examples) along the US–Mexico border. The complex interplay between Latinidad and queering sexual desire and identities has provided the material for sophisticated philosophical analyses by both scholars. Muñoz (2009: 18) "offers a theory of queer futurity that is attentive to the past for the purposes of critiquing a present." Referring to Kevin McCarty's portraits of empty club performance stages, particularly at La Plaza – a queer bar in Los Angeles – leads to the conclusion that "the aesthetic fuels the political imagination" (Muñoz 2009: 106). The aesthetic dimension is all too often ignored in politics, and yet from Muñoz' account, it is precisely at the visual, artistic, and aesthetic levels that futurities of Latinidad are envisioned.

In general, the ways in which queer Latinidades are conceptualized is directly related to whether queer individuals, folks, or communities are conceived of as distinct from society or aiming at integration.

"Integrationist accounts of queer theory ... attempt to respond to the challenges posed by the multiplicity of identity that separatist accounts avoid ... integrationists advocate for queer theory as a way to address the multiple relations among race, gender, class, and sexuality" (Hames-García 2011: 24). For instance, in the conversation around gay marriage, the integrationist approach would attend to differences between Latino and White gay men's views toward same-sex marriage. In contrast, a very general call for same-sex marriage or, similarly, a call to transcend misogynistic institutions (like the very institution of marriage), in order to form different social formations and reconceptualize intimate partner relations along polyamorous or radical sexual politics lines (regardless of race or class), would espouse more separatist views. "The proponents of separatist accounts for queer theory focus on the articulation of sexuality (sometimes, but not always, understood as only lesbian or gay sexuality) as distinct from gender, race, and class" (Hames-García 2011: 22).

The individualism that deeply informs not only some approaches to queer studies, but often White queer studies more generally, is very different than queer Latindades, which more often define identities as social relations and queer culture as collectivities. As Rodríguez (2014: 11) notes of José Esteban Muñoz' work, "Muñoz counters the antisocial impetus with a queer articulation of utopia that is always on the horizon and decidedly committed to futurity and 'an understanding of queerness as collectivity' ... Muñoz connects sociality to futurity, where sociality becomes the means and the condition for the possibility of collective futures." The varieties of approaches and empirical referents can be thought of along the lines suggested in table 5.1.

Since the majority of queer Latinidades are analyzed along the sociality/collectivity dimension, an example may help to illuminate how this approach operates. In Karma Chavez's *Queer Migration Politics*, the understanding of social relations and sociality is understood in terms of coalitional activist politics. "[C]oalition enables a different understanding of activists' rhetorical intervention as they discover and innovate responses – creative and sometimes mundane – to predominant rhetorical imaginaries" (Chávez 2013: 7). With the goal of creating more livable

Table 5.1 Queer theory and positioning Latinidad

	Anti-relational/Singular	Sociality/Collectivity
Separatist		
Integrationist		

Source: Author's own

worlds by centering queer migrants in often disparate and disconnected politics of queer activism and immigrant activism, coalitions serve the purpose of challenging anti-immigrant or xenophobic politics. "Queer women of color feminist approaches begin from the flesh to explicate the present conditions of material and symbolic oppression. From that realistic place, those explications aid in using available material resources and available means of persuasion to enact social change" (Chávez 2013: 149). The focus is on the quotidian, the daily practices of resistance to acts of oppression, from mundane to exceptional. From the building of protective mental armor to on-the-ground community activist responses to heteropatriarchal, neoliberal nativism, connecting the struggles of marginalized groups is a primary aim of undocuqueer (discussed in the next section) and related QTPOC politics.

Finally, Hurtado and Sinha (2016) and Guttman (2006) offer more nuanced understandings of masculinity in Latino culture. The long-standing stereotype of Latino men as exhibiting machismo is challenged by the heterogeneity of men's responses to gender roles. Guttman roots their analysis in the experiences in Santo Domingo, Mexico City, whereas Hurtado and Sinha focus on Latino men in the United States. They state,

> Examining the views of gay Latino men toward gender is especially important, given the manner in which culturally dominant forms of masculinities function in the United States. Because of their sexuality, gay men are many times explicitly excluded from the category of "real" men ... [G]ay men are subordinated to heterosexual men and relegated to an inferior social position because of their sexuality; race, ethnicity, and social class can further complicate this ranking. (Hurtado and Sinha 2016: 12–13)

I am not sure that "ranking" is the best way to conceive of privilege and oppression in the formation of intersectional identities, but their main point that social inequalities are manifested along lines of sexuality is a useful line for future inquiry.

Conclusion

Though it may appear, based on the above presentation, that the focus of Latina feminist theory and queer Latinidades is more abstract, I end the chapter with two direct applications of the ideas developed above. The first is in relation to a major change that occurred early in the development of the Young Lords Party. Negrón-Muntaner (2015: 18) notes that the presence of women in the Young Lords Party had a major impact in terms of both governance and guiding philosophy. One of the key manifestations was rewriting point number (5) of the thirteen-point program.

> By June 1970, the Young Lords' women won a series of victories that substantially altered their status ... Among these were the elevation of two women [Denise Oliver-Velez and Gloria Fontanez] to the central committee and other positions of power, and the complete overhaul of point number 5 in the party program, the only item that the Lords amended while an active organization. Whereas before the Young Lords argued in their platform that "machismo must be revolutionary and not oppressive," the new point number 5 now read: "We want equality for women. Down with machismo and male chauvinism" ... For the Lords' women, rationale for the amendment was simple. In the words of [Denise] Oliver[-Velez], "machismo was never gonna be revolutionary. Saying 'revolutionary machismo' is like saying ... 'revolutionary racism'."

The fundamental shift in politics, from venerating machismo to equality for women, is more than mere semantics. The shift represents a major, early contribution to intersectional politics that centered Puerto Rican struggles in gender and race while fundamentally shifting the power dynamics away from reinforcing misogyny and patriarchy.

Thinking on the politics of intersectionality today finds its boldest and clearest statement in the undocuqueer movement, consisting of social media campaigns, activist art, and on-the-ground protests and organizing. The artist behind the "I Exist" collection, Julio Salgado, titles each poster in the collection "I am undocu-queer."

> Immigration and LGBTIQ [Lesbian, Gay, Bisexual, Transsexual, Intersex, and Queer] issues are controversial topics that have gained prominence in political and social circles throughout the nation and at the ballot boxes. These are not parallel movements, but intersecting ones in the fight for social justice. This is true for those who are undocumented and identify as queer, but also for those who are in one or the other (or neither) because of the interconnectedness of all those fighting for human rights.[2] (Julio Salgado 2012)

It is precisely at the intersections that contemporary politics finds expression. One of the art projects by Salgado (a set of posters, sometimes assembled by Salgado's internet fan base) is on *lotería* cards (essentially Mexican bingo with cultural referents), to connect with Latina/o communities familiar with the game, but the images can also be found on billboards. Social media are the main venue for the movement, and the images have their own life online and connect members via the hashtag #undocuqueer. The movement, very much in formation, is currently working on DREAMer rights campaigns (named after the failed bill and Obama-era executive order that provided deportation relief or Deferred Action for Childhood Arrivals [DACA]) and highlighting the vulnerability of queer undocumented immigrants currently undergoing deportation hearings.

6

Latina/o Cultural Studies: From Invisible to Hypervisible

A 2016 University of Southern California Annenberg School study of inclusion in television and film, entitled *Inclusion or Invisibility*, notes that only 5.8 percent of roles with speaking parts are filled by Latinos (Smith, Choueiti, and Piper 2016: 7). They refer to media as perpetually "whitewashed," and in summary, "our findings show that an epidemic of invisibility runs throughout popular storytelling" (Smith et al. 2016: 9). As the media become the only reference point for the racial diversity of the nation, in a largely segregated society, representation that accurately reflects demographic composition truly matters. As the mass media continue to equate "typical Americans" with Whiteness, the lack of accurate representation impacts Latinos in particular due to their relatively recent growth as the nation's largest minority in addition to a longstanding complete lack of representation, accurate or not. This chapter focuses primarily on Latina/o representations in popular culture. The juxtaposition of invisibility with hypervisibility allows Latina/o Studies scholars to sift through hegemonic representations of Latina/o stereotypes and make sense of how mass-mediated significations are received by audiences and countered by Latina/os.

Hyper(in)visibility

When Latinos are visible, they are often hypervisible when representations coincide with negative stereotypes. For many years, the only Latinos who were widely recognized in scholarly works were in a burgeoning set of studies on youth gangs. Gangs invoke the negative stereotypes of Latinos as prone to crime, drugs, and illicit behaviors. The main representation of Latinos in popular culture was a gang culture inhabiting urban ghettos. Recall that *West Side Story*, the first motion picture associated with Nuyoricans, is a story about two warring gangs – Sharks and Jets. Gangs and crime are hypervisible in, among others, Piri Thomas' *Down These Mean Streets* (1997 [1967]), James Diego Vigil's *Barrio Gangs* (1994), Philippe Bourgois' *In Search of Respect: Selling Crack in El Barrio* (2003), Luis Rodriguez' *Always Running* (2005), Martin Sanchez-Jankowski's *Islands in the Street* (1991), and Victor Rios' *Human Targets* (2017) and *Punished* (2011). Many of these books are most often trying to dispel myths and negative stereotypes to identify that gangs are not what they seem: gangs often involve a great deal of social organization and integration, and offer alternatives to poverty in a context where extra-legal means are one of very few methods of advancement. Yet these books outlive typical shelf lives and are some of the most widely read nonfiction works on Latinos because, in the end, they focus on a group that reinforces the stereotype that Latinos are prone to crime, delinquency, and gangs.

Yet, more often, invisibility is the norm in terms of (non-)representation. On the one hand, it has only been very recently that Latina/o stories have found their way into television programs and motion pictures. In addition, a handful of actors stand in for Latinos, regardless of their national origin. This results in Panamanian actor Rubén Blades often playing Mexican characters, and when the movie about late Tejana pop star Selena Quintanilla was cast, it was Puerto Rican actor Jennifer Lopez who played the Mexican American icon. When a few stories break through, it's through a process of Latino conflation that stories are re-told. The diversity of the Latino label is lost when the idea is promulgated that any well-recognized Latino can stand in for characters from any Latino subgroup. On the other hand, reigning discourses about race in the United States allow Latina/os to be "missed by commentators well-schooled in ignoring populations and cultures made invisible by the continuing hegemony of the black/white binary within the national narrative" (Brady 2002: 203). Race relations in the United States, and media representations of said relations, have incorporated African American history, literature, experiences, and stories to a much larger degree. Yet the majority of US citizens are not aware that California, Arizona, Nevada, Utah, New Mexico, Texas, and parts of Colorado and Oklahoma were once the northern territories of Mexico or that Puerto Rico is a commonwealth territory of the United States. Who Latinos are would simply not be discernible if one relied solely on media representations and, more recently, political rhetoric.

Invisibility includes not only the lack of recognition that Puerto Ricans are US citizens, but all too often the assumption that only Cubans reside in South Florida, Dominicans in Washington Heights, Puerto Ricans in El Barrio, and Mexicans in the Southwest. The vital roles that Latinos play in the economy are often hidden in favor of stereotypical representations of Mexican immigrants stealing jobs from US citizens. The industries of agriculture, residential construction, landscaping, hotel and restaurant services, janitorial, and childcare, and professional occupations such as teaching (from pre-kindergarten to higher education), increasingly rely exclusively on Latino laborers. Treating Latino laborers as disposable people is not just a contemporary issue. The reality is this has been going on a very long time and on a mass scale, since the US–Mexico Bracero Program (1942–64), the first guestworker program, which embodies in particular how the Mexican population residing in the United States was driven even further into obscurity, despite the fact that their labor was responsible for putting food on the table of US residents. *Braceros* (manual laborers) were rendered invisible because the agricultural program resulted in more than 4.5 million work contracts being signed, and provided large-scale agriculture with a steady stream of labor for over twenty-two years, yet operated unknown to the vast majority of US citizens. My research details how these workers persevered under circumstances that have profoundly influenced their subjective evaluations of their experiences, made invisible by US society (Mize 2016b).

Demonizing Latino immigrants: the hypervisibility of criminalization

Leo Chavez has done more to document the demonization of Latino immigrants than any other scholar (Chavez 2001, 2008, 2012). Their conceptualization of the "Latino threat narrative" becomes the modality by which Latino immigrants are made hypervisible due to their criminalization. As a result, Latina/o Studies scholars see instances of this in California's Proposition 187 (banning health and social services to undocumented immigrants), Arizona's State Bill (SB) 1070 (racial profiling of immigrants), and House Bill (HB) 2281 (Arizona ethnic studies ban), to name just a few of the local and state immigration laws designed to target immigrants as the source of social and economic problems. Even though Chavez' work on the Latino threat narrative precedes the current administration, the threat characterization is most visible in the political rhetoric of President Trump, Attorney General Jeff Sessions, and Presidential Advisor Stephen Miller. "The Latino Threat Narrative is a social imaginary in which Latinos are 'virtual characters'. They exist as 'illegal aliens', 'illegitimate recipients of organ donations', 'highly fertile invaders', and 'unassimilable separatists bent on a reconquest of the Southwestern United States'" (Chavez 2008: 42). Similarly, Otto Santa Ana (2002: 260) refers to the metaphors of nation as body and as house that require protection or sanitation from the immigrant as animal or invader, to "express the anxiety at the apparent loss of Anglo-American cultural hegemony."

In their prescient analysis of California's Proposition 187, the so-called "Save our State" initiative, Chavez discusses the attempt of California voters, approved in 1994, to deny access to public benefits to undocumented immigrants residing in the state. It began a groundswell of anti-immigrant rhetoric in the mid-1990s that has taken on a renewed momentum in the twenty-first century. Chavez (1997: 73) notes that "the current wave of immigration reform proposals reflects a nationalist response to this transnational challenge." All Latina/o Studies scholars have to recognize that in many ways our celebration of transnationalism has a response in the form of nationalist backlash. Chavez' work was written before Proposition 187 was dismissed by state courts and subsequently superseded by two federal acts in 1996 (the welfare reform act, known officially as the Personal Responsibility and Work Opportunity Reconciliation Act of 1996, and the Illegal Immigrant Reform and Immigrant Responsibility Act – IIRIRA). Starting with Proposition 187, anti-immigrant forces were clearly defining their battle along racial lines, and as a result set their sights on a range of proposals to overturn the federal Bilingual Education Act of 1974 (Proposition 227-1998), end affirmation action (Proposition 209-1996), make English the official language (Proposition 63-1986), require Latinos to carry identification cards to verify legal residence (connected to the 2010 racial profiling SB1070 in Arizona), and amend the US Constitution to end automatic citizenship for those born on US soil (reintroduced by Nathan Deal, Republican Governor of Georgia, as the Birthright Citizenship Act of 2009, H.R.1868). What Chavez first identified in 1997 is clearly the blueprint for anti-immigrant legislation circa 2018.

The debates in the 2016 US presidential election campaign also placed immigrants in the limelight as squarely to blame for not only their own lot but the US nation's lot as a whole. Republican presidential candidate Donald Trump stated most vociferously in 2015: "The Mexican Government is forcing their most unwanted people into the United States. They are, in many cases, criminals, drug dealers, rapists, etc. ... They're sending us not the right people. It's coming from more than Mexico. It's coming from all over South and Latin America, and it's coming probably from the Middle East" (Walker 2015). Doubling down on his anti-Muslim, anti-immigrant linkage following the 2015 workplace shooting in San Bernardino, California, he went one step further to call for "a total and complete shutdown of Muslims entering the United States." In addition, he has justified and promised more torture, a database to register all Muslims residing in the United States, and the surveillance and potential closure of mosques, all the while praising the illegal internment of Japanese Americans during World War II. There is simply no better example of the fear-mongering xenophobia than Donald Trump's campaign rhetoric and subsequent presidential actions (including the Muslim ban subsequently referred to as a "travel ban" but challenged in federal court at the time of writing, continuing the rhetoric of building a wall between the US and Mexico with prototypes currently constructed in San Diego, rescinding the Deferred Action for Childhood Arrivals program – also caught up in the courts – and calling for a refusal of Department of Justice funding to sanctuary cities).

This rhetoric is based on how Latina/o immigrants are often reduced to a cost–benefit debate where the benefits are slighted by the constant media presence of anti-immigrant scholars and policy wonks such as George Borjas, Mark Krikorian, Stephen Moore, and those affiliated with the Center for Immigration Studies. This means that the costs school has ready access to political pundits, talk shows, and news media, and an eager audience – regardless of the actual facts. Immigration politics do not easily divide into liberal or conservative, Democrat or Republican, though the vitriolic hatred and fear-mongering market is pretty well cornered by the Far Right. There is basically a new Washington consensus on immigration: both parties highlight the negative costs, in spite of the evidence to the contrary, and all agree to comprehensive immigration reform in the abstract.

The reality is that in a nation of 323 million people, 11 million undocumented immigrants or 3 percent of the population could not possibly be responsible for ruining an entire economy or draining government services. Nor could they be responsible for saving the economy or spurring all economic growth. Yet in the news media, immigrants are consistently treated as criminals even though their single offense of residing in the nation without proper documentation is a misdemeanor.

Legislation at the state level is the main expressions of today's nativism. At the national level, the impasse over comprehensive immigration reform has not stemmed the tide of border militarization and mass deportations, resulting from a fear of foreigners or xenophobia. The political rhetoric of Donald Trump and his campaign promise to "build a wall" are the logical policy outcome of this racist language of immigrant-bashing.

Anti-immigrant legislation found its first major state-level expression in California's Proposition 187. This inspired 164 anti-immigrant state laws passed between 2010 and 2012. Since President Trump took office, a new wave of anti-immigrant bills is being considered in many states, as well as laws at the state level that bar localities from defining themselves as "sanctuary cities." Arizona's 2010 racial profiling SB1070 law emboldens law enforcement to verify the citizenship documents of anybody detained if there is "reasonable suspicion" that they may be in the state without proper documents. The clear mandate for racial profiling of those deemed "illegal aliens" is in determining reasonable suspicion, as it constitutes an explicit penalty for driving while Brown or speaking to an officer with an accent. SB1070 is steeped in trumped-up fears of a reconquest or multicultural invasion characterized as threats to national security (a concern only heightened in a post-9/11 era), and racially define the contours of the battle over who is or should be an "American." Even when the decision was successfully challenged in the courts, Maricopa County Sheriff Joe Arpaio continued to enforce the law, leading to his indictment for contempt of a court order, only for him to be pardoned by President Trump. When immigrants are treated as if they are criminals, even by law-breaking police officers, their presence in the United States can only be described as hypervisible.

Latina/os in popular culture

It's no mistake, and no mere coincidence, that some of the strongest literary and scholarly voices to come out of Latino/a Studies are those of journalists or former journalists. The list, by no means exhaustive, includes Maria Hinojosa (*Latino USA*), Juan Gonzalez (*Democracy Now!*), Hector Tobar (*Los Angeles Times*), Luis Alberto Urrea (*San Diego Union Tribune*), Roberto Cintli Rodriguez y Patrisia Gonzales (*Column of the Americas*), and David Bacon (*In These Times*). Two key texts in the formation of Latino Studies, Juan Gonzalez' *Harvest of Empire* and Hector Tobar's *Translation Nation*, were penned by journalists. There is no question that the field of border studies has been immeasurably improved by first the new journalism of Luis Alberto Urrea (*Across the Wire, By the Lake of Sleeping Children*, and *The Devil's Highway*) and then his fictional accounts of migration and US–Mexico connections (*Into the Beautiful North* and *The House of Broken Angels*). And it is certainly no coincidence that both the rise and fall of the Chicano Movement in Los Angeles found expression and particular voice in the writings and words of slain journalist Ruben Salazar, as their murder at the hands of the police for some made them a martyr of the waning movement.

Moving from news media to media more generally, and therefore to analyses of popular culture, many Latina/o Studies scholars look to visual studies. This draws widely from fields such as art and literary criticism, media and communications studies, cultural studies, theater and performance studies to fully reflect the range of representations analyzed by Latina/o Studies scholars. For instance, in the analysis of Chicana/o art, Peréz (2007: 4) describes their project:

> What began to emerge for me, through the work of the more than forty visual, performance, and literary artists examined here, was a picture of a politicizing spiritual hybridity, sometimes accompanied on the formal level by alternative, culturally crossed artistic languages which joined Western and Euroamerican canonical and popular literary and visual art dialects with those of Mexican American popular, folk, and Native American art, and with the social imaginaries or worldviews within which these were shaped.

We will discuss the relationship between Latina/os and hybrid cultures in the next chapter, but the key takeaway here is defining the various relationships between aesthetics and politics, formal and informal, high art and popular folk.

The "Hispanic market" is assumed to be a unified, homogenous segment like the "tween" or "double income, no kids (DINK)" market segments. "The homogenization of a heterogeneous population into a single 'Latino' market, for instance, while increasing the visibility of Latino populations, coincides with larger processes of partial containment and recognition of ethnic differences that are at play in other spheres of contemporary U.S. society" (Dávila 2001: 8–9). As Latinos become more visible to, first, advertisers and then the overall US population, particularly through mass-mediated representations, Dávila identifies in their follow-up work the character of said representations, in discussing "Latinidad, highlighting the move from deficiencies in terms of recognition, economic gains, and political standing, to the more marketable paradigm, where Latinos are presented as preeminent regenerators of all things 'American'" (Dávila 2008: 4). The double-edged sword of Latino "culture," all too often defined in terms of "values," may render Latinos a readily identifiable market segment (in terms of language or familialism) but it also serves as a marker of difference that reinforces negative stereotypes. And all too often these markers take the form of objectifications. Negrón-Muntaner analyzes the "queer hips" of Ricky Martin and "buttocks" of Jennifer Lopez to demonstrate how Puerto Rican bodies are specifically and uniquely represented, due to the "shame of specifically boricua and blanquito racialization" (2004: 237, 247–8).

Juan Flores established the analysis of popular culture in their 2000 book *From Bomba to Hip-Hop*. Taking musical representations typically thought of as quintessentially Puerto Rican (bomba) and juxtaposing them with the key Puerto Rican originators of a style of music more often considered African American (hip-hop), Flores begs the field of popular culture studies to think of cultural expressions as sites to better understand how Puerto Rican identity and culture in the diaspora and in Puerto Rico are mutually constitutive. The study of popular culture is deeply informed by intersectional analyses. "Popular culture constitutes a terrain where not only are ethnic and racialized, as well as gender, identity contested, reproduced, and transformed, but also the struggle for and against social inequality is engaged" (Habell-Pallán 2005: 5). One of the chapters in Michelle Habell-Pallán's book identifies the development of Chicana theater in the context of New American Theater. They write about Chicano playwright Luis Alfaro, who currently serves as a professor of dramatic arts at the University of Southern California and former resident playwright at the Oregon Shakespeare Festival, where their newest play, *Mojada: A Medea in Los Angeles*, was performed in 2017. "As both a Latino and a gay man living in twenty-first-century Los Angeles, Alfaro creates work that pushes against multiple oppressions that censor discussions about his identity in both communities. Alfaro's struggle for visibility takes places in multiple arenas" (Habell-Pallán 2005: 84). A prolific playwright, Alfaro takes Greek tragedies and other forms of classical theater and places them in Chicana/o Los Angeles contexts, drawing on diverse sources, from his personal family to Chicano iconography.

A great example of analyzing popular culture as it is most often conceived of is the work of Isabel Molina-Guzmán (2010: 2), who analyzes representations of Latina bodies in the news coverage of Elián González, the movies *Maid in Manhattan*, *Spanglish*, and *Frida*, and the television program *Ugly Betty*. They provide case studies from which to elaborate how "Latina bodies in the media landscape [operate] as both culturally desirable and socially contested, as consumable and dangerous." Television and movies are sometimes the only time that White citizens see Latinos, given the residential and social segregation endemic to US society. As mentioned before, it is when negative stereotypes of Latina/os are reinforced that we view Latina/os in their hypervisible context. "The hypervisibility of ethnically and racially ambiguous Latina bodies in the media is illustrative of demographic shifts and global media transformations … setting up Latina/o identity and culture as inherently exotic, foreign, and consumable" (Molina-Guzmán 2010: 7). The reality is that many Latina/o actors – marked as non-citizens, regardless of actual citizenship status rates, and objectified sexually as exotic and desirable, regardless of the actual variety of Latina/o body types, and in the end all objects to be consumed – are simply not in control of their own representations and find roles most often where negative stereotypes predominate.

In contradistinction, music is a genre where self-expression can find a cultural expression much closer to how artists define themselves and their communities. Unfortunately, to sell music, the commodification of the Hispanic market equivalent is the production of Latin music. The genre of Latin music is a catch-all for the various styles of music originating in Latin America but consumed in the United States. Rumba, bachata, salsa, bolero, samba, merengue, cumbia, punta, mariachi, norteño, Tejano, banda, ranchero, bomba, son, bossa nova, tango, reggaeton, *rock en español*, palo de Mayo, Garifuna, and hip-hop are just a smattering of the musical styles that fit under the umbrella. The Latin Grammy awards have done the most to introduce the genre to North American, English-speaking listeners. Those who study the field note: "a causal relationship between the segregation of Latino musics from the world beat market and U.S. mainstream music and the linguistic difference and social marginality of U.S. Latinos" (Aparicio and Jáquez 2003: 3).

Studies of Tejano pop star Selena (Paredez 2009) and Colombian pop star Shakira (Cepeda 2010) have elicited book-length treatments. "Selenidad continues to provide an organizing anthem for latinidad, a performative realm for articulating Latina/o citizenship, and a visual icon for marking Latina/o geographies and budding Latina sexuality" (Paredez 2009: 189–90). They go on to note that Selena represents not only the cheering-on of young Latinas to reach their dreams but also the honoring of the dead. Cepeda places Shakira in the context of both the Latin music boom of the 1990s, rooted in Miami, and the political crisis in Colombia. "I trace Shakira's somewhat contradictory representation as an idealized transnational citizen at a pivotal moment in the (re)configuration of *colombianidad* and, in a broader sense, *Latinidad* itself" (Cepeda 2010: 15). Born to a Lebanese father and a Catalan mother, relocating to Miami to pursue their musical career, Shakira's role as a transnational citizen is fully reflected in their eclectic, hybrid music that draws from Middle Eastern instrumentation, Spanish and English, Miami Latin pop, rock, Colombian cumbia, and rap.

Flores identifies the shift from invisibility to visibility in rap music as Latinos moved from nonexistence in a Black/White binary narrative to being viewed basically as oddities: "The disbelief and strategic invisibility that surrounded Latino participation in rap performance in the early years gave way to a fascination with something new and different" (Flores 2000: 125). With emerging rap-inspired genres such as reggaeton, Latina/o musical artists are finding their unique voice and developing their market niche in the contemporary era of digital downloads.

Finally, the link to performance studies brings us to Lawrence La Fountain-Stokes' *Queer Ricans*, which focuses on how "the social performance of effeminate manhood is *necessary* for other men's successful enactment of virile masculinity to work, as it is performed in perfect counterpoint. To put it simply, in this relational system, there can be no *macho* if there is no *loca* or *maricón*, perhaps in the way there can be no virgin if there is no whore" (La Fountain-Stokes 2009: 1). From drag performances to activist art, gay pride parades, and film, the terrain of cultural expression is more fully illuminated when considering the hypervisible/invisible dimensions.

7

New Approaches: The Logic of Comparisons, Connections, Bridges, and Borders

Longstanding and emerging methodological approaches are reshaping how Latina/o Studies operates today in more comparative, intersectional, and engaged forms. No longer is it assumed that a particular Latino community operates in a bubble, when it is in fact in connection with other communities (both in solidarity and in conflict) that shape it as much as it does in and of itself. I identify examples of Latina/o alliances and struggles with other racialized communities, in addition to Latina/o multiracial identities and experiences. But first, I discuss the longstanding participatory action research model, which arose concomitantly with Chicano and Puerto Rican Studies, and how the contemporary discussion of engaged scholarship is embedded within this long and conveniently ignored history. Emergent scholarship on comparative Latinidades and multi-racialities also marks new directions for the field of Latina/o Studies. New methodologies and analytical approaches, such as the importance of *testimonios* to Latina *feministas* and the rise of LatCrit in legal and education studies. The ascendancy of border studies interrogates how both socially constructed physical and mental borders are shaping Latina/o identities.

From participatory action research to community-based engaged research

The origins of Chicano and Puerto Rican Studies are clearly indebted to the communities from which they sprang. Communities are defined as geographically bound groups of similarly situated folks – in the case of Chicano and Puerto Rican communities, folks who share common oppression and mount collective resistance. *El Plan de Santa Barbara* (CCCHE 1969: 14) states,

> The premises for Chicano programs are: that the colleges/universities must be a major instrument in the liberation of the Chicano community; colleges/universities have a threefold responsibility: education, research, and public service to the Chicano community; only by comprehensive programs instituted and implemented by Chicanos, for Chicanos that focus on the needs and goals of the community will the larger purposes of the academic institutions and the interests of the Chicano community be served.

What research would look like was always in relationship to teaching, curriculum, and public service. Many professors in Chicano Studies referred to themselves as educators to not only recognize that threefold role but also to break down barriers and hierarchies among different levels of teachers. The educators who sought to systematize how to conduct research with Chicano communities referred to participatory action research (PAR) as the guiding methodology. A comparison of early PAR approaches and contemporary discussions of engaged research will be made later; conducting research with, and not on, communities is a hallmark of Chicano, Puerto Rican, and Latina/o Studies.

What we refer to today as community-based engaged research relies upon the insights of one scholar and on institutional recognition of them. The Carnegie Classification of Institutions of Higher Education, Community Engagement Classification (a voluntary accreditation system where colleges and universities submit materials to be designated as "engaged" institutions), builds on the publication of Ernest Boyer's (1990) *Scholarship Reconsidered*. Distinguishing the science of discovery (how universities normally define research success) from the science of engagement (responsiveness to community needs), community-engaged scholarship is currently all the rage with college and university administrators. The Carnegie recognition and engaged universities are positioning themselves to demonstrate university endeavors as public goods (defined extremely widely to include entrepreneurship opportunities to monetize basic science discoveries, industry partnerships, applied research, land grant university extension programs, and, often lastly, marginalized community engagement).

The notion that universities should be in contact with communities that partially fund them, send their children to study at them, and house their staff and faculty is in direct opposition to the idea of ivory towers where erudite, cloistered knowledge is constructed in isolation, to further the intellectual development of the anointed few with the proper credentials and privileged insular social networks. It should be obvious by now that Latina/o Studies would never flourish in the ivory tower model.[1] When Latina/o Studies first arrived on the scene, it was during a time of massive democratization of knowledge and expanded access to higher education as a result of social protest. From its very inception, Latina/o Studies was always already "engaged," and models of research and community advocacy, deemed novel in this current wave of engaged scholarship, were in fact first developed and deployed by Chicano and Puerto Rican Studies scholars. Community-based PAR was one of the first methodologies explicitly developed in Chicano Studies. One of the first defenses and best summaries of a rationale for PAR was published in 1974:

> The research reported here was consciously designed to benefit the poor and the powerless, who can least afford to fund research, and whose interests may in many cases be opposed to those of dominant elites. It is research in the service of the community, intended to provide the essential knowledge base from which more effective social and political action can be mounted. (Barrera and Vialpando 1974: 2–3)

Dr. Ernesto Galarza was one of the first (Paul S. Taylor, Carey McWilliams, George I. Sanchez, and possibly but problematically Manuel Gamio were others) to conduct community-based research. Writing originally in 1949, he established the PAR agenda. "Bibliographically, at least, the Mexican minority has come of age. But now the time has come for this minority to find the connection between the library card index and life. In the living and working conditions of this group certain problems have been isolated, defined, studied, and analyzed" (Galarza 2013: 34). With a doctorate from Columbia University, Galarza never held a full-time university position but spent his professional life as a community activist, labor organizer, and prolific author.[2] His organizing work with the National Farm Labor Union during the Bracero Program led to the publication of two key books: *Strangers in Our Fields* (1956) and *Merchants of Labor* (1964). These two books are often credited with souring informed public opinion on the Bracero Program and the intolerable, exploitative conditions that *braceros* faced as the nation's first "guestworkers." The program ended in 1964. Galarza's life, a life in struggle, established the pathway from community-based research to the formation of what we recognize today as Latina/o Studies.

When considering Latina/o Studies from PAR to community-based engaged research, the field can be boiled down to five central features:

1   no preconceptions/no boundaries;
2   community advocacy;
3   liberatory knowledge;
4   anti-elitism;
5   goal of bridging.

"No preconceptions" and "no boundaries" signal that interdisciplinary, comparative, multidisciplinary, even transdisciplinary studies are at
home in Latina/o Studies. Though some fields tend to predominate (say,
history and literature in Chicano/a Studies), at the end of the day it is the
subject matter and focus on community that create the space for inquiry
not beholden to a single theoretical tradition, methodological approach,
or anticipated finding.

Community is not an abstract concept in Latina/o Studies; it is the
very basis for its existence. What this means is that the research process
is often the exact opposite of the scientific method where the researcher
goes into a situation with a pre-formed set of hypotheses to test. Communities are not variables and test subjects to Latina/o Studies, often
because Latina/o Studies scholars come from the communities they
engage. Advocating for one's community means that the community
most often sets the research agenda; they know their collective wants and
needs, and Latina/o Studies scholars are expected to invert the research
process so they provide useful information, skills, tactics, and knowledge
that allow marginalized communities to advocate on their own behalf.

Liberatory knowledge asks the hard questions of whose knowledge is
valued and validated. Traditional distinctions of local versus scientific,
traditional versus organic, street smart versus book smart, community
versus academe are not diametric opposites in Latina/o Studies but most
often mutually informed. The breaking down of barriers comes down to
the very core of knowledge formation.

The project of Latina/o Studies is unabashedly one of radical democracy, and an explicit call to tear down ivory towers. Elitism has only
served those in power to reproduce their legacy, and breaking in as
tokens or charity cases will never challenge those structures of power.
Democracy and equality are not lofty ideals and faraway hopes in
Latina/o Studies but the central mechanisms for reaching the goals
of the social justice movements that often gave birth to them. In the
end, Latina/o Studies exists and persists to bridge theory and praxis,
campus and community, normative and empirical; and even though
bridges are often the first things to be burned during times of war,
Latina/o Studies by its very existence must operate to heal wounds and
divides. Contrary to social conservatives' characterizations, the emanci-
patory aims of Latina/o Studies are both universal and transcendental
when actualized.

Testimonio

If PAR was the guiding methodology of the 1970s, Latina feminism developed the ascendant methodology of the twenty-first century to ask the difficult questions of who constitutes the community, who is included and who is excluded, and in the process turned to methodological developments in Latin America to recover a critical storytelling tradition. The Latin American origins of *testimonio* are crucial in understanding how Latina *feministas* made the *testimonio* methodology their own. Women in Latin American resistance movements found voices in "the *testimonio* … inscribed and sanctioned as a literary mode since the 1970s, in large part as a result of the liberation efforts and the geopolitical resistance movements to imperialism in Third World nations" (Blackmer Reyes and Curry Rodríguez 2012: 526). From June Nash's *We Eat the Mines* via the work of Elena Poniatowska, chronicler of Mexico's recent radical history (1979, 1998), to *I, Rigoberta Menchú*, the shared approach of *testimonio* places the most neglected voices at the center of storytelling. The ensuing controversy about Rigoberta Menchú Tum was whether she actually experienced what she detailed in her life story, even though her purpose was to tell a larger story of Indigenous women in her community. Though plagiarism is a serious charge, Menchu's *testimonio* still holds sway because it not only identified a political struggle against military repression in Guatemala but also provided pathways forward. "Testimonio has been critical in movements for liberation in Latin America, offering an artistic form and methodology to create politicized understandings of identity and community" (LFG 2001: 3). The focus on everyday oppression and resistance demonstrates how liberation movements operate in micro-locales.

Blackmer Reyes and Curry Rodríguez (2012: 526) identify *testimonio* as a unique expression of the methodological use of spoken accounts of oppression. There is an explicit politics of thinking of storytelling as a form of resistance. "Testimonio, as a genre, is about the claiming of 'lived experience.' In staking this claim, those who testify bear witness to the dehumanizing processes to which their communities have been or are subject. Testimonio is inherently political, a vehicle to counter the hegemony of the state and to illuminate the repression and denial of human rights" (Cuadraz Holguin and Flores 2017: 5).

The IUPLR provided funding to a group of scholars, named the Latina Feminist Group (LFG), interested in thinking about the tradition of Latin American *testimonio* and applying it to contemporary Latina feminism. The "Telling to Live" coalition of eighteen writers (Luz Del Alba Acevedo, Norma Alarcón, Celia Alvarez, Ruth Behar, Rina Benmayor,

Norma E. Cantú, Daisy Cocco De Filippis, Gloria Holguín Cuádraz, Liza Fiol-Matta, Yvette Giselle Flores-Ortiz, Inés Hernández-Avila, Aurora Levins-Morales, Clara A. Lomas, Iris O. López, Norma Quintanales, Eliana Rivero, Caridad Souza, and Patricia Zavella), through a series of writing retreats, collectively penned the landmark contribution to US-based Latina *testimonios*. They see the methodology as a "[c]rucial means of bearing witness and inscribing into history those lived realities that would otherwise succumb to the alchemy of erasure" (LFG 2001: 2).

As scholars from Mexican American, Puerto Rican, Cuban American, Cape Verdean, Dominican, and other Latina and Native American identities, the authors embodied Latinidad in practice by not only finding the points of conjuncture and disjuncture among themselves, but also charting a project for how Latina/o communities, families, and selves negotiate the convergences and closures in the stories we tell. "Testimonio was critical for breaking down essentialist categories ... we gained nuanced understandings of differences and connections among us ... Through testimonio we learned to translate ourselves for each other" (LFG 2001: 11). Anti-essentialism, to be discussed in the later section on LatCrit, assumes just intent to critically interrogate the variety of daily lived experiences and social identities that embody Latinidad in its various congruent/discordant forms, with the willful intent of honest translation and well-intended, active listening practices. Building community through critical storytelling, translating, and listening is the opposite of assuming a unitary, singular definition of what it means to be Latino.

As the use of *testimonios* enters the new era of communications, access to stories is increasingly just a click away. Benmayor (2012: 508) notes "digital storytelling offers students and teachers a compelling way to discuss and understand social identities, positionalities, and inequalities." The author draws from their classroom experiences where students develop their own life stories and share their *testimonios* through web-based platforms. "Digital testimonio gives urgent and powerful voice to individual and collective Latin@ experiences and allows for broader, more democratic authorship, dissemination, and reception" (Benmayor 2012: 508). The idea of sharing stories openly and freely greatly facilitates and eases access to *testimonios*.

Comparative Latinidades and multiracialities

We discussed visibility and invisibility in the previous chapter, but one issue not discussed was how the mass media relish portraying Black–Brown strife and discord (the points of conflict between African

Americans and Latina/os). CNN coverage of inflammatory comments by ultraconservative Iowa state representative Steve King in 2017 serves as one of many concocted examples. When the media publish the headline "Steve King: Blacks and Hispanics 'will be fighting each other' before overtaking whites" (Massie 2017), the conflict raised in King's narrative goes unquestioned and unchallenged. In response to the demographic changes in US society, King claims that minorities will not become the majority because Black–Brown conflict will reverse demographic patterns as the two groups apparently kill each other off. The news report does not cite alternative views, it simply serves as a bullhorn for King's unsubstantiated, unfounded claims. Clearly, bigots like King think that driving a wedge between minority communities will allow White supremacist logic to reign unabated.

But the issue has important consequences within Latino communities. Flores notes, in *The Afro-Latin@ Reader*, "It is rare to see Latin@s of African descent on Spanish-speaking television or in the movies … Spanish-speaking television has portrayed Latin@s of African descent and indigenous people as uneducated, lazy, sex driven, violent, sloppy, and untrustworthy" (Flores in Jiménez Román and Flores 2010: 324). Anti-Blackness across the spectrum in Latino communities is a very real and serious issue and will likely serve as a fecund source for future inquiry, but scholars studying comparative racializations have more often chosen to focus on the spaces of hope, the places where coalitions and networked politics bring Black and Brown communities together.

A significant focus on multiracial relations is in Southern California, particularly Los Angeles (see Pulido 2006, Kun and Pulido 2014, López-Garza and Diaz 2001). The basis for coalitions can be found in expressive culture, but economy and politics also serve as home to multiracial coalitions, conflicts, and synergies. Whereas Pulido focuses on a range of multiracial coalitions and the edited collection of Kun and Pulido focuses on Black–Brown relations, the edited collection of López-Garza and Diaz focuses specifically on Asian American and Latino relations, given the two groups are fast growing in the region. Pulido (2006) analyzes three organizations – Bert Corona's CASA (*El Centro de Acción Social y Autónomo*), the Black Panther Party, and East Wind – to demonstrate how Chicano, Black, and Japanese leftists together advocated for radical change in Los Angeles and united movements across racial lines to pursue economic justice. A hallmark of recent radical politics is coalition building, so it is not as if these organizations operated in isolation, but building solidarities across communities of difference proved exceedingly difficult in Los Angeles. The point is coalitions are happening; the hard work of solidarity is being invested in to effect positive social change.

Ruthie Gilmore Wilson, prison abolitionist scholar-activist, has detailed the work of the Mothers Reclaiming Our Children (Mothers ROC) organization, who have fought the criminalization of Black and Latino youth in California with challenges to the three-strikes law (required life sentences for those convicted of three felonies), mandatory minimum sentencing (removing judiciary discretion), war on drugs (targeted enforcement in Black and Brown communities), and targeting of Black and Brown youth for increased police surveillance.

> A small, poor, multiracial group of working-class people, mostly prisoners' mothers, mobilize in the interstices of the politically abandoned, heavily policed, declining welfare state. They come forward, in the first instance, because they will not let their children go. They stay forward, in the spaces created by intensified imprisonment of their loved ones, because they encounter many mothers and others in the same locations eager to join in the reclamation project. (Gilmore Wilson 2005: 248)

Working-class people and communities living in poverty tend to be the focus of studying multiracial politics, but there is clear evidence that solidarities and multiracial relations are playing out in relatively affluent suburbs as well. Monterey Park is a middle-class, multiracial suburb seven miles east of downtown Los Angeles. Horton (1995) and his colleagues/graduate students José Zapata Calderón, Mary Pardo, Leland Saito, Linda Shaw, and Yen-Fen Tseng developed a multi-year, multi-site ethnographic project to study the complexities of daily living. Pardo, Saito, and Calderón all went on to write books based on their ethnographic research, with Pardo (1998) expanding their analysis to the *barrio* of East Los Angeles to compare women's activism in the two communities, Saito (1998) focusing on multiracial politics in Monterey Park, and Calderón (2015) identifying and analyzing their role as an insider and activist in the community. For instance, the case of redistricting in the San Gabriel Valley (where Monterey Park is located) afforded opportunities for Latinos (primarily Mexicans) and Asians (primarily Chinese) to build interracial coalitions. Four reasons were (1) similar histories of discrimination; (2) common interests including "immigration legislation, bilingual education, employment discrimination, and hate crimes; (3) increased efficacy due to combined population size and resources; and (4) a history of working together" (Saito 1998: 178–9). Pardo (1998) compares two organizations: Mothers of East Los Angeles (MELA), which fought the siting of a prison and toxic incineration dump in unincorporated East LA, and Concerned Parents and Residents of Monterey Park, which fought the siting of a parole office. Pardo records the challenges, difficulties, and opportunities of organizing across racial, class, gender, citizenship, and language lines.

As much as we might be inclined to assume multiraciality is a contemporary phenomenon, or at the very least a post-1965 "new" immigrant response, scholars inspired to work in this arena note that a history of multiracial relations goes back much further. Alvarez (2008: 5) notes:

> African American, Mexican American, Asian American, and white zoot suiters shared fashion trends, listened to the latest jazz and big band music, and danced the jitterbug or Lindy Hop together. By sharing a style and public spaces, including dance halls, movie theaters, and street corners, they not only showed that different races in the wartime United States sometimes lived, worked, or played together but also challenged the segregated sensibilities of 1940s America.

A burgeoning literature on Latina/o indigeneities has developed to detail the longstanding impact of colonization on Latina/o communities and Latin American nations, the recent influx of Indigenous migrants from Mexico and Central America to the United States, and the relationship between Latina/o Indigenous immigrants and Native Americans. Taking those three in order: the theoretical intervention is most often defined in relation to coloniality. "Latin American structures of coloniality and racial domination interface with US racial and economic hierarchies and settler colonial structures. When two systems of indigeneity and racial/class hierarchy hybridize in the process of migration, they create ... hybrid hegemonies" (Blackwell, Boj Lopez, and Urrieta 2017: 128). Indigeneity marks in this usage a specific form of colonized subjugation that intersects with race, class, gender, sexuality, illegality, and other systems of oppression.

The second way indigeneity operates is the recognition of new waves of migration by Indigenous Latina/os, and is most often focused on Indigenous migrants from Oaxaca, Michoacán, and Puebla in Mexico, or Mayan communities fleeing violence in Guatemala. Since the 1980s, we have seen a major transformation in terms of the increasing number of Indigenous migrants moving to the United States (see Bacon 2013, Fink 2003, Fox and Rivera-Salgado 2004, Smith 2006, Stephen 2007, Velasco Ortiz 2005). Even though colonialism sought to undermine indigeneity as a way of life, Mixteco Indigenous communities in Oaxaca vivified language and kinship bonds: "just as the family kept the indigenous language alive, the community was where the sense of *parentela* [big family] and territorial belonging was reproduced throughout the years" (Velasco Ortiz 2005: 32).

Turning to the third point: unlike Latin American nations that often negate Indigenous identity by promoting *indigenismo* or assimilation to an equally shared mestizo (mixed) identity, where all can supposedly trace their roots to Indigenous ancestors as citizens of the nation, the US federal recognition of native nations relies on fraught processes that in the end give the US government ultimate authority in determining who is and who isn't Native American. "For US natives, tribal membership is tightly controlled through blood quanta and tribal enrollments, and thus the politics surrounding these historical practices, rather than mestizaje, have shaped their experiences as colonized people" (Bianet Castellanos, Gutiérrez Nájera, and Aldama 2012: 6–7). The focus so far has most often been on the conflicts between Indigenous Latino communities and Native American tribal nations. What is still lacking in the scholarly discussion is a positive relationship between Indigenous immigrants and Native Americans. Longstanding alliances between, for instance, the American Indian Movement (AIM) and the Chicano organization Crusade for Justice in Denver, and other Native–Chicano/a alliances in urban areas such as San Francisco and Los Angeles, point to a more complicated picture than the imposed antagonisms of the two groups vis-à-vis statuses imposed by respective nation-states.

One last example of cross-racial alliances can be found in the Smithsonian's "Many Voices, One Nation" exhibit. A papier-mâché statue created by Kat Rodriguez is based on the Statue of Liberty, but in her hands are a bucket of tomatoes and a single tomato raised. The base of the statue has the words of African American poet Langston Hughes, "I too am America," and was used in the 2000 March for Dignity, Dialogue, and a Fair Wage led by the Coalition of Immokalee Workers (CIW). The march brought together "diverse, interracial groups including agricultural workers, environmentalists, and community organizers, to negotiate for better working conditions and higher wages in the agricultural industry."[3] As exhibit curator Salazar-Porzio (2014) notes, "Rodriguez painted the statue's bronze skin tone to reflect her own and the racial diversity of the mostly Mexican, Haitian, Mayan, and Guatemalan agricultural workers and CIW labor organizers." As the CIW farmworker movement created a national stage to highlight the poverty-level working conditions and modern-day slavery in Florida's tomato fields, they deftly invoked images associated with immigration (such as the Statue of Liberty) to more accurately reflect the challenges facing today's multiracial farmworker alliances.

Often just below the surface in the aforementioned studies is a critical analysis of political economy and how Latina/os are often concentrated and exploited in segmented labor markets. Though maybe not as explicit as early Latino Studies analyses of economic restructuring effects and international development (see Morales and Bonilla 1993), current studies call for direct challenges to neoliberalism (Córdova 2016) and the problematic linkage between North American consumption practices and labor migration from Mexico to fulfill production demands (Mize and Swords 2010). Another way in which political economy finds expression in Latina/o Studies is in the analysis of law and society.

Law and society: the development of LatCrit

The origins of LatCrit or Latina/Latino Critical Legal Theory can be traced back to movements in the legal academy in the 1980s and 1990s to diversify both its ranks and its intellectual frameworks. Some, particularly Kimberlé Williams Crenshaw, trace the origins of critical race theory (CRT) to pioneering legal scholar Derrick Bell and their resignation from Harvard Law School due to its unwillingness to hire any African American women, citing the conclusion that no qualified candidates existed (Harvard Law currently has six African American women on their faculty). As Bell was one of few law professors to teach about race and the law, that departure left a personnel and curricular hole that students organized to fill (Crenshaw 2002: 12). Harvard law students protested, and out of the tumult came an organizational plan to convene law students and faculty of color to discuss more widely the law environment's lack of minority representation. Several meetings of law faculty of color occurred in conjunction with Critical Legal Studies (CLS) conferences. These meetings, as Crenshaw notes, pointed out the continuing problems of the lack of diversity and the liberal, individual-rights tendency of the main progressive approach to law at the time, namely CLS. In response, the first CRT workshop was held, by invitation only, in 1989 with twenty-four participants at the University of Wisconsin, Madison (Crenshaw 2002: 20). Conveners included Kimberlé Crenshaw, and the very naming of CRT came from three aims: "We would signify the specific political and intellectual location of the project through 'critical', the substantive focus through 'race', and the desire to develop a coherent account of race and law through the term 'theory'" (Crenshaw 2002: 19).

A second origins story traces CRT, as detailed by Cho and Westley (2002), to the nationwide general strike at law schools that they identify as a progeny of the Third World Student Strike. The Boalt Coalition for a Diversified Faculty was formed in the mid-1980s to challenge what at that time was a faculty comprised of 46, 42 of whom were White males, 3 White women, and 1 African American male (Cho and Westley 2002: 41). The law faculty were actually less diverse than the previous decade, when, in 1978, of the 42 Boalt faculty, 37 were White men, 3 White women, 1 African American male, and 1 Asian American woman (Cho and Westley 2002: 40). The charge of tokenism (asking one faculty member to represent an entire race) would have been a severe understatement. Students explored all formal options to no avail, so they voted to strike in 1988 to protest this profound lack of diversity. But the following year, the Boalt student coalition organized a nationwide strike to address the lack of diversity in the nation's law schools. Not coincidentally, law schools started hiring minority faculty in 1990, and at Boalt in particular, diverse representation can be directly traced to the student protests of the late 1980s.

University of Houston law professor Michael Olivas brought this issue of lack of diversity to Latino communities by publishing what came to be known as the dirty dozen list. "This List, comprised of the top twelve U.S. law schools located in high Latina populated areas but lacking a single Latina professor on the faculty, served to increase awareness of the lack of diversity at some of the nation's top legal institutions, as well as 'shame' these schools into remedying the dearth of diversity within their faculties" (Román and Carbot 2008: 1238). At the time of their writing, 87 law schools in all four status tiers did not have a single Latina/o faculty member, Latina/os represented 1.6 percent of the legal academy, and of the top 20 programs, 9 did not have a single Latina/o faculty member (findings remarkably similar to Olivas' earlier dirty dozen list) (Román and Carbot 2008: 1248).

What developed in CRT was a significant focus on the Black/White binary, and race relations falling outside of that frame found themselves intellectually and pragmatically out of the conversation. As the CRT workshops dissipated over the years, in CRT's place has developed, thanks to a group of Latina/o law professors (including Francisco Valdes, Elisabeth Iglesias, Margaret Montoya, George Martinez, Steven Bender, Gilbert Carrasco, Kevin Johnson, and Richard Delgado) and many non-Latinos, a framework for analysis that focuses on Latino experiences, to be sure, but also provides an open forum for all marginalized groups to find expression and common cause – what Mari Matsuda (1987) refers to as outsider jurisprudence.

Many point to one of the first Latino law professors in the nation, Richard Delgado, and his critical storytelling methodology (certainly acknowledged as being indebted to CRT's founder Derrick Bell and their fictional foil, the character they created named Vanessa Crenshaw) as evidenced in their *Rodrigo Chronicles* and *The Coming Race War* (Delgado 1995, 1996). "Stories, parables, chronicles, and narratives are powerful means for destroying mindset – the bundle of presuppositions, received wisdoms, and shared understandings against a background of which legal and political discourse takes place" (Delgado 1989: 2413). Critical storytelling challenges legal studies to re-conceptualize how law is taken for granted, facially neutral, assumed to operate in a vacuum, and reified to the point that to challenge legal logic and laws is deemed almost blasphemous.

The main contention of CRT is that racism is central to US law, and for LatCrit scholars the racialization of Latina/os finds its origins and contemporary manifestations in law as well. There is a certain degree of hopefulness in this formulation as it also means that the law can be used to undo racism, protect classes (groups officially recognized by law as legally cognizable) from discrimination, or at the very least provide compensatory damages to those subject to discrimination.

Angela Harris, in their seminal critique of White feminist law professor Catharine MacKinnon, invokes anti-essentialism to understand how MacKinnon's "dominance" theory places gender inequality and patriarchy at the center of analysis, to the detriment of understanding intersectionalities.

> MacKinnon assumes, as does the dominant culture, that there is an essential "woman" beneath the realities of differences between women – that in describing the experiences of "women" issues of race, class, and sexual orientation can therefore be safely ignored, or relegated to footnotes. In her search for what is essential womanhood, however, MacKinnon rediscovers white womanhood and introduces it as universal truth. In dominance theory, black women are white women, only more so. (Harris 1989–90: 591–2)

There is no universal definition or identification of womanhood. The experiences of White privileged women were obscuring or disregarding the experiences of non-White women (see chapter 5). The unintended consequence of the argument is that dislodging a unified subject, challenging the idea of a singular axis subject, led to conservative African Americans with agendas very opposed to African American civil rights and Black power agendas claiming their Blackness as a form of discriminatory treatment by fellow African Americans (claims made explicitly by Supreme Court Justice Clarence Thomas and Housing and Urban Development Secretary Ben Carson). For instance, Thomas claimed he was subject to a "high-tech lynching for uppity Blacks" for his refusal to adhere to liberal beliefs on Black civil rights, even though his accuser Anita Hill was calling out Thomas for their pattern of sexual harassment. For LatCrit, anti-essentialism is better conceptualized as a multidimensionality that does not deny the existence of Thomas and Carson, but links anti-essentialist understandings to political commitments if the project of understanding multiple identities is to have social justice aims and goals. Theorizing race from the perspective of Latina/os, as a LatCrit project, identifies the diversity of Latina/o experiences and identities. To avoid the past mistakes of CRT, LatCrit practices what they refer to as "de-centering," which is one necessary element in solidarity work among progressive communities. Coalitional politics means Latina/o interests like DACA may take the back seat to addressing, for instance, Donald Trump's Muslim ban or the overturning of protections from discrimination for transgender students.

LatCrit topics of inquiry include reparations, legally cognizable identities (Martinez 1997), ethnic studies (Delgado 2013, Mize 2014, Stefancic 2014), culture wars (Venator Santiago 2005, Mize 2014), global development (Carrasco 1996), immigration law (Johnson 2003b), civil rights (Delgado 1989), international human rights regimes (Hernández-Truyol 1996), gender and sexuality (Montoya 1994, Hernández-Truyol 2008, Valdes 1995), hate speech acts (Matsuda et al. 1993, Delgado and Stefancic 2004), microaggressions[4] (Lawrence 2008, Solarzano, Ceja, and Yosso 2000), and dog-whistle politics (Haney López 2015). When I began participating in LatCrit around 2005, sociologist Mary Romero and political scientist Charles Venator Santiago were the only non-law professors attending LatCrit conferences. Most recently, a large contingent of education scholars attend the conferences.

In the United States, the long history of racialization is deeply connected to the institution of chattel slavery and the distinction between freedom and unfreedom. The resultant one-drop (just one drop of "Black blood" made someone Black) or hypodescent (all offspring of mixed race couples take the status of the subordinate race) rules were designed to unequivocally distinguish Black from White as the dominant legal and social categories of separate and unequal. The point was to avoid gray areas; admixture was only proof of inferiority, and the racial hierarchy of White over Black left little room for definitions of in-between or outside. As a result, Haney López (2006) notes in *White by Law* the fifty-two cases that mixed race, Asian, Latino, or Middle Eastern litigants sought to use the legal system to be counted as White and receive all the accruements embodied within full citizenship rights.

Finally, LatCrit has developed a new following and an emerging scholarship in schools of education, as already mentioned. CRT entered into education circles with a pioneering article penned by Gloria Ladson-Billings and William Tate (1995), with Latino education scholars Daniel Solorzano and Tara Yosso soon taking the concepts of CRT and applying them to Latina/os in education systems. Yosso (2005) identifies the Chicano education "pipeline" and finds that there is a 1 in 100 chance of a Mexican American earning a terminal degree (PhD, MD, JD) and that particularly at every transition point, from middle school to high school to community college to four-year university, there are major leaks in the pipeline. This accounts for the relatively high rate of high school non-completers and the disproportionately low number of Chicano college graduates. Solorzano et al. (2000: 60) effectively analyze the role that microaggressions play in shaping the experiences of minority youth in education systems. They identify "microaggressions as the subtle insults (verbal, nonverbal, and/or visual) directed at people of color often automatically or unconsciously." The field of LatCrit in education is burgeoning (see recent contributions by Malagon, Perez Huber, and Velez 2009, Pacheco and Velez 2009), which should come as no surprise given public education's close relationship as a state actor alongside the legal system and the longstanding presence of CRT in critical education studies.

Border Studies

The final approach we will discuss is defined less in terms of a single methodology and much more as rooted in a specific geographical formation that is the result of US–Mexico geopolitics – the border. Anzaldúa's insights often serve as the alpha and omega for where the border begins and ends. "The U.S.–Mexican border *es una herida abierta* where the Third World grates against the first and bleeds" (Anzaldúa 1999: 25). This open wound they refer to is very much historically constructed and a lived contemporary reality. Profound inequalities persist along the border, even if the terminology of First and Third World holds less resonance.

> 1,950 mile-long open wound
>   dividing a *pueblo*, a culture,
>   running down the length of my body,
>   staking fence rods in my flesh,
>   splits me   splits me
>   *me raja   me raja.* (Anzaldúa 1999: 24)

Rather than being one monolithic border, that nearly 2,000-mile stretch is home to at least 12 million to 31 million residents (depending on the way one measures population relative to distance from the border), most of whom reside in the fifteen major pairs of sister cities that straddle the border.[5] The population is expected to double by 2030. As the present-day border has been in place since 1848 (with the southern portion of Arizona added in 1853 as a result of the Gadsden Purchase), the longstanding presence of Mexicana/os on both sides of the border has resulted in specific cultural formations and the unique lived experiences of feeling split and divided, though varying as a generational phenomenon.

One of the first authors to write about life on the border was Texas folklorist Américo Paredes. Their most widely recognized work is *With His Pistol in His Hand*, which was originally published in 1958, and details the various stories, *corridos* (songs in a specific style), and ballads about Mexican American folk hero Gregorio Cortez. One version of the story goes like this: a man, Cortez, hunted by the Texas Rangers for a crime he did not commit tragically dies at the hands of the Rangers, with his pistol in his hand. Paredes analyzes the variations of the *corrido* textually in addition to conducting a historical analysis to compare the versions of the border ballad with the historical record. In both, they recognize a particular set of themes that arise. "The *corrido* of border conflict assumes its most characteristic form when its subject deals with the conflict between Border Mexican and Anglo-Texan, with the Mexican – outnumbered and pistol in hand – defending his 'right' against the *rinches* [Texas Rangers]. The *corrido* of border conflict follows a general pattern, out of which emerges the Border concept of the hero" (Paredes 1996 [1958]: 147). For Paredes, history and the remembrance of history were categorically matters of social aesthetics, formalized as folklore, as vernacular local knowledge, and in the stories, legends, songs, customs, and beliefs of a particular place and time (Salvídar 2006: 24). Paredes spent his career understanding "Greater Mexico" from the vantage point of the Texas–Mexico borderlands.

> Inventing the idea of Greater Mexico as an imaginary social space consisting in transnational communities of shared fates, Paredes allows us to make sense of the new geographies of citizenship in an era of the emerging globalization of capital with its intensified flow of ideas, goods, images, services, and persons. He allows for the possibility of a theoretical repositioning of modern citizenship in new multicultural versions. (Salvídar 2006: 59)

Paredes, Jovita Gonzalez, and other anthropologists began the study of border folklore that directly inspires and mentors the study of Mexican South Texas by anthropologists José Limón (1994, 1999) and Richard Flores (1995, 2002). More widely, border ethnographies have since come to dominate the scholarly discussion of the US–Mexico border region. Devon Peña (1997) analyzes *maquiladora* (global assembly factory) workers in Cuidad Juaréz, while Miranda Cady Hallett (2012) discusses the ways in which Salvadoran immigrants have to negotiate boundaries as poultry workers in Arkansas. Josiah Heyman

(2008) and Nicholas De Genova (2005), in their respective works, identify how the border can be conceptualized in terms of militarization, illegality, surveillance, securitization, and virtual walls that result in the border being felt and experienced in Chicago as much as it is along the actual border.

> More narrowly, the virtual wall involves applying advanced surveillance and computer technologies to border law enforcement ... More broadly, the virtual wall points to the massing of police forces, including military and intelligence agencies, in the border region, which presents a web of obstacles to northward movement of illegalized people and goods, obstacles that usually are overcome, but at great risk and cost. (Heyman 2008: 305)

Along with this conceptualization, the width and breadth of the impacts of the border can be identified along the border strip, border area (encompassing the area 100 kilometers north of the US border and 300 kilometers south of the Mexico border), and transborder region of all ten states traversing the US–Mexico border.

Yet Pablo Vila and current anthropological border ethnographers also want to limit the border metaphor to identify that there is no singular border experience, but specific experiences in the Cuidad Juaréz–El Paso region, which constitute a set of unique interactions with the border. "Current border studies suffer from two contradictory and equally problematic tendencies. The first essentializes the differences it finds in any border encounter, and the second ignores the differences" (Vila 2003: 313). The El Paso–Cuidad Juárez border is not the same border as the Cuidad Juárez–El Paso Border, let alone the San Diego–Tijuana border or the US–Mexico border or any nation-state border, at least in terms of how the border is lived. Border as metaphor is simply not the same thing as living on the border in local, concrete, daily experiences.

Themes that stem from Vila's two-volume approach to the Texas–Chihuahua sister city include in the first volume "the discourses of national identity and with it, region, ethnicity, and social constructions of race" (Vila 2000: vii). In Vila's follow-up, themes include religious identities (Catholic Mexicanness in addition to the rise of Mexican Protestantism), gender (given the relevance of the Juárez femicides),[6] and class discourses on both sides of the border.

> The goal of my own research on the border was neither to exemplify with a geographical region what the theorists of postmodernization were advancing in their highly abstract writings (the sin of most American border studies practitioners), nor to ease Mexican anxieties about

the possible pernicious cultural and identitarian effects of NAFTA [North American Free Trade Agreement]; rather, it was to investigate the complex processes of identification that, in some way or another, actually organize the behavior of border actors in the Cuidad Juárez–El Paso area. (Vila 2005: 5)

I liken the criticisms of Vila and their colleagues to research I conducted in the South San Diego region. I worked at an educational supply company (filling orders by school teachers who ordered their supplies by the company catalog), and the organization of work was very much gendered according to job task. The company's San Diego headquarters consisted of an office and a warehouse. The office contained all the managers, secretaries, receptionists, and customer service representatives. The managers were all male. Their secretaries, as well as receptionists, order takers, and customer service agents, were female. In the warehouse, all of the workers were male. Twice a year, the full-time staff and a few of the temporary agency employees were required to work on a Saturday to conduct an inventory count in the Tecate, Mexico, *maquiladora*. The San Diego-based warehouse employees claimed they had to do inventory twice a year because the female, Mexican workers, according to the full-timers, could not count. The inventory count shed light on the possibilities and limits in terms of cross-border unities and organizing. All of the full-time warehouse employees were either 1.5- (sons of Mexican immigrants) or second-generation Mexican Americans. Most grew up in South San Diego, Chula Vista, or San Ysidro, which are cities less than five miles from the border. The articulations of *el otro lado* or the other side that were expressed by the predominantly young, male Mexican Americans reinforced nearly every stereotype of Mexico as dirty, Mexicans as lazy or stupid and thus deserving of $5 per day, and Mexican women as easily controlled by male managers.

Working in the US distribution centers often requires at most a high school degree. Many counterculture Chicano youth, derisively referred to as *vatos* or *cholos*, find few other employment options open to them. Their working conditions are often extensions of inferior schooling conditions, and filling the bottom end of the labor market might potentially encourage them to seek out similar counterparts to build alliances and resist those conditions. Yet, even in the same company that employed exploitative practices on both sides of the border, the Mexican American male distribution workers most often naturalized the differences between themselves and their Mexican female counterparts in terms of gendering relations (assembly is women's work), nationalizing working conditions (Mexicans deserve to work in substandard workplaces for little pay), and claiming a slice of superiority at the expense of those below them on the wage scale (for more information, see Mize 2008: 150–1).

The field of borderlands history traces the origins of sister cities and other relevant phenomena to major shared events in US and Mexico history that play out uniquely in the border region. Major themes vary from the various actors and social groups who comprise the border to state violence and lynchings (particularly in Texas and Arizona) (Truett and Young 2004, Villanueva 2017). A plethora of topics inform borderlands history, but recent analysis of the longstanding Chinese immigrant presence on the border is particularly noteworthy. The US Chinese Exclusion Act of 1882 barred further migration from China, and the hostile environment generated by the act impelled many Chinese residing in Southern California and Arizona to cross the border and take up residence in Sonora and Baja California. Delgado (2013) traces merchants who made it possible for Chinese Mexicans to thrive in Sonora, whereas Martinez (2008) identifies the longstanding impact of this group as evidenced in the sheer number of Chinese restaurants and Chinese-Mexican-owned businesses currently operating in the border town of Mexicali.

Explorations in literary theory more often conceptualize the border as metaphor, but the works of Brady (2002) and Salvídar (2006) locate their analysis along the physical, albeit socially constructed, border. Definitely harkening back to Anzaldúa, they describe border politics as shaping immigrant and border resident experiences, in addition to bringing forward the relevance of space to

> challenge the ongoing efforts of the U.S. government to further militarize borders of all sorts and to demonize those who cross them. The border, of course, brings together the temporal and the spatial, the metaphorical and the material at multiple, imbricated, and sliding scales, a mezclada that Chicana spatial theorists … challenge and mine as they construct the terrains of a radical mestiza praxis. (Brady 2002: 206)

The biggest farce of neoliberalism is that of the laissez-faire state, when in reality the state becomes the preferred labor contractor in the service of global capital. Andreas (2000) argues that boundary enforcement along the US–Mexico border during the 1990s stemmed from political factors and pressures to gain control of the border. Additionally, they assert that enforcing the boundaries of the United States is less about curtailing the flow of drugs and undocumented migration than about setting the symbolic territorial boundaries of the nation-state, as the state has in the past failed to implement immigration policies that would deter the movement of undocumented immigrants along the boundary.

The symbolic representation of the border as a wall or fence in need of further fortification only serves to place the problems associated with illegal immigration as a burden on those deemed illegal. Lost in the equation are the employers who are illegally employing workers without papers, consumers who benefit from cheap products and services, and politicians on both sides of the aisle who criminalize immigrants for their own political gain. And it is clear that the rising tide of nativism coincides with economic downturns and uncertainties (see Mize and Swords 2010: ch. 5, Mize and Peña Delgado 2012: ch. 6). Nativism, xenophobia, and racism are the main impediments to immigrant incorporation in the early years of the twenty-first century.

8

New Perspectives:
Theorizing (Post)Coloniality
and Racializations

When we think about the theoretical contributions that stem from the development of Latina/o Studies, we often come back to the question that began our discussion: who is a Latino? Viego (2007: 121) asks us to consider

> Latino as a term outside and beyond ontologies of race and ethnicity, not because it appears to point to the postraciological but rather because in fact it is a term that is first and foremost remarking on questions of temporality ... Latino as a term is resignifying temporality, not just race and ethnicity; it should affect how we will tell the time and the history of the Americas in the future.

What it means to be Latina/o is very much a product of living simultaneously in the United States and the Américas in these times. In a book that is much more about Lacan than Latino Studies, the syncretism Viego calls for is demonstrated best by their Anzaldúa/Lacan articulation:

> This link couples Lacan with Anzaldúa, grafting Lacan's *sinthome* to Anzaldúa's *mestiza* to create the term *sinthomestiza*, an antipsychologistic reading of Chicano and Latino identity that stays alive to the effects of language as structure on the speaking organism as well as staying sharply attuned to the cultural and historical particularities of Chicano and Latino experience in the twenty-first century. (Viego 2007: 160)

So, on the one hand, being Latino is a temporal marker, one that places those who identify as such in a particular time and space. On the other hand, the question is also very much a matter of what we mean when we talk about race and ethnicity. We begin our discussion with thinking about Latina/os in the twenty-first century, particularly in a post-9/11 US context. Then, we visit the various approaches to seeking Latinidad through a shared history of and contemporary struggle with colonization. Finally, we discuss how theories of race are very much articulated distinctly from Latina/o engagements with the social and historical construction of race.

Brown threats, Brown bodies

Certainly, an emerging way of conceptualizing Latinidad is in relation to other communities experiencing racialization, immigrant restriction, and negative stereotyping (in this case, terrorism) since September 9, 2011. "Since 9/11, the ethos and pathos of nationalism and nationhood have changed in the United States, where brown has become a *malleable identification* that neonationalist discourses use as a ranking logic of belonging that re-creates a hierarchy of nationalist belonging" (Silva 2016: 49). Nationalism, or in this very specific case who is considered an "American," is constantly changing and new groups find themselves excluded from incorporation by historical, social, and demographic conjunctures. As Christopher Rivera (2014: 45) also notes, in a post-9/11 US context, the conflation of Latino (predominantly Mexican) with Arab, Middle Eastern, and Muslim immigrants and refugees conjoins the "twin processes of racialization and securitization, the construction of Latina/os and Muslims in dominant culture as posing a 'Brown Threat' in the post-9/11 American imagination."

"Essentially, though 9/11 is instrumental as shorthand for producing brown anxieties, these anxieties are also fed by the outsourcing of jobs *to* brown spaces, immigration *from* brown spaces, and economic challenges *by* brown spaces, especially South Asia" (Silva 2016: 163). I would contend that US residents from the Middle East, South Asia, and Latin America all find themselves defined as unacceptably Brown, at a time when US citizenship, or being "American," is conflated with Whiteness. There is certainly a contradiction in place, though, as so many products for US consumption are fully reliant on Brown bodies providing the necessary labor to exploit and culture to appropriate. "And whereas the materiality of brown, in the form of commodity culture, can freely cross the border for pleasurable consumption, the brown body itself, as it is currently produced, is a site of fear and loathing" (Silva 2016: 163).

Attraction/repulsion is a longstanding narrative in Latina/o history but it plays out very differently in this post-9/11 context. Education scholar Cindy Cruz asks us to reflect back on Latina feminist thought to understand how Brown bodies not only pay the costs of such fear and loathing, but also are the sites for radical social change and praxis-based theorizing. "Situating knowledge in the brown body begins the validation of the narratives of survival, transformation, and emancipation of our respective communities, reclaiming histories and identities. And in these ways, we embody our theory" (Cruz 2001: 668).

It is within this context, and the even more repressive post-9/11 era of reducing civil liberties and restricting the rights of immigrants, that tireless activists have continued the movement for amnesty begun in the previous era of the 1980s and broadened it across the entire United States. In many ways, a shared opposition to the US Patriot Act (the state's response to terrorist threats that severely curtailed all US residents' civil liberties) and the promotion of cities and states as sanctuaries have united Latino advocacy organizations, refugee and immigrant service providers, labor unions, socially conscious church groups, and members of all racialized communities (Black, Latino, Arab, Middle Eastern, Muslim, Asian, and Native American).[1]

Efforts by lifelong Latina activist Emma Lozano in Chicago certainly exemplify cross-racial organizing and advocacy. A former staffer in the Harold Washington mayoral administration, Lozano has worked tirelessly to develop three organizations working on behalf of amnesty and immigrant rights. They are founder and president of the community-based membership organization Pueblo Sin Fronteras and two related non-profits, Centro Sin Fronteras and Sin Fronteras. They were recognized by the Cook County Board of Commissioners for their work on educational reform, legal advocacy for undocumented immigrants, and union representation regardless of citizenship status, and as one of the national leaders in the amnesty movement. In the 2000s, they shared the stage with Middle Eastern and African American leaders to not only push the Chicago city council to urge the federal administration to repeal the Patriot Act, but also identify and challenge the increased use of racial profiling as a result of the far-reaching powers of the Act. Lozano is on the front lines and a recognized leader of sanctuary politics as well.

From this activist response to trumping up fears, Silva theorizes that the unity of Brown politics relies upon transcending past and present, old and new, identity and nationalism.

This convergence of historical brown [Chicano/Latino] with "terrorist" brown [post-9/11 Muslim, Middle Eastern, Arab, South Asian] produces a process of identification that simultaneously rejects and relies on past racisms. Converging multiple vectors of identities, both old and new, under discourses of security and securitization effectively animated a form of securitized nationalism that hinged on two interrelated concepts: (1) to secure the homeland from threats and (2) to identify and separate those considered a threat from those who belonged within the secured perimeters of the nation-state. (Silva 2016: 27)

Conversations about building a wall across the full expanse of the US–Mexico border are much more legible when we see they are rooted in a nationalism fully governed by fear of those deemed un-American and therefore an enemy of the state – the condition of being Brown in twenty-first-century US society.

Colonization: de-, post-, internal, power, settler

The origins of Chicano Studies, as discussed in chapter 3, are deeply intertwined with the internal colony theory. A nation-based approach, the idea that racial minorities constitute nations within the nation represents the first attempt to engage how colonization shapes the lived experiences of Latina/os. More recently, a key contribution to the interest in Latina/o Studies in theorizing colonization as central to Latinidades is Emma Pérez' *The Decolonial Imaginary*. Their central premise is: "I believe that the time lag between the colonial and postcolonial can be conceptualized as the decolonial imaginary" (Pérez 1999: 6). What they refer to as the decolonial imaginary is the spaces in between, the liminal sites where most everything, even meaning, is contested. It is these "interstitial gaps, the unheard, the unthought, the unspoken" that comprise the "third space where I find the decolonizing subject negotiating new histories" (Pérez 1999: 5). The notion of the hybrid or third space can be traced back to one particularly influential book. Néstor García Canclini's *Hybrid Cultures* (1995) relies on a high–low cultural hybrid to study contemporary Latin American (primarily Mexican) culture. They refer to the hybrid of high and low art and the hybrid of the First and Third Worlds (North–South) to tangentially discuss what are thoroughly racialized issues. But García Canclini deflects attention away from the racialized nature of social relations within Mexico as well as between the United States and Mexico. This may be a result of the materials they chose to analyze: museum displays, high art and literature, monuments, and statues in addition to *brief* mentions of the "low" art of billboards, cartoons, and Tijuana tourist representations. García Canclini notes that these materials are decontextualized from the social relations from which they arise. For example, "[t]he antique objects are separated from the social relations for which they are produced; ... the objects are converted into *works* and their value is reduced to the formal game that they establish through their proximity to others in that neutral space – apparently existing outside of history – that is the museum" (García Canclini 1995: 118–19, emphasis in original). At times, for García Canclini, the hybrid is simply a combination of two elements and a blurring of distinctions. For others such as Bhabha (1994), Soja (1996), and Grossberg (1997), the hybrid is a new entity unto itself. "[T]he subaltern is neither one nor the other but is defined by its location in a unique spatial condition that constitutes it as different from either alternative" (Grossberg 1997: 359). For Soja (1996), following the lead of Bhabha, the hybrid constitutes a "thirdspace" in defining the postcolonial moment. Bhabha (1994) is primarily concerned with how the subaltern defines itself after the colonial empire has left or been forced out. The vestiges of colonial relations weigh heavily upon the minds of those attempting to escape the definitions imposed from above. Even though Bhabha draws on the work of Chicano performance artists and African American authors to demonstrate their vision of the thirdspace, Bhabha's interests remain rooted in throwing off the shackles of the imperialist legacy. The conflation of postcolonial relations and contemporary US race relations as constituting the same space, defined by its hybridization with other forms, misses the specificities of both sets of relations and explains the former better than the latter. But Bhabha moves hybrid cultures closer to a historically delimited group in a way that the use of the hybrid as redefining culture does not.

Another scholarly group theorizing colonization operate from primarily South American and Puerto Rican contexts to articulate the coloniality of power approach. Many are associated with the State University of New York at Binghamton, but the foundational work is offered by Peruvian scholar Anibal Quijano. As they state, "the coloniality of power based on the imposition of the idea of race as an instrument of domination has always been a limiting factor for constructing a nation-state based on a Eurocentric model" (Quijano 2000: 569). Rather than distinguishing colonialism from race, the point from their perspective is that race thinking (the dividing of groups into biologically marked superior and inferior groups) was part and parcel of the colonialist project. Both operated in the service of power. Quijano (2000: 552) notes:

This resultant from the history of colonial power had, in terms of the colonial perception, two decisive implications. The first is obvious: peoples were dispossessed of their own and singular historical identities. The second is perhaps less obvious, but no less decisive: their new racial identity, colonial and negative, involved the plundering of their place in the history of the cultural production of humanity.

Dehumanization is the clear end result of racialization, and Latin America, as first a Spanish colony and second subject to US imperialism, has felt the full effects.

In many ways, the coloniality of power theory has its roots in the Puerto Rican experience (see Grosfoguel 2008), broadened to the Americas by Anibal Quijano and Walter Mignolo, and very much tied to theorizing the linkages among race, colonization, capitalism, and modernity. Performance studies have been influenced by the theory: for example, the editors of *Performing the US Latina and Latino Borderlands* write "since the term 'colonization' points to the imposition of hierarchical powers through the cannibalization of meaning by imperialistic meaning, the volume editors understand *de*-colonization as an affirmative process of reversing, releasing, and altering an established coloniality of power" (Aldama, Sandoval, and García 2012: 5).

But the position is not without critics. It is clear that gender drops out of the analysis of the relationship between race and class in coloniality of power analyses.

> I think this understanding of gender is implied in both frameworks in large terms, but it is not explicitly articulated, or not articulated in the direction I think necessary to unveil the reach and consequences of complicity with this gender system. I think that articulating this colonial/modern gender system, both in large strokes, and in all its detailed and lived concreteness will enable us to see what was imposed on us. It will also enable us to see its fundamental destructiveness in both a long and wide sense. The intent of this writing is to make visible the instrumentality of the colonial/modern gender system in subjecting us – both women and men of color – in all domains of existence. (Lugones 2007: 189)

Less a dismissive critique and more a necessary elaboration and expansion of coloniality of power, what María Lugones offers is a centering of gender systems in the enactment of colonial powers. The applications are just as relevant in the contemporary context as historical analysis. "To understand the relation of the birth of the colonial/modern gender system to the birth of global colonial capitalism – with the centrality of the coloniality of power to that system of global power – is to understand our present organization of life anew" (Lugones 2007: 187).

The last approach to colonialism is the burgeoning literature on settler colonialism. It begins with the widely recognized and validated assertion that the United States is first and foremost a nation of genocide, with the clearing of Native Americans from their lands to establish White, European supremacy. Scholars who discuss settler colonialism (Smith 2010, Wolfe 2006) are often writing from this historical formation. The further development and the application to Latino communities come from Berkeley scholar Evelyn Nakano Glenn. "I describe U.S. settler colonialism as a race-gender project. By that I mean that it transplanted certain racialized and gendered conceptions and regimes from the metropole but also transformed them in the context of and experiences in the New World. What emerged out of the settler colonial project was a racialized and gendered national identity that normalized male whiteness" (Nakano Glenn 2015: 60).

The impact this has on Latina/os is they are then subject to containment (segregation and labor market segmentation), erasure (forced assimilation), terrorism (state and vigilante violence), and removal (mass deportations). Manifest Destiny shapes how

> the confrontation between Anglo settlers and Mexicans in the American Southwest was a continuation of U.S. settler colonialism's restless expansion. As in the case of settler colonial takeover of Indian land, Anglo takeover of northern Mexico was a race-gender project. In the settler imagination, a feminized and backward Mexican race was giving way to a freedom-loving, democratic progressive Anglo-Saxon or "American" race. Anglo settlers viewed Mexican men as weak, pusillanimous, and above all, lazy. (Nakano Glenn 2015: 63)

Though Nakano Glenn does not talk about Puerto Rico and the rest of Latin America, it is clear that the logic of settler colonialism disproportionately impacts the island with the Treaty of Paris in 1898, Foraker Act of 1900, Insular Cases of 1901, and Jones Act of 1920, which severely restrict the sovereignty and citizenship rights of Puerto Ricans, unlike those that were uniformly extended to Mexicans residing in the United States after the signing of the 1848 Treaty of Guadalupe Hidalgo. It would be remiss to not note that this conversation about post-, de-, internal, settler, and power is meaningless for the world's longest-standing colony – Puerto Rico. For Puerto Ricans, it's simply a matter of colonization, regardless of the window dressing of commonwealth status.

Racializing Latinidades

The historical construction of race in the United States rests on a very different set of assumptions than racial constructions in Latin America.

As distinct from the White/Black paradigm, Latin America's engagement with race thinking has been rooted in the notion of cultural hybridity or racial *mestizaje* since first contact between Europeans, Africans, and Indigenous peoples. In every nation that grappled with the imposition and vestiges of Spanish or Portuguese colonialism, what became valorized was a history not of segregation and separation but of mixture and combination, in spite of the shared genocidal impulses of all European conquerors (see Candelario 2007b). The long history of defining race as a mixture embodies Latin American encounters with *mestizaje*, creolization, mulattoes, mixed bloods, and the cultures of hybridity. In contemporary discussions of race in relation to Latina/os in the United States, "the mantra-like 'race is a social construct' seems to preface almost every serious discussion ... it is accompanied by both scholarly and popular invocations regarding the benefits of hybridity ... Latina/os are constructed as the main embodiment of racial mixture and as carriers of a framework of theoretical legitimacy" (Jiménez Román 2007: 326).

For instance, the confluence of the Indigenous (original inhabitants of Latin America) and the Spanish conquerors of the region in the formation of the mestizo population means different things to Mexicans of Mexico than Mexicans of US descent. The mestizo category that views Mexicans as truly "mixed" and unproblematic is a view restricted, more often than not, to Mexican Americans north of the border. The melding of Spanish and Indigenous is more problematic in Mexico, where class and urban/rural differences often coincide with sharp distinctions between those who view themselves as *Hispano* and therefore White, and those viewed as "Indians" or non-White. Sandra Cisneros' wonderfully textured *Caramelo* highlights these distinctions in stark terms when discussing the Reyes family's convoluted relationships with their servants in Mexico City. Hybridization is confined to those privileged groups in Mexican society that have the power to make and remake themselves in the elite forms of culture. Viewing the Mexican population as *la raza cosmica* is exactly the type of distortion that Mexican elites have foisted upon the general population to both hide their own colonizer roots and deny the general coloniz(er/ed) relationship (and the accompanying social segregation) that persists to this day (see Vasconcelos 1997 [1948]).

Moving beyond a hybridization approach, the developments in Latino education studies and the latest book by Puerto Rican/Latino studies pioneer Juan Flores are the main conduits for introducing Latina/o communities as diasporas. Wortham, Murillo, and Hamann (2002) refer to the "New Latino Diaspora" sixteen times in the first two pages of their introduction, to assert the concept by repetition with very little substantive discussion about why new Latino destinations constitute diasporas. Flores is more critical of this recent turn from a term specific to the long Jewish exile and the dispersal impacts of the slave trade on Africa.

> But nowadays, as of around 1990, anything can be a diaspora, from a food club to a graduating class to a far-flung viewing audience, such that only the minimal sense of dislocation and displacement, as suggested in the etymological metaphor of scattering or sowing seeds (-*sperien*) across space (*dia-*) seems to circumscribe in any way this sprawling and variegated semantic field. Appropriately, there has also been contestation over the very relativism and indeterminacy of such displaced, scattered usages. (Flores 2009: 15)

The diaspora metaphor is often problematically applied to include all migrations, and though distinctions between voluntary and forced (particularly those who migrate for their economic betterment) might be overstated, the uncritical application of the diaspora signifier to all immigrant communities hollows out the analytical power of diasporic studies. Rooting the Latino or Puerto Rican diaspora in Flores' concept of Créolité may make literary sense, but this and its preceding concept of Négritude are often bound to the cultural nationalist impulses of bygone generations and embedded in biologistic reductionisms (from blood mixing to longstanding denigrations of strategic essentialist identities – as Jean-Paul Sartre described them, "anti-racist racisms"). "Furthermore, because the creolizing process has traditionally had central reference to African cultural groundings and to the saliency of blackness, this guiding theoretical concept, more so than alternatives like transculturation, mestizaje or syncretism, lends due attention to the dimension of race and racial identity" (Flores 2009: 29). Unfortunately, terms like creole, mulatto, mestizo, mongrel, and coyote may connote the transracialized origins of contemporary Latinos but they are not easily excised from their biologistic origins, which defined race mixing as producing inferiorities, most often in contradistinction to the equally problematic concept of *blanqueamiento* (see Candelario 2007a for a more detailed discussion of the Dominican experience with "Whitening" or the purging of Blackness and any connections to Haiti).

Furthermore, it is never explained how new destinations for Latino immigrants constitute the conditions necessary to deem them diasporic communities (see Wortham et al. 2002). The decontextualization of the "diaspora" metaphor means it represents, as Quiroz (2006) notes, the movement of Latino "newcomers" to "new destinations" but does not capture the continuities in the racialized treatment of Latino immigrants to new or longstanding destinations; nor does it adequately describe the experiences of schooling, identity formation, or Latino responses to racist treatment. "So too does the researcher who, when portraying that system, clearly describes such racism, yet fails to name it for what it is" (Quiroz 2006: 341).

Moving away from hybrid or diasporic approaches to racialization, and exemplifying the metaphor of difference to explain Latina/o racializations, is De Genova and Ramos-Zayas' (2003) comparative analysis of Mexican–Puerto Rican relations in Chicago. Their stated intent is "to examine how the construction of differences – whether 'cultural' or 'biological' – between Mexicans and Puerto Ricans, *as groups*, operates within a larger social framework of racialized inequalities of power and opportunity" (De Genova and Ramos-Zayas 2003: 2). Their analysis of intra-Latino racializations is unique in both its empirical content and its theoretical application of race as difference.

> Mexican migrants often generalized from the allegation that Puerto Ricans were "lazy" to posit variously that they were likewise untrustworthy, deceptive, willing to cheat, disagreeable, nervous, rude, aggressive, violent, dangerous, and criminal. In constructing these racialized images of the character of Puerto Ricans as a group, Mexicans were implicitly or explicitly celebrating a sense of themselves as educated, well-mannered, and civilized. (De Genova and Ramos-Zayas 2003: 83)

Unfortunately, differences are conceptualized at the level of mutual racializations or stereotypes, so the authors' analysis never moves beyond these surface representations. A shared project of Latinidad, in opposition to Anglo racism is sacrificed to the commitment by the authors to solely analyze and investigate racializations between the two Latino communities.

De Genova embeds most of their work in theories of difference, whether they are talking about markers of cross-national difference (i.e., borders) or racialization as difference (e.g., constructions of Mexican immigrants as "illegal aliens"). Differentiating between spatialized and racialized forms, De Genova frames their "illegality" concept as invoking the nation-state, citizenship, governance, militarization, law, and identity. "The legal production of Mexican (and also Central American) migrant 'illegality' requires the spectacle of enforcement at the U.S.–Mexico border for the spatialized difference between the nation-states of the United States and Mexico (and effectively, all of Latin America) to be socially inscribed upon the migrants themselves" (De Genova 2002: 437). Yet, at the same time as borders represent spatial difference, "the sociopolitical category 'illegal alien' itself – inseparable from a distinct 'problem' or 'crisis' of governance and sovereignty – has come to be saturated with racialized difference and indeed has long served as a constitutive dimension of the racialized inscription of 'Mexicans' in the United States" (De Genova 2002: 433). The point is that difference stands in to do much of the analytical work of constructing everything from identities to nation-state contradictions.

The final manner in which race is theorized in Latina/o studies is in the metaphor of Latina/os as the Other. In their critical interrogation of *mestizaje*, Pérez-Torres comes closest to situating the Othering process in Anglo racializations of Chicanos. "The incorporation of the Mexican Other into American national consciousness birthed the Chicano as a racial being" (Pérez-Torres 2006: 8). Attempting to move the "race as Other" metaphor into Latino racializations, the idea is that race is imposed upon particular Latino groups and the response to that racialization is what Pérez-Torres refers to as critical *mestizaje*.

On a similar imposition, Rocco's (2004: 12) examination of the citizenship literature (particularly the work inspired by Will Kymlicka's multicultural liberalism) results in their positing that Latinos occupy the status of perennial "foreigner." Prefiguring contemporary citizenship debates and therefore not addressing the explicitly "Other"-ed citizenship approach of Benhabib (2004), Rocco notes: "But it is precisely this conception of political community that has been challenged in the last few decades by the various consequences of processes of globalization, particularly the very significant growth in the immigrant, or 'foreign' populations in traditionally Euro- and Anglo-centric societies" (Rocco 2004: 13). The Latino as Other informs the relationship between citizenship and imposed definitions of identity.

> Theories of otherness, on the other hand, assume that difference itself is a historically produced economy, imposed in modern structures of power on the real. Difference as much as identity is an effect of power ... Rather they begin with a strong sense of otherness that recognizes that the other exists, in its own place, as what it is, independently of any *specific* relations. But what it is need not be defined in transcendental or essential terms; what it is can be defined by its particular (contextual) power to affect and be affected. (Grossberg 1997: 351, emphasis in original)

Race thus becomes the underlying logic of Eurocentrism where the images of Europe are as the most technologically advanced, modern, sophisticated, cosmopolitan, rational center that is the culmination of centuries of progress. The rest of the globe is thought to have been inhabited by savages stuck in their traditional, primitive, backward, parochial, irrational cultures. The modernization project puts forward the claim that the undeveloped world is only in need of a little Western assistance to modernize their previously non-scientific ways of viewing the world, their uncultured ways of evaluating it, and their economically backward ways of living. Culture of poverty causal explanations easily stem from this modernization approach.

Recent advances in racial formation theories have been challenged by Barrera (2008), abandoning an earlier, nation-based, internal colony analysis of class and race in the Southwest for an ethnic approach to Latino identity that is consonant with mainstream sociological approaches to Latino immigrant communities. Barrera (2008: 315, 318) notes:

> [m]y own writing and that of Almaguer followed Blauner's lead in using "racial" terminology, but neither of us had a clear or sophisti-cated concept of "race." We differed largely on the importance assigned to class interests in structuring ethnic relations ... Overall, I do not see what is added here by including a racial terminology. It seems that the essence of the relationship can be straightforwardly described as an ethnic relationship in which discrimination does or does not occur and leave it at that.

Yet Barrera's dismissal of the racial formation paradigm shift in Latino studies, ethnic studies, and the sociology of race and ethnicity stems from their etymological reductionism of anything referencing the word "race" as inherently biological and thus inherently racist, even when they consider critical interrogations of the social and historical con-struction of racializations (e.g., Omi and Winant 1994). This sleight of hand of deeming all racial words as inherently racist (including deep interrogations of racialization and anti-racist thought) has been called out by scholars such as Bonilla-Silva (2001, 2006) who notes that defining race as ethnicity, or, similarly yet more popularly, via the "color-blind" ethos of the post-civil rights era, has become exceedingly obfuscating.

Notwithstanding Barrera, recent theories of "race" all agree on the social construction argument. Biological explanations of racial differ-ences do not suffice to explain the persistence of racism. This is where Barrera's ethnicity-based analysis falls short in its imputation of race solely as biology.

> Since there exists now a scholarly consensus that "races" in the bio-logical sense of so-called scientific racism do not exist, it follows that Latinos cannot be a racial minority. I would argue that Latinos are for the most part not a "racialized" minority either, because prevailing discourses about Latinos in American society are not about "race" in the above sense. (Barrera 2008: 316)

But the most important aspect of the social construction argument is that when understandings of the world, groups, or social relations are defined as real, they are very much real in their consequences. Race is no more (or no less) real than class or gender or any other form of social inequality because ascription is always imputed, and most often arbitrarily and contextually as if it is natural or inevitable. The biological is in the end the least relevant to the interests, power relations, and inequalities that mark said distinctions.

In complete agreement with the finding that there is a lack of clearly definable phenotypes that could define racial groups by a set of universal categories, I contend that racist logics are essentialist representations of groups (referring to biological markers, though just as often invoking cultural, linguistic, religious, citizenship, behavioral, attitudinal, and other identifiers). They represent a set of power relations whereby a dominant group imposes definitions on subordinate groups to construct and defend unequal lived experiences. When a group is essentialized to its set of perceived common racial characteristics, it is quite appropriate to talk about race in order to challenge that racism. Rendering racial groups invisible, by denying the use of the term "race," is not a particularly viable solution for the representations of Chicanos/Latinos, Asian Americans, Native Americans, Blacks, or any other group that experiences racism. It is from this theorization of race as racism that we can begin to understand how the concept of race is deployed to shape the lived experiences of racialized communities.

A view of race and its social construction that is more expansive than the hybrid, diaspora, difference, or Othering approaches is offered by theorists who specifically work from the vantage point of non-White groups that do not align along the Black/White color line. "The racialization of Latinos … also entails their incorporation into a white-created and white-imposed racial hierarchy and continuum, now centuries old, with white Americans at the very top and black Americans at the very bottom. Thus, one can speak about the intense racialization of daily life, including health, housing, education, work, friendship, and marriage patterns" (Cobas, Duany, and Feagin 2009: 1). It is not necessarily the characteristics of the racialized group that define race, but rather the perceptions and underlying interests of dominant groups that define subordinate racial groups. Racism is embedded within specific histories that relate to specific subordinate groups. The historical process of the racialization of Puerto Ricans, Dominicans, and Chicanos differs considerably from that of African Americans in the United States and their experiences of slavery, Chinese and Japanese immigrants and their shared indentured servitude and the latter's internment during World War II, and the genocidal treatment of Native Americans.

How the United States Racializes Latinos

For scholars in Latina/o Studies who are working on the historical and social construction of racializations and race, Cobas et al.'s *How the US Racializes Latinos: White Hegemony and its Consequences* is key to our contemporary understandings of theorizing race from Latina/o subject positions. Featuring both established and emerging scholars in the social sciences, the book has as its central analytical framework Feagin's "white racial frame," defined as: "An organized set of racialized ideas, stereotypes, emotions, and inclinations to discriminate ... Critical to the white racial frame is an interrelated set of cognitive notions, understandings, and metaphors that whites have used to rationalize and legitimate systemic racism" (Feagin 2006: 25, 28; Cobas et al. 2009: 3). Couched in this understanding, substantive chapters focus on Census (mis)categorizations of Latinos, urban locales and racial dynamics, linguistic racism, transnational dimensions of White racial frames, Latino interracial relations with Blacks and Haitians, racial violence, articulations with panethnicity, and the specter of Samuel Huntington. The book chapters focus primarily on Latino racializations of Cubans, Dominicans, Mexicans, Chileans, Central Americans, and Puerto Ricans.

A key unifying thread in the collection is the principle that race is a process, not a thing, and thus the verb "racialize" is consistently deployed throughout. In the editors' introduction, they point to the pervasive naturalization of race and oppression (often by invoking the West's greatest and racist thinkers – Immanuel Kant, David Hume, Thomas Jefferson, and Herbert Spencer). Yet they do not amass equivalent examples on the specificities of Latino racializations (other than John C. Calhoun's infamous statements in an 1848 speech opposing the settlement terms of the US–Mexico War)[2] and, albeit quite unintentionally, their introduction can potentially be read as legitimating White racial frames with their attempt at claiming the all-pervasiveness of race. The substantive chapters are much more effective in directly countering White supremacist logics and practices (for example, Gomez' discussion of *mestizaje* versus hypodescent, Carrigan and Webb's lost history of lynched Mexican Americans, and Purcell's analysis of Chileans subjected to racial violence and nativist laws, such as California's Foreign Miners' Tax).

"White over Latino" is most often the main racialized relation analyzed in the book, but Bada and Cardenas' discussion of Black–Latino relations in Los Angeles and Chicago, Perez' comparison of Cuban racializations on the island and in the diaspora, Duany's comparisons of Haitians in the Dominican Republic and Dominicans in Puerto Rico, and

Roth's analysis of countering/absorbing US racializations in those same places point to some of the complexities that define the transnationalization of racialization. Anglo–Latino relations are in many ways easy, uncomplicated examples of racialization in the service of White supremacy, but Valdez' interviews with Houston's Latino restaurant owners and one Chilean's racialization of local Mexican restaurant owners as keeping dirty kitchens point to some of the complexities marking intra-Latino racializations.

The historical specificities of Latino racializations are well represented by Purcell's discussion of racial violence against Chileans during the California Gold Rush, Gomez' familiar interrogation of Manifest Destiny and the uneasiness of one-drop rules as applied to Mexican American history, and Carrigan and Webb's discussion of lynching – the most serious manifestation of racial violence – which identifies the nearly 600 Mexicans who were subjected to the act in the Southwest. Duany's chapter briefly touches upon Trujillo's *blanqueamiento* campaigns to eradicate Haitian, Black bodies from the Dominican Republic.

The geographic specificities of racializations are well noted when considering the relevance of race in global cities such as Miami, Houston, Chicago, and Los Angeles (New York is strikingly absent). It is important to focus on the immigrant gateway cities, where Sassen (2005) identifies Latino "serving classes" who are increasingly present to cater to the needs of affluent post-Fordist producers. Yet the new (and frankly not-so-new) destinations, such as meatpacking towns, resort towns, large-scale agricultural regions, suburbs, and mid-size cities like Dalton, Georgia (Gutiérrez 2004), are undergoing major demographic transformations that are increasingly met with a racial backlash. The chapters by Garcia and Hill discuss the specific process of linking Latino racial identities with linguistic identifications. Hill's provocative discussion of mock Spanish, both Hill's and Garcia's interrogation of Official English as the kinder, gentler version of English-Only, and Garcia's tracing of the political incorporation of bilingualism are important contexts for understanding an essentializing process that links Latinos in their shared fate as perennial US non-citizens, and oftentimes foreigners in their native lands.

Given the new empirical terrain and novel analytical framework that are represented by this book, it is understandable that it contains a few inaccuracies. For instance, only a presentist perspective would inform the claim that 1850s California was marked by raising Hispanic American "Race" consciousness; it is probably more accurate to describe early Chilean–Mexican solidarities as constructing a "Hispanic American" race. In negotiating the complicated terrain of anti-racist work that challenges biological determinism on the one hand and the idea of race as a social and historical construction on the other hand, there are times when the analysis slips into phenotypical and biological essentialisms, and other times when "socially constructed" is equated with myth or fabrication. But most of the chapters remain rooted in the idea that racialization is a social and historical process that is pernicious in its outcomes, regardless of its arbitrary biological categorizations (that is, the old Thomas dictum that if we define situations to be real, they are real in their consequences).

Conclusion

Drawing on relevant components of the new race theories, I seek to develop a theory of race specific to its relationship with racism. I contend that it is a disservice to divorce the race concept from the social conditions that construct races. Race is a product of racism. Races are constructed to legitimate, justify, or naturalize racist actions and institutions. Race is a category that both informs and transcends the Black/White dichotomy. Though race is historically variant, groups that face racism today in the United States have experienced it for the better portion of the nation's existence. Discussions about the "new" racism or "new" nativism disregard the historical roots of racial oppression. When race is defined in terms of racism, inferior identities are imposed by those who view themselves as superior. New terms must be employed in order to articulate the active resistance of those deemed inferior in the racialization process.

Viewing race as racism predisposes one to view racial identities as imposed upon subgroups. In fact, the construction of races is embedded in specific unequal relations that require a rationale for why particular privileged communities live, work, and even die in relative affluence. It is especially important in demonstrating how that relative affluence is at the expense of other groups who are subjected to dirty, dangerous, difficult, and undesirable jobs; expected to live in urban and rural ghettos, *barrios*, and *colonias*; and at certain times in history are murdered, buried in mass, unmarked graves, have their corpses burned en masse, or are not allowed to be buried in Whites-only cemeteries. Living, working, and dying with dignity are markers of privilege, not a basic inalienable right, as evidenced by the history of racialization in the United States.

The forms of racism that each subgroup actively resists differ at the *level* of discriminatory practices. As Omi and Winant (1994: 56) point out, race "is a matter of both social structure and cultural representation." In a separate essay (1993), they demarcate two dominant trends in "race" theorizing that view race as an ideology or race as an objective condition that they juxtapose to their racial formation thesis.[3] Rather than saying the formation of racial groups (i.e., racism) is this or that, for Omi and Winant the reason why racism is so naturalized is that it works at multiple levels. Racism is a set of ideological beliefs; a way of thinking about the world in terms of superior and inferior groups that justifies unequal social conditions. Racism is a historical process that patterns racial segregation in housing, employment, education, health, and leisure activities. Racism is also a set of attitudes and actions that are deployed on the level of interpersonal relations and have very real effects on how people deal with one another. The deployment of stereotypes, hate speech, microaggressions, discriminatory attitudes, and racist behaviors at the interpersonal level is often what instigates violence, denigration, elision, and internalized feelings of inferiority on the part of those racialized. It is at all these levels that the term "racism" is appropriate to describe why racially defined minority groups are systematically excluded from the benefits of US capitalist, White-privileged society.

Theorizing forms of institutional racism, Haney López (1997, 2000) has moved Latino Studies, and the legal academy's LatCrit project, farthest along in considering the relevance of race and law. Yet Haney López erroneously conflates the institutional racism of Stokely Carmichael and Charles Hamilton, which seminally influenced Robert Blauner's (1972) internal colony/structural approach to racism, with the New Institutionalism of organizational sociology, which is decidedly Weberian in its historico-processual analysis of the iron cage of bureaucracy. Similarly, Haney López mistakenly conflates existing race theories and, less problematically, equal protection jurisprudence with rational choice theory to elevate their ethnomethodological approach to institutional actors involved in decision making. "Intentional action has since emerged as a core concept in equal protection jurisprudence, and in theories of racism more generally. In particular, purposeful action is the defining element in discrimination models employing rational choice theory" (Haney López 2000: 1757). Yet purposive action need not be always rational. I fully agree with the judicial analysis by Haney López, who questions the strict scrutiny standard that relegates equal protection only to those subject to purposive discriminatory action. But I depart from Haney López' compulsion to dismiss the interpersonal forms of in-your-face racism in order to establish the institutional paths and scripts for racism's insidious naturalizations. The two levels are not mutually exclusive, nor is one reducible to the other. Racism is both a matter of interpersonal relations governing daily interactions and an institutional process that shapes the boundaries of large-scale social relations.

As Lipsitz (1998: 4–5) notes, "There has always been racism in the United States, but it has not always been the same racism. Political and cultural struggles over power have shaped the contours and dimensions of racism differently in different eras." For Latinos, racism is not only encountered in the United States but also lived out in Latin America. Yet these nuances are lost in the US racialization of Latinos, itself fraught with historical variations. Once the concept of race has been theorized in both its interpersonal and institutional dimensions, it then becomes much easier to explore how race articulates with other forms of domination and resistance. Rather than substituting race for colonialism or nationalism or diaspora or class or ethnicity, one can explore how race articulates with colonialisms, nations, diasporas, classes, and ethnicities. We do not understand race better by conflating it or replacing it with other terms.

9

Conclusion: The Future of the Latina/o Studies Field

Quite simply, the future of the United States and the Américas writ large is inextricably bound up with the fate of Latina/os. In this conclusion, I discuss likely future trends that Latina/o Studies must deal with to remain relevant. I also identify the major themes within Latina/o Studies scholarship that will only grow and develop into the future. With a burgeoning field such as ours, this conclusion ends on hopes and aspirations for the future of Latina/o Studies as well as some warning signs for both dangers ahead and avoiding roads previously traveled that turned out to be dead ends.

The plurality of Latina/o experiences and the sheer complexity of varied Latina/o lives require polyvocality as the *modus operandi* of Latina/o Studies. Multiple voices, multiple experiences, none reducible to the other, is simply the way forward if Latina/o Studies is to remain responsive to the diverse communities it serves. No single discipline will ever suffice to account for Latina/os' relevance to US society so we will continue to need history, literature, sociology, political science, anthropology, geography, visual studies, performance studies, cultural studies, ethnic studies, gender studies, education, and new disciplines to inform Latina/o Studies.

Similarly, there is also a need for a new language on race, racism, ethnicity, colonialism, and nationalism. The conversation on Latinx indigeneity gets us one step closer to that new language (see Blackwell et al. 2017). Resistance to racism by subordinate groups requires a new set of terms that transcends "race." We may talk of "strategic essentialism" or "reverse racism" to explain how solidarities or reactionary politics are formed to mount a resistance to the imposed definitions to which sub-groups are subjected. But rather than saying members of subgroups do not think in racial terms, my contention is solely that the effect this has is qualitatively different than the effects of Anglo racism. Anglo racism is linked to a system of institutions and privileges. The benefits of the system are not equally shared by everyone who can claim Whiteness, but the system certainly furthers the enjoyment of privilege by a few.

A new language to describe the resistance to racism is offered by cultural studies icon Stuart Hall's delineation of "new ethnicities." For Hall, it is ethnicity that enables them to talk about self-identification of Blacks in the face of racism.

> If the black subject and black experience are not stabilized by Nature or by some other essential guarantee, then it must be the case that they are constructed historically, culturally, politically – and the concept which refers to this is "ethnicity." The term ethnicity acknowledges the place of history, language and culture in the construction of subjectivity and identity, as well as the fact that all discourse is placed, positioned, situated, and all knowledge is contextual. (Hall 1996: 446)

The improvement I find in Hall's discussion is the adoption of a new – anti-racist yet non-racialized – language to capture the "politics of self-clarification." Hall's formulation of new ethnicities solves the dilemma of the contemporary responses to racism on the part of negatively racial-ized groups. The question becomes: where do the repertoires of repre-sentation, the cultural materials that comprise the building blocks of resistance, originate? Are they simply imagined? Are they simply fictive representations of the past?

History matters – cultural materials and shared lived experiences do have, at different levels of adherence, an ancestry. Ancestry is not the same as viewing ethnicity as an antique to be preserved intact through-out the ages. Rather, ancestry is very much the story of social rela-tions that connect past and present, while bounding the trajectories of future possibilities. Ancestry must be conceptualized at different levels of lived relations as they are based on family, community, time, space, and place.

Distinguishing ethnic formations from racializations[1] is precisely the way to define the specificity of racialized identities as imposed from above (even when they are marked as a Census-imposed ethnic cat-egory) as distinct from signifying Latina/o from below. This distinguish-ing consists of new ethnicities embedded in the shared lived experiences that define Latinidades embedded in grassroots panethnic associations, transnational community formations, and political projects.

Understanding the processes of racialization, from the perspective of lived experiences, allows one to complexly understand both how race is deployed at the level of everyday practices and how discrimination is deployed at the interpersonal level, as well as how everyday lives are structured by the institutionalization of racialized thoughts and actions to construct a system of racial oppression. At this level of contextualized generality, one can begin to understand race as a comparative and meaningful signifier – both within Latina/o communities and in relation to non-Latinos. This allows for an understanding of how Latina/o identities are informed by multipositionalities, an acknowledgment of the plurality of subject positions that inform social identities in terms of race, class, gender, sexuality, coloniality, nation, and citizenship. No two Latina/os occupy the exact same subject position, so the logic of anti-essentialism drives the understanding of Latina/o identities. This is actualized most fully in the return to community-based research and advocacy scholarship. Listening to life stories, documenting *testimonios*, and activating narratives to humanize Latina/os, both individually and collectively, will counter the negative stereotypes, criminalizations, and demonizations. Whether it be the stories of undocumented students (Gonzales 2015, Perez 2009, 2011), youth who have returned to Mexico as either deportees or following deported family members (Gándara 2016), or the heterogeneous, including Indigenous Latino, population residing in Oregon (Mize 2016a, Stephen 2007), the stories told and lives experienced are barometers of the overall climate for Latina/o incorporation or repulsion in the United States.

Future trends

The rise of anti-immigrant forces holding federal power is a danger sign for the future of Latina/o stability in this era of xenophobic backlash shown by President Donald Trump, Attorney General Jeff Sessions, and Kansas Secretary of State Kris Kobach. Eight themes, which are not going away soon, represent the immediate future trends in Latina/o Studies:

1 demographic futures;
2 new Latina/o destinations;
3 citizenship and undocumented immigration;
4 health issues;
5 housing;
6 economic factors;
7 education;
8 political representation.

These organizing features of Latina/o lived experiences will continue to shape what the field of Latina/o Studies must deal with going forward.

1 Demographic futures

The current size of the Latina/o population and its future growth trends ensure Latina/os will be a formidable force in all aspects of US society. "Latinos are the engine of the US population. Indeed, the Latino population is driving the demography of the US. The future of the US will depend greatly on the fortunes of the Latino population" (Sáenz and Morales 2015: 228). The reality is that many in the United States are unwilling to face a demographic inevitability that will make the White majority the minority as early as 2037 or, more conservatively estimated, by 2042. "The Latino population grew 58 percent between 1990 and 2000 and increased 43 percent between 2000 and 2010" (Fraga et al. 2012: 29). The US Census estimates that by 2060, Latinos will comprise nearly 30 percent of the total population. The relative youth of Latina/os and their status as US citizens or permanent legal residents all but guarantee their future numbers will rewrite who we think about when we ask the question: who's an American? In this demographic context, the sharp inequalities that many Latina/os face will only be exacerbated if current trends hold true. Inequalities in health outcomes, educational success, social mobility, income and wealth, access to full citizenship rights, language rights, political incorporation, civic engagement, and space (land, housing, gentrification) constitute major future dilemmas.

2 New Latina/o destinations

As Latinos migrate to all fifty US states, new Latino destinations have recently resulted in a vast increase of Puerto Ricans in Florida, Mexicans in every state, and Central Americans in the meatpacking and poultry towns of the Midwest and South. New Latina/o communities include Dominican, Central American, and South American immigrants moving into traditional Latino destinations as well as settling in new destinations (e.g., the rise of Salvadorans in the DC metro area, Columbians and Ecuadorans in Jackson Heights, Puerto Ricans in central Florida, and Dominicans in Providence). Demographics in the future and the reality of an imminent White minority and Latino majority in several key cities and states will either be reconciled with current patterns of inequalities and inequities or require a substantial revision of the current US social contract – a Latino nation separate and unequal. Previous research has identified that Latina/

os are dispersed across all US states, and their historical concentrations in specific regions (Mexicans in the Southwest, Cubans in South Florida, and Puerto Ricans in New York City) have been partially superseded by migration to non-traditional or "new" destinations in rural, suburban, and urban areas of, particularly, the South and Midwest (Eckstein and Peri 2018, Kandel and Cromartie 2004, Marrow 2011, Massey 2008, Millard and Chapa 2004, Mize and Peña Delgado 2012, Mize and Swords 2010, Singer, Hardwick, and Brettell 2008, Zúñiga and Hernández-León 2005). As new geographies and labor markets adapt to Latina/o presences, the field must incorporate the diversity of experiences these changes represent.

3   Citizenship and undocumented immigration

Immigration politics stem from what is a profoundly broken immigration and citizenship system. Wait times are in the decades, non-citizens face bureaucratic nightmare scenarios, and immigrant admittance policies in no way match the profile of immigrants who come to the United States. The only "solution" proffered from Washington politics is more borders, more securitization, and more militarization. That decision has proved downright deadly for the thousands of border crossers who have lost their lives traversing *la linea*. Failed comprehensive immigration reform (it has been over twenty years since the last immigration overhaul) creates new categories such as DREAMers. Current politics on immigration reform come directly from those DREAMers who see firsthand the hypocrisies in the system, particularly when President Trump struck down the DACA executive order, then subsequently claimed it was the humane thing to do. A growing number of deportees, well into the millions, are pressing both the Mexican and US governments to reckon with their presence in Mexico, many with little to no prior experience of living in Mexico. Given the current US deportation state of the nation, this problem facing the nation's 10–11 million undocumented immigrants will only worsen in Mexico and the rest of Latin America and the Caribbean. In the next section, on the dangers ahead, I will detail the seismic shifts in contemporary immigrant politics.

4   Health issues

The impact that the immigration debate, deportation threat, and racialized politics have on the mental health of Latina/os will continue to be a source of inquiry. Rumbaut (2008) finds in their research and review of the health sciences literature: "Immigrants are also healthier than natives, that is, until Americanization becomes hazardous to their health. As immigrants become more acculturated over time and generation, their rates of obesity, mortality, and mental and physical health problems actually rise." Scholars such as Sáenz and Morales (2015) refer to the Latina/o epidemiological paradox, which finds that low-income Latina/o immigrants tend to have better health outcomes than those with more racial and economic advantage. These two findings together are not contradictory but point to some clear protective factors that immigrants cultivate to remain healthy, whereas becoming "American" is, all too often, in fact bad for one's health.

5   Housing

Latina/os experience high rates of residential segregation; they are the second most segregated minority group behind African Americans. In particular areas, they also experience hypersegregation, which means they rarely come into contact with non-Latinos due to the overwhelming concentration of Latina/os in their neighborhoods (often *barrios* and *colonias*). Latinos have also been hit hard by the 2008 housing crisis and a longer history of home loan denial and predatory loaning practices that pre-date that crisis. In the post-2008 context, the gentrification of Latino neighborhoods in desirable areas of major cities also builds upon historical precedent. Spatial analysis of Latina/o residential patterns was first called for by Ernesto Galarza in 1973. What scholars today refer to as urban renewal and gentrification, Galarza defined more accurately as barriocide.

> Social scientists have not concerned themselves seriously with its socio-logical significance to the Mexican ethnic group itself, its connection and relationship to the deep currents of American life that do not originate in the barrio but do destroy it physically and culturally. To understand it would require particular studies of what has already happened in Los Angeles, Albuquerque, Phoenix, Fresno, Sacramento, San Antonio and San Diego, to mention only some of the instances of barriocide. (Galarza 2013: 101)

More recently, Latina/o Studies scholars of gentrification differentiate among the policies and periods of urban renewal (Avila 2014, Padilla 1987), White flight and subsequent suburbanization (Avila 2006), and gentrification (Betancur 2011, Dávila 2004). In Latina/o Chicago and Puerto Rican New York, particularly El Barrio, the forces of gentrification have been well documented by John Betancur (2002, 2011) and

Arlene Dávila (2004). Yet most major cities find Latina/os facing soaring rents and property values, no-cause evictions, foreclosures, and re-zoning to attract high-end establishments in California's Bay Area, Los Angeles metropolitan area, and San Diego as well as cities such as Houston and Denver. Gentrification is not about only wealthy Anglos moving into working-class Latina/o neighborhoods; it is also about Latina/os actively resisting their displacement and claiming rights to the city.

6   Economic factors

Barriers to socio-economic mobility, labor market concentration, poverty, and income and wealth inequality are also major issues for Latina/os that will not be remedied adequately or quickly. In the United States, Latina/o "immigrants work in distinctive labor market niches where they account for a high percentage of those employed. In some instances, they replaced earlier immigrants within the niche. Others carved out new niches of their own, often providing products and services not previously available" (Eckstein and Peri 2018: 3). Both exploitation and entrepreneurship are shaping the experiences of Latino/as in the US labor market. The future of Latina/o Studies will have to focus not only on the rise of new destinations, but also on Latina/o laborers in the meatpacking towns of Dodge City, Kansas, Garden City, Kansas, Guymon, Oklahoma, Postville, Iowa, Lexington, Nebraska, Greeley, Colorado, and Tar Heel, North Carolina. Metropolitan areas such as Houston, Washington, DC, Providence, Raleigh, Atlanta, Las Vegas, San Diego, and Nashville will join Miami, Chicago, New York, and Los Angeles as future sites of inquiry to explore immigrant labor niches and entrepreneurship. Economic restructuring is a longstanding focus of Latino Studies scholars but, as Córdova (2016: 69) notes, "since the rise of the regime of neoliberal policies, socioeconomic indicators reveal increased poverty both within the United States and throughout the world." Transnationally, the forces of globalization and free-trade zones displace laborers from their homes as well as draw them to economic centers (both within their nations of origin and across nation-state borders). To keep up with the rapid economic changes, Latina/o Studies must be nimble in its transnational work to account for new, linked, and informal labor markets.

7   Education

One sees how closely related educational inequities perpetuate a state of blocked opportunities in the employment sphere. The study investigators of the 2006 Latino National Survey interviewed Latina/o parents nationwide and found they hold high aspirations and high expectations for their children and the schools they attend, are highly involved in their children's education, and generally view public schools in a favorable fashion; yet this must be squared with "the reality that Latino students have low high school completion, college attendance, and particularly low college graduation rates" (Fraga et al. 2012: 404). One factor informing this conundrum is the long history of schools failing Latina/o children, which blocks future economic opportunities. There are at least 800,000 children, many US citizens, some deportees, and many in mixed-citizenship-status families, who currently find themselves in Mexico due to the US deportation state of the nation (a development that earned President Obama the label deporter-in-chief). A recent binational conference organized by University of California Los Angeles professor Patricia Gándara has led to changes in Mexican law to facilitate the entry of these children into Mexico's public education system, but no solutions are in place to address, for instance, the large number of monolingual English students trying to navigate an educational system in a language they do not speak.

8 Political representation

Finally, given the relative youth of the Latino population, they are becoming an increasingly important voting bloc every election year, and despite Republican attempts to dilute their voting power through gerrymandering and voter suppression efforts, Latina/os are increasing their political representation at all levels of government and challenging barriers to register to vote. There is a consistent argument in the popular press that a Latino voting bloc is a "sleeping giant" ready to be awakened, but never seemingly woke. But as Fraga et al. (2012) and Mize (2016a) note, many Latina/os are not yet eligible to vote. "Although 87 percent of Latinos younger than eighteen are U.S.-born citizens and will be immediately eligible to vote when they reach adulthood, only 60 percent of Latino adults are citizens, and many of those are among the young, another group with historically low participation" (Fraga et al. 2012: 250). Similarly, a report on the State of Latina/o Oregon I conducted for the Oregon Latino Agenda for Action found:

> Even though Latina/os represent more than 12 percent of the state's population, the voting bloc that Latina/os constitute is only 4.9 percent of the voter eligible population. This is primarily due to the youth of the population, not due to immigration or citizenship status. Even

though the number of Latinos is 473, 729, only 164,670 are over the age of 18, native-born or naturalized citizens ... Clearly, in the upcoming years, even with no immigration reform and continued blocked pathways to naturalization, the current Latino voting bloc of 4.9 percent will double and become much more representative of the overall percentage of Latinos in the state. (Mize 2016a: 55–6)

Even with diluted representation, the voting power of Latina/os is starting to be felt in places like heavily Latina/o Woodburn and Salem, Oregon. In 2016, area voters elected State Representative Teresa Alonso Leon (Democrat, House District 22) to represent them, as the first Purépecha (Mexican Indigenous woman) to hold state office in the United States.

Latina/os care not only about immigration politics but about issues such as the economy, education, and healthcare, which consistently poll at the top of lists of Latina/o policy concerns. In the wake of Hurricane Maria in 2017, the island of Puerto Rico was left facing a prolonged environmental disaster of a magnitude unseen by any other US territory or state, which only highlights both its status as the world's oldest colony and the impact of a neoliberal debt crisis blocking basic public infrastructure and citizen access to potable water, electricity, food, and other forms of disaster relief. More political representation and civic engagement have the chance to alter the current crisis in Puerto Rico and head off the dangers that Latina/os face.

Dangers ahead

It is important to note the following dangers that lie ahead for Latina/o incorporation into the United States:

- nationalism;
- migrants, transnationalism, and cosmopolitans vs. US-centrism;
- authenticity policing;
- who's in, who's out;
- finding Latino/a identities in multiraciality;
- colorism – making "White Hispanics";
- assimilation/acculturation;
- Trumpism.

Nationalism has been used to not only restrict access to Latina/o social movements but also define Latina/os as perpetual foreigners in their places of birth. The political language of "putting America first" is precisely the language designed to exclude Latina/os from their rightful place. There is the possibility of global citizenship, but the pressures of nationalist backlash make US-centrism a serious challenge for the well-being of

Latina/os. All too often, communities turn in on themselves when trying to make sense of external threats, and both the definitions of who we are and who we are not and the policing of who's the most Latino – the politics of authenticity – are internal dilemmas that have the ability to destroy the Latina/o Studies intellectual project from within. Externally, the changing nature of multiracial relations itself makes complex identities across racial lines a question of what it will mean to be Latina/o in the near future, or whether multiracial identities will shape questions of social identities. Colorism is an issue within Latina/o communities, to be sure, but the aspect I think of as most problematic is the "white Hispanic" category created by demographers and US Census categorizations. A remnant of the way the US Census struggles to understand how Latina/os self-identify, racially and otherwise, it has quickly become a reified demographic social fact that the category is to be distinguished from non-White Hispanics and analyzed as a distinct group. Finally, the external dangers that most Latina/os face today are the pressures to assimilate and the deleterious effects of assimilation, even as Latina/os find themselves increasingly unwelcome in Trump's America. One final example should suffice.

Arizona has become the epicenter for anti-immigrant sentiments and ensuing legislation. Decisions made at the national level have created fewer viable border crossings. Today, Arizona is the main siphon for undocumented immigrants entering the United States. The two laws aimed at vilifying Latina/os are SB1070, the immigrant profiling law (enforced by Maricopa County Sheriff Joe Arpaio even after it was struck down by the courts, resulting in first his indictment for contempt and then his pardon by President Trump), and SB2281, the Mexican American ethnic studies ban (most recently overturned in a federal court).

Yet these tactics of exclusion and vilification have been in place for over twenty years. With the passage of IIRIRA in 1996, Provision 287g allowed the then Immigration and Naturalization Service to deputize local police forces as federal immigration officers. Romero and Serag (2005) investigated the 1997 joint operation between the Border Patrol and Chandler Police Department to target working-class, Chicano neighborhoods in the Phoenix metropolitan area. In what has come to be known as the Chandler Round-Up, the detainment and inspection of papers of those who looked like "illegals," or were of Mexican ancestry, certainly represents racial profiling. The Round-Up also deployed class profiling, by targeting neighborhoods slated for redevelopment and by stopping pedestrians in public shopping areas, residential streets, and bus stops, and by unannounced house-to-house visits.

The situation has only worsened since the 1997 Chandler Round-Up. The tactic of stopping anybody who looks like an illegal immigrant, particularly with no probable cause, became standard police practice under Sheriff Arpaio (and emboldened by the passage of SB1070 in 2010).[2] Meghan McDowell and Nancy Wonders interviewed Mexican migrant women and immigrant service providers in Phoenix and Tucson to ascertain the impact of surveillance and racial profiling.

> Maricopa County Sheriff Joe Arpaio emerged as one of the most powerful representations of the complex interplay between surveillance and enforcement rituals as a disciplinary force in the lives of migrants ... [H]e is the "mobile, elastic border," the "gaze of surveillance," and the myriad enforcement rituals that (re)inforce migrants "illegality" and vulnerability as a disposable source of labor. (McDowell and Wonders 2009)

SB1070 "Support our Law Enforcement and Safe Neighborhoods" continues the longstanding practice of racial profiling in an increasingly police state.[3] This bill extends recent legislation in Arizona that emboldened these racist agendas: making English the official language of the state (Proposition 106 in 2006); English immersion for limited English proficiency public school students in 2000 (English for the Children – Proposition 203); nearly unilateral rejection of the federal recognition for the Dr. Martin Luther King Jr. national holiday;[4] rogue racial profiling and targeting practices by Sheriff Joe Arpaio; and most recently SB1070, which encourages law enforcement to verify the citizenship documents of anybody detained who with "reasonable suspicion" may be in the state without proper documents. The clear mandate for racial profiling of those deemed "illegal aliens" is in determining reasonable suspicion, as it constitutes an explicit penalty for driving while Brown or speaking to an officer with an accent.

Often not discussed in the passage of ethnic studies ban HB2281 is that the original impetus for the creation of ethnic studies programs in Tucson was a direct response to federal desegregation orders. The linkages between anti-immigrant sentiments and banning ethnic studies should be readily apparent to anyone knowledgeable in Chicano Studies. The linkage, according to Saucedo and Mootz (2012), is best evidenced by Tom Horne, who is making his political career stoking anti-Mexican, Chicano, and immigrant fears as one. "Horne continues to link ethnic studies programs with support for illegal immigration as he makes his case for restrictive state legislation to protect the country from a Mexican invasion." On the other side, what Horne, Pearce, and John Huppenthal (Horne's successor as Arizona Superintendent of Public Instruction) see as being under threat is exactly what the 1980s Kulturkampf (culture struggle) fighters feared: loss of American exceptionalism, challenges to Western rational superiority, and an end to natural law and rights of individuals. Yet this group goes one step further and claims that the United States itself is under threat.

Kobach, former Vice-Chair of President Trump's ill-fated 2017 Commission on Election Integrity and current Kansas Secretary of State, was the architect of Arizona's SB1070 and similar state-level anti-immigration laws. A "smoke 'em out" proponent, Kobach, as legal counsel for the Immigration Law Reform Institute and FAIR, sees state governments as essential in turning up the heat to make undocumented immigrants so miserable that they have no choice but to leave. SB1070, with US Supreme Court approval, allows Arizona law enforcement to racially profile those they suspect of "looking illegal." Similar laws in Alabama, such as HB56 passed in 2010, seeking to supersede federal immigration law have also been crafted and litigated by Kobach. The far right line, very often White nationalist, on immigration is currently holding sway in the Trump White House. In addition to Kobach, Attorney General Jeff Sessions and his former aide Stephen Miller (current Trump senior policy advisor) have espoused the most vitriolic forms of immigrant-bashing over their careers. In the first year of the Trump presidency, we have seen executive orders, and rescissions of past orders, to attack sanctuary cities by proposing the cutting of federal funding; talk of building Trump's wall along the 1,950-mile border; rescission of DACA; enforcement of a Muslim travel ban; ending of Temporary Protected Status for Haitians and Salvadorans; calls to end the diversity lottery; new attacks on legal immigration through family reunification provisions deemed "chain migration"; calls for more immigration from Norway and less from "shithole countries"; and ramping up deportation orders to extend into areas previously deemed "safe." The years ahead can stand to learn something from the US history of using White supremacist logic to inform immigration policy.

For instance, the US state's role in using violence to enforce border and immigration law has a very long history. Lytle Hernández' *Migra! A History of the U.S. Border Patrol* notes of agents that "They used the monopoly on violence granted them as immigration law-enforcement officers to both maintain and manipulate the world in which they lived [Texas–Mexico borderlands] by policing Mexicans as a proxy for policing illegals. In the process, they filled the caste of illegality with Mexican Browns and introduced a unique site of racialization to the U.S.–Mexico borderlands" (Lytle Hernández 2010: 69). As a result, "the border has become a place where immigrant life is being disavowed to the point of death" (Inda 2006: 26). Political decisions are having downright deadly consequences and the level of indifference is jarring to those paying attention. This restriction on the free movement of people, even as goods and services freely traverse borders, is most often discussed as a matter of national security. Specifically, it is the threat of terrorism that governs policy. "[S]ubsequent to the 9/11 attacks, terrorism has generally come to be regarded as the greatest threat facing the nation. And since all the 9/11 hijackers were foreigners who somehow managed to get into the United States, the movement of people in and out of the country has become indissociable from this threat" (Inda 2006: 117). It is clearly the politics of Brown exclusion that link terrorism to immigration, and though Latina/os are not the only group impacted, the narrative that governs their exclusion is clearly the most developed. Though these issues are most pronounced in the era of Trump, they clearly have very long antecedents that will take a long time to rectify.

Hope and promise

Yet Latina/os have had to tap deep reserves of resiliency in the face of such challenges and it is only appropriate that I end on a positive note. Two sets of collective action, one a burgeoning movement and the other a humanitarian act of courage, represent at least some hope in navigating the threats to Latina/o communities. In Latina/o Studies, we often focus on the immigrant rights movement, given it was the largest social protest since the Vietnam War era. Clearly, immigrant rights are being violated daily on the border, in interior enforcement practices, in the rise of deportations, and by the White House. Yet a movement for the right to stay home is increasingly challenging neoliberalism, globalization, and US control over immigration. Particularly in Oaxaca, Indigenous communities are at the head of such movements, increasingly articulated and refined by the Frente Indígena Organizaciones Binacionales (FIOB). "As communities assert their right to not migrate, they are challenging the basic way this international system functions ... challenging the way the economic system is geared to produce displaced people and make migration a matter of survival" (Bacon 2013: 284). Asserting the right to stay home challenges the neoliberal geopolitics that put people in the service of the economy and state.

The second case is a group of women in the small town of Las Patronas, Veracruz,who are actively creating a sense of Latinidad daily with Central American migrants/refugees. *La Bestia* (the Beast) is the cargo train that runs from Central America to the United States through Mexico, and the documentary *Llévate Mis Amores* (Villaseñor et al. 2014) describes the relationship between the male riders of *La Bestia* and the women, *las patronas*, who feed them by handing off and throwing bags of food they prepare to the passengers of the speeding, dangerous train.

> [The documentary provides an] intimate view of *Las Patronas*, a group
> of women living in the Veracruz town of Guadalupe La Patrona on
> the banks of the tracks through which passes the Beast, the danger-
> ous freight train in which hundreds or thousands of migrants travel,
> most of them Central Americans, heading for the United States. Since
> 1995 these women have been preparing, transporting in wheelbarrows
> and delivering food paid for by themselves to those migrants who are
> trying to find a better life in the country of the north. This documen-
> tary shows us a clear example of the love, solidarity, empathy and
> humanitarian commitment of this popular organization.[5]

The documentary is heart-wrenching, but out of the despair comprising
the conditions of travel on *La Bestia*, the willingness to sacrifice time and
resources to help out those even worse off is a testament to the staying
power and fortitude of building Latinidades. It is these forms of resistance and resiliency in political coalitions of Latinidad that can fuel voter
drives, social movements, alternative economies, mutual assistance, and
progressive social change.

Notes

1 What's in a Name?

1 Later in this chapter, we will discuss terminology and labels more fully, but one of the terms that seems to have a longer half-life and the one most often used here is "Latina/o" to identify that the standard use of Latino is very gender restrictive, even though Spanish-language convention requires masculine "o" to stand in for both "o" and feminine "a." The decision to use the term "Latino" is limited and intentional, most often referring to US government definitions or early alternatives to "Hispanic."

2 To respect inclusivity, this book does not refer to scholars by gendered categories but instead uses the gender-inclusive "they" pronoun.

3 US Census. "Hispanic Origin." https://www.census.gov/topics/population/hispanic-origin.html

4 Frank Valdés (1996), in a defense of Latina/o categorizations, has been cited by Norma Cantú and María Fránquiz in their defense of Latin@ labels. "The recent proliferation of outsider or perspective jurisprudence has brought with it questions and critiques of identity and community, of sameness and difference. This sameness/difference multilog, as the works presented in this Colloquium attest, remains open-ended for and among Latinas/os as well. In fact, these works suggest that sameness/difference discourses are compelling to Latinas/os because the category 'Latina/o' is itself a conglomeration of several peoples from varied cultures and localities, all of which have managed to become thoroughly embedded in American society through different yet similar experiences. These group experiences include, but are not exclusively about, Mexican-American, Puerto Rican, and Cuban-American communities. Each of these (and other) Latina/o sub-groups not only comprises 'different' national origins and cultures but also diverse spectrums of races, religions,

genders, classes, and sexualities. Given these multi-textured groups, and their wide ranges of overlapping experiences vis a vis the dominant culture of this Euro-American society, issues of sameness and difference must be a source of fascination and dissection for Latina/o legal scholarship – they are exactly the issues with which any conception or practice of coalitional Latina/o pan-ethnicity in the United States must grapple."

5 Latinidad refers, in this usage, not only to the lived embodiment of Latino identities that transcend definitions of "Hispanic" imposed from above, but also to the separate national origins that internally divide Latina/os. Most often a political project to align power through coalition building and shared interests, it also refers to emerging Latina/o communities where what it means to "be Latina/o" is experienced on a daily basis, and where no one national-origin group presides.

6 The Corona neighborhood in Queens is home to Ecuadorans, Chileans, Salva-dorans, Venezuelans, Argentineans, Bolivians, Uruguayans, Cubans, Domini-cans, Puerto Ricans, and Mexicans.

7 The Pew Center Hispanic Trends study (October 8, 2013) noted: "When asked which term they use most often to describe themselves, 54% use Hispanic origin terms such as Mexican, Cuban, or Dominican and 23% say they use the term American. Another 20% say they use the more broad terms, either 'Hispanic' or 'Latino'" (Lopez 2013).

8 Organizing farmworkers in the Central Valley of California is well docu-mented. Galarza (1970) began organizing on behalf of the National Farm Labor Union during the Bracero Program and became one of its most vocal opponents. AWOC was sponsored by the recently merged American Federa-tion of Labor-Congress of Industrial Organizations (AFL-CIO) and the local branch in Delano represented Filipino farmworkers, many of whom arrived in the Central Valley during the 1910–30 migration wave. At the same time, César Chávez and Dolores Huerta were organizing Mexican farmworkers in Delano under the auspices of the National Farm Workers Association. When Filipinos called for a grape strike in 1965, the NFWA followed suit on August 22, 1966, and forces were combined to form the UFW.

2   Historical Groundings

1 Financed voyages include Columbus' four trips (1492–1503), the colonization of Cuba by Diego Velázquez de Cuéllar in 1511, and expeditions ordered by Velázquez to the Yucatan peninsula in 1517 and 1519 by Francisco Hernández de Córdoba and Juan de Grijalva, to eventually finance Hernan Cortes' mis-sions beginning in 1519, culminating in the invasion of Tenochtitlan in 1521. In addition, the crown financed two circumnavigations of the globe by Elcano and Magellan in 1521 and several explorations of Caribbean islands and South America in the same time period – including those by Amerigo Vespucci (1497–1504), Juan Garrido (multiple campaigns 1502–30: Hispaniola, Puerto Rico, Cuba, Florida, Mexico), Diego de Nicuesa (1506–11: Panamá), Juan Ponce de

León (1508: Puerto Rico, 1513: Florida), Vasco Núñez de Balboa (1510–19: Panamá), Juan Díaz de Solís (1516: Uruguay), Pedro Arias Dávila (1519: Colombia), and Pedro de Alvarado (1519–21: Mexico).

2 My sincerest thanks to Yolanda Flores for referring me to *Our Lives Are the Rivers*.

3 In many ways, Martí was goaded into the 1895 Cuban independence movement. Fellow revolutionary Enrique Collazo Tejada penned an open letter published in an 1892 edition of a Cuban newspaper: "If the hour of sacrifice comes again, we may not be able to shake your hand in the Cuban *manigua* [difficult terrain] – undoubtedly not, because you will be giving the Cuban emigrants lessons in patriotism under the shadow of the American flag" (Martí 2002: 335).

4 Author's translation; original Spanish speech in Juárez (1905 [1862, December 4]: 265).

5 Similar sentiments accompany a bust of Juárez in Mexico's National Palace. The quote on the wall plaque reads in Spanish: "Todo lo que Mexico no haga por sí mismo para ser libre, no debe esperar, ni conviene que espere, que otros gobiernos u otras Naciones hagan por él" ("Everything that Mexico does not do for itself to be free, must not wait, nor should it wait, otherwise other governments or other nations will do it for her").

6 The original reads: "A los revolucionarios más jóvenes, especialmente, recomiendo exigencia máxima y disciplina férrea, sin ambición de poder, autosuficiencie, ni vanaglorias. Cuidarse de métodos y mecanismos burocráticos. ... En la nueva era que vivimos, el capitalismo no sirve ni como instrumento, es como un árbol con raíces podridas del que solo broton las peores formas de indiviualismo, corrupcion y disegualdad."

3   Origins of Latina/o Studies

1 See the conclusion of chapter 5: the language of point (10) became a major source of contention by Puerto Rican women who refused to venerate machismo, and this was eventually revised to read "We want equality for women. Down with machismo and male chauvinism." The full text of the platform can be found in Vázquez and Torres (2003: 342–7).

2 http://www.cwu.edu/~mecha/documents/plan_de_aztlan.pdf. A KCET web program on *El Plan* can be located at https://www.kcet.org/history-society/defining-chicanismo-since-the-1969-denver-youth-conference.

3 In the introduction to *This Bridge Called My Back* (1981: xxiii), Moraga and Anzaldúa identify that "how it all began" was in response to a national feminist writers' organization devoted solely to "white middle-class women" that divided feminists, treated them as tokens, and invited "incidents of intolerance, prejudice and denial of differences within the feminist movement."

4 Orozco (1997: 267) elaborates by calling for gender inclusion as: "we revise 'El Plan de Santa Barbara' to encompass the feminist voice it lacked in 1969. We have appropriately called it 'El Plan de Santa y Barbara' since it is a

proposal written to Chicano studies across the nation in hope that feminism will reemerge in strength. ... [T]he self-determination of the female community is now the only acceptable mandate for social and political action; it is the essence of Chicana commitment."

5 First published in 1989; the University of New Mexico imprint in 1991 is most often referenced. The 2017 revised and expanded edition includes two more women (Cherríe Moraga and "French scholar" [p. 13] Elyette Benjamin-LaBarthe) but the basic structure of the collection remains intact, and the defense of cultural nationalism is even more strident.

6 In 2012, *Occupied America* was one of several books banned in Arizona as a result of the enforcement of H.B. 2281, the anti-Mexican American Studies (MAS) bill. Tucson Unified School District (TUSD) was forced to remove books from classrooms: "following the State's decision, at least seven books that the State deemed 'racist propaganda' were physically removed from TUSD MAS classrooms" (https://digitalcommons.law.seattleu.edu/cgi/viewcontent. cgi?referer=&httpsredir=1&article=1001&context=korematsu_center).

7 Arizona State University, Bakersfield College, California State University (Channel Islands, Dominguez Hills, Fresno, Fullerton, Long Beach, Los Angeles, Northridge, San Diego, San Francisco, San Jose, Sonoma), Claremont Colleges, Colorado State University-Pueblo, Contra Costa College, East Los Angeles College, Eastern Washington University, Fresno City College, Fullerton College, Los Angeles City College, Loyola Marymount University, Mesa College, Metro State College of Denver, Our Lady of the Lake University, San Diego City College, San Diego Mesa College, Santa Barbara City College, Southern Methodist University, Southwestern College, Stanford University, Sul Ross State University, University of Arizona, University of California (Berkeley, Davis, Irvine, Los Angeles, Santa Barbara), University of Minnesota-Twin Cities, University of New Mexico, University of Texas (Austin, El Paso, Pan American, San Antonio), and Washington State University. The majority have maintained their Chicano Studies nomenclature but a few have included Latino Studies or Transborder Chicana/o Latino/a Studies, as at Arizona State University. The University of California, Santa Barbara, is the only PhD-granting program in Chicano Studies, a feat partially due to a very public and litigated discrimination case in the department's refusal to hire an originator of Chicano/a Studies, Rodolfo "Rudy" Acuña (see Acuña 1998, 2011, Martinez 1998: ch. 16).

8 Brooklyn College City University of New York (CUNY), Hunter College CUNY, and Lehman College CUNY. Most also identified as Puerto Rican and Latino Studies, though the vast majority of Puerto Rican Studies programs only offer minors and have transitioned to Latino or Caribbean Studies programs (such as Wayne State University and University of Connecticut).

9 City University of New York (Baruch College, City College, John Jay, Queens College), Columbia University, Connecticut College, Dartmouth College, DePaul University, Fordham University, Iowa State University, Mount Saint Mary College, New York University, Northwestern University, Oberlin College, Rice University, Rutgers University, Smith College, State University of New York (Albany, Oneonta), Syracuse University, Texas A&M University,

University of California Santa Cruz, University of Connecticut, University of Illinois (Chicago, Urbana-Champaign), University of Nebraska-Lincoln, University of Northern Colorado, and University of Notre Dame. Some are combined with Latin American and/or Caribbean Studies and a couple are named Hispanic Studies. The total did not include programs identified as solely American, Latin American, Caribbean, Spanish, Southwestern, or Ethnic Studies even though many of these programs house Chicano/Puerto Rican/Latino professors, students, and coursework, including the University of California Santa Cruz' doctoral program in Latina/o and Latin American Studies. The NACCS Directory can be accessed at: https://www.naccs.org/naccs/Directory1. asp. I cross-checked the directory with PRSA and IUPLR directories and found a handful of discrepancies, so updated information is provided as available.

4   The Arrival of Latina/o Studies

1 "Frank Bonilla, In Memoriam: 1925–2010, *El Boletín*, http://centroweb. hunter.cuny.edu/sites/default/files/pictures/frank_final.pdf
2 In their seminal account of Dominican racial identities, Ginetta Candelario (2007a: 10) refers to Duany's report as "a groundbreaking study of Dominican transnational identity in Washington Heights" and frames their work as answering Duany's call to systematically interrogate race in relation to nation and identity.
3 https://cri.fiu.edu/about
4 This Latinidad ethnography speaks to me personally as I spent my undergraduate college career at the University of Colorado Boulder working as a quite solitary custodian in its Macky Auditorium to pay for college.

5   Latina Feminism, Intersectionalities, and Queer Latinidades

1 Coatlicue is the mother of the gods, the goddess who gave birth to the moon and stars. She also bore Huitzilopochtli, the god of the sun and war, and Coyolxauhqui, the goddess of the southern stars, who was killed and dismembered by her brother. Her body was strewn across the world to make the lands. Xochiquetzal is the goddess of agriculture, fertility, beauty, and female sexual power, who protects young mothers and is the patron of pregnancy, childbirth, and women's handicrafts.
2 https://equalityarchive.com/issues/undocuqueer-movement

7   New Approaches

1 Though Latina/o Studies departments are quite prominent in major public universities across the country (though clearly concentrated in the Northeast and

Southwest), elite private universities (both Ivy League universities and liberal arts colleges) have been quite reluctant to expand ethnic studies classes and programs beyond token faculty and minor offerings. All too often, Latina/o Studies finds itself subsumed under American Studies or retains the perennial "program" status, sparsely populated by faculty in precarious joint appointments to ensure disciplinary primacy.

2 What Galarza offers is a subtle but effective take-down of the culture of poverty thesis. "It is rather an important clue to what may be termed the systems resistance of the poor, of which reluctance to give information is a manifestation. The resistance operates in varying degrees against administration, supervision, enforcement, policing and inquiry. There is among the poor a sort of collective privacy, the invasion into which is resented. There is good reason for this resentment. Privacy is the last refuge of pride and self-respect. It is the condition in which choices can be made or changed without risk of ridicule or punishment. It is also the chance to weigh those choices and their effect on personal security before they are expressed in words or actions. The Mexican-Americans in Oakland may be buffeted rather than helped by urban renewal if all the reasons for their resentment are ignored. It is sometimes held that ghetto and slum dwellers are in that condition because they have a limited range of urban-life skills. The contrary is true. But their skills are of a different order than other urban dwellers. They possess survival skills imposed by individual and collective deprivation of long standing. The 'research gap' will begin to close when planning proceeds by stages sensitive to the priorities that the target community itself accepts. Progress will stimulate the community when it feels and sees movement toward community priorities. Both require organization from within and for the group" (2013: 84).

3 http://americanhistory.si.edu/many-voices-one-nation/new-americans-continuing-debates-1965–2000/marching-liberty

4 The term "microaggressions," as deployed by legal scholars working in the CRT and LatCrit traditions, identifies the exceedingly small but grinding forms of everyday racism that include not only the deployment of stereotypes but also the normalization of white privilege and the taken-for-granted denigration of non-whites. A related political program of Lat Crit is its anti-essentialist position, which denies a unitary, homogenous, one-dimensional account of all Latinos as if the members of the group are all the same.

5 Data are from the United States–México Border Health Coalition, http://www.borderhealth.org/border_region.php. Wilson and Lee (2013) offer more up-to-date data but use a larger catchment area in defining the border to come up with the larger estimate.

6 In Cuidad Juárez, a number of unsolved murders of women *maquiladora* (global assembly factory) workers are frequently referred to as femicides. The critically acclaimed and influential documentary by filmmaker and actress Lourdes Portillo, *Señorita Extraviada* (2001), examines the murders in the context of a complete lack of law enforcement, governmental, or industry concern. The documentary details Portillo's two-year search for the truth behind the murder of *maquila* women and why they are so often viewed as disposable bodies. The marginalization of gendered labor in the *maquilas*

coupled with a lack of state enforcement of the human rights of poor Mexican citizens (on both sides of the border) is implicated in the murders of over five hundred women in the El Paso–Juárez border region.

8 New Perspectives

1 This is precisely why the Trump administration characterizes sanctuary as harboring criminality and defying law and order. Sanctuary is a genuine threat to those who vilify immigrants for their own xenophobic political ends.

2 http://teachingamericanhistory.org/library/document/conquest-of-mexico

3 Similarly, Bonilla-Silva's (2001, 2006) survey of race theories points out that the insidious character of race is due to its operation at multiple levels. Their notion of "racialized social systems" avoids the metaphors of the new race theories while identifying that: "This term refers to societies in which economic, political, social, and ideological levels are partially structured by the place of actors in racial categories or races" (2001: 36). The overemphasis on the structural is the key point of contention here, as I view race as more processual in its social and historical shaping of lived experiences, even though I also find it problematic that "races" tend to be reduced in Bonilla-Silva's analysis to the Black/White binary as a result of the race theories they seek to criticize.

9 Conclusion

1 Interpreting these same dilemmas through the lens of hybrid cultures, Torres-Saillant (2003: 124) takes the hybrid to a new "ethnoracial" level by combining race and ethnicity in the discussion of the category of "Hispanic" or "Latino": "As a 'hybrid category' that entered 'the ethnoracial imagination of American social life' just over a quarter of a century ago, the classification 'Hispanic' remains as pliable as the very texture of race has proven to be." Their analysis of the amalgamated category "Hispanic" or "Latino" not only represents a hybrid category to be deconstructed to its national-origins bases; more problematic is how the hybrid of ethnicity and race is uncritically deployed as fulfilling the identities constituted within national origins.

2 "For any lawful contact made by a law enforcement official or agency of this state or a county, city, town or other political subdivision of this state where reasonable suspicion exists that the person is an alien who is unlawfully present in the United States, a reasonable attempt shall be made, when practicable, to determine the immigration status of the person. the person's immigration status shall be verified with the Federal Government pursuant to 8 United States Code Section 1373(c) (1: 20–26)" (https://www.azleg.gov/legtext/49leg/2r/bills/sb1070s.pdf).

3 Johnson (2003: 331–3). Recalled state Senator Russell Pearce introduced "Homeland Security Bill" SB1108 and SB1070, though he is often not credited with its authorship. Leading the anti-immigrant charge is Kris Kobach, Kansas Secretary of State, who has provided counsel to immigration-restriction groups

the Federation for American Immigration Reform (FAIR) and the American Legislative Exchange Council (ALEC). An NPR story identifies Kobach as the SB1070 author and identifies Pearce's sponsorship of the bill as problematic in its benefiting of private prison companies. The language of what would eventually become SB1070 was presented at a December 2009 meeting of ALEC, where Pearce and private prison company Corrections Corporation of America (CCA) jointly attended.

4 "[A]ll three Arizona House Republicans including current Senator and former presidential candidate John McCain, voted against the bill in 1983. The state did not vote in favor of recognizing the holiday until 1992, not only rejecting pleas from Reagan and then Arizona governor Evan Mecham but also losing the NFL's support when the league moved Super Bowl XXVII from Sun Devil Stadium, in Tempe, to California in protest" (Romero 2010).

5 Original documentary description: "Visión íntima de Las Patronas, grupo de mujeres que vive en el pueblo veracruzano de Guadalupe La Patrona a la orilla de las vías por las que pasa La Bestia, el peligroso tren de carga en el que viajan cientos o miles de migrantes, en su mayoría centroamericanos, rumbo a Estados Unidos. Desde 1995 estas mujeres preparan, transportan en carretillas y entregan alimentos pagados por ellas mismas a aquellos migrantes que intentan encontrar una vida mejor en el país del norte. Este documental nos deja ver un claro ejemplo del amor, la solidaridad, la empatía y el compromiso humanitario de esta organización popular."

References

Acuña, Rodolfo. 1998. *Sometimes There is No Other Side*. Notre Dame, IN: University of Notre Dame Press.

Acuña, Rodolfo. 2011. *The Making of Chicana/o Studies: In the Trenches of Academe*. New Brunswick, NJ: Rutgers University Press.

Acuña, Rodolfo. 2014. *Occupied America: A History of Chicanos*, 8th edn. Boston, MA: Pearson.

Alamillo, Jose M. 2006. *Making Lemonade out of Lemons: Mexican American Labor and Leisure in a California Town 1880–1960*. Urbana: University of Illinois Press.

Albizu Campos, Pedro. 1980 [1930]. "Observations on the Brookings Institution Report," pp. 173–80 in *The Intellectual Roots of Independence: An Anthology of Puerto Rican Political Essays*, edited by Iris M. Zavala and Rafael Rodríguez. New York, NY: Monthly Review Press.

Aldama, Arturo J., Chela Sandoval, and Peter J. García. 2012. *Performing the US Latina and Latino Borderlands*. Bloomington: Indiana University Press.

Almaguer, Tomás. 1984. "Racial Domination and Class Conflict in Capitalist Agriculture: The Oxnard Sugar Beet Workers' Strike of 1903," *Labor History* 25 (3): 325–50.

Almaguer, Tomás. 1994. *Racial Fault Lines: The Historical Origins of White Supremacy in California*. Berkeley: University of California Press.

Alvarado, Stephanie J. 2014. *Queer Latinx Feminist Futurism: F.K.A. Latina Reproductive Justice*. Unpublished Master's thesis, Emory University.

Alvarez, Luis. 2008. *The Power of the Zoot: Youth Culture and Resistance During World War II*. Berkeley: University of California Press.

Alvarez, Wilfredo. 2013. "Finding 'Home' in/through Latinidad Ethnography: Experiencing Community in the Field with 'My People'," *Liminalities: A Journal of Performance Studies* 9 (2): 49–58.

Anaya, Rudolfo, and Francisco Lomeli, eds. 1989. *Aztlán: Essays on the Chicano Homeland*. Albuquerque: University of New Mexico Press.

Anderson, Jon Lee. 1997. *Che Guevara: A Revolutionary Life*. New York, NY: Grove Press.

Andreas, Peter. 2000. *Border Games: Policing the U.S.–Mexico Divide*. Ithaca, NY: Cornell University Press.

Anzaldúa, Gloria. 1987. *Borderlands/La Frontera: The New Mestiza*. San Francisco, CA: Aunt Lute Books.

Anzaldúa, Gloria, ed. 1990. *Making Face, Making Soul/Haciendo Caras: Creative and Critical Perspectives by Feminists of Color*. San Francisco, CA: Aunt Lute Books.

Anzaldúa, Gloria. 1999. *Borderlands/La Frontera*, 2nd edn. San Francisco, CA: Aunt Lute Books.

Anzaldúa, Gloria. 2009. *The Gloria Anzaldúa Reader*, edited by AnaLouise Keating. Durham, NC: Duke University Press.

Anzaldúa, Gloria. 2015. *Light in the Dark = Luz En Lo Oscuro: Rewriting Identity, Spirituality, Reality*, edited by AnaLouise Keating. Durham, NC: Duke University Press.

Anzaldúa, Gloria, and AnaLouise Keating, eds. 2002. *This Bridge We Call Home: Radical Visions for Transformation*. New York, NY: Routledge.

Aparicio, Frances R. 1998. *Listening to Salsa: Gender, Latin Popular Music, and Puerto Rican Cultures*. Middletown, CT: Wesleyan Press.

Aparicio, Frances R., and Cándida F. Jáquez, eds. 2003. *Musical Migrations: Transnationalism and Cultural Hybridity in Latin/o America*. New York, NY: Palgrave Macmillan.

Arana, Marie. 2013. *Bolívar: American Liberator*. New York, NY: Simon and Schuster.

Aranda, Elizabeth M., Sallie Hughes, and Elena Sabogal. 2014. *Making a Life in Multiethnic Miami: Immigration and the Rise of a Global City*. Boulder, CO: Lynne Rienner.

Arias, Arturo. 2003. "Central American-Americans: Invisibility, Power and Representation in the US Latino World," *Latino Studies* 1 (1): 168–87.

Arias, Arturo, and Claudia Milian. 2013. "US Central Americans: Representations, Agency and Communities," *Latino Studies* 11 (2): 131–49.

Arreola, Daniel, ed. 2004. *Hispanic Spaces, Latino Places: Community and Cultural Diversity in Contemporary America*. Austin: University of Texas Press.

Avila, Eric. 2006. *Popular Culture in the Age of White Flight: Fear and Fantasy in Suburban Los Angeles*. Berkeley: University of California Press.

Avila, Eric. 2014. *The Folklore of the Freeway: Race and Revolt in the Modernist City*. Minneapolis: University of Minnesota Press.

Baca Zinn, Maxine. 1993. "Feminist Re-Thinking from Racial-Ethnic Families," pp. 303–14 in *Women of Color in U.S. Society*, edited by Maxine Baca Zinn and Bonnie Thornton Dill. Philadelphia, PA: Temple University Press.

Bacon, David. 2013. *The Right to Stay Home: How US Policy Drives Mexican Migration*. Boston, MA: Beacon Press.

Baker, Beth F., and Ester E. Hernández. 2017. "Defining Central American Studies," *Latino Studies* 15 (1): 86–90.

Balderrama, Francisco E., and Raymond Rodríguez. 2006. *Decade of Betrayal: Mexican Repatriation in the 1930s.* Albuquerque: University of New Mexico Press.

Barrera, Mario. 1989. *Race and Class in the Southwest: A Theory of Racial Inequality.* Notre Dame, IN: University of Notre Dame Press.

Barrera, Mario. 2008. "Are Latinos a Racialized Minority?" *Sociological Perspectives* 51: 305–24.

Barrera, Mario, and Geralda Vialpando. 1974. *Action Research: In Defense of the Barrio.* Los Angeles, CA: Aztlán.

Barreto, Matt, and Gary M. Segura. 2014. *Latino America: How America's Most Dynamic Population is Poised to Transform the Politics of the Nation.* New York, NY: PublicAffairs (Perseus Books).

Beltrán, Cristina. 2010. *The Trouble with Unity: Latino Politics and the Creation of Identity.* New York, NY: Oxford University Press.

Benhabib, Seyla. 2004. *The Rights of Others: Aliens, Residents, and Citizens.* Cambridge: Cambridge University Press.

Benmayor, Rina. 2012. "Digital Testimonio as a Signature Pedagogy for Latin@ Studies," *Equity & Excellence in Education* 45 (3): 507–24.

Bennett, Claudette. 2000. "Racial Categories Used in the Decennial Censuses, 1790 to the Present," *Government Information Quarterly* 172: 161–80.

Betancur, John J. 2002. "The Politics of Gentrification: The Case of West Town in Chicago," *Urban Affairs Review* 37 (6): 780–814.

Betancur, John J. 2011. "Gentrification and Community Fabric in Chicago," *Urban Studies* 48 (2): 383–406.

Bhabha, Homi. 1994. *The Location of Culture.* New York, NY: Routledge.

Bianet Castellanos, M., Lourdes Gutiérrez Nájera, and Arturo J. Aldama, eds. 2012. *Comparative Indigeneities of the Américas: Toward a Hemispheric Approach.* Tucson: University of Arizona Press.

Blackmer Reyes, Kathryn, and Julia E. Curry Rodriguez. 2012. "*Testimonio*: Origins, Terms, and Resources," *Equity & Excellence in Education* 45 (3): 525–38.

Blackwell, Maylei. 2011. *¡Chicana Power! Contested Histories of Feminism in the Chicano Movement.* Austin: University of Texas Press.

Blackwell, Maylei, Floridalma Boj Lopez, and Luis Urrieta Jr. 2017. "Introduction: Critical Latinx Indigeneities," *Latino Studies* 15 (2): 126–37.

Blauner, Robert. 1972. *Racial Oppression in America.* New York, NY: Harper and Row.

Bolívar, Simón. 2003. *El Libertador: Writings of Simón Bolívar.* New York, NY: Oxford University Press.

Bolívar, Simón. 2008. *Simón Bolívar: Essays on the Life and Legacy of the Liberator,* edited by David Bushnell and Lester D. Langley. Lanham, MD: Rowman and Littlefield.

Bolívar, Simón. 2009. *Hugo Chavez Presents Simón Bolívar: The Bolívarian Revolution.* New York, NY: Verso Books.

Bonilla, Frank. 1985. "Ethnic Orbits: The Circulation of Capitals and Peoples," *Contemporary Marxism* 10: 148–67.

Bonilla, Frank. 1997. "Brother, Can You Paradigm?" *Inter-University Program for Latino Research* 1: 1–10.

Bonilla-Silva, Eduardo. 2001. *White Supremacy and Racism in the Post-Civil Rights Era.* Boulder, CO: Lynne Rienner.

Bonilla-Silva, Eduardo. 2006. *Racism Without Racists: Color-Blind Racism and the Persistence of Racial Inequality in the United States,* 2nd edn. Lanham, MD: Rowman and Littlefield.

Bourgois, Philippe. 2003. *In Search of Respect: Selling Crack in El Barrio,* 2nd edn. New York, NY: Cambridge University Press.

Boyer, Ernest. 1990. *Scholarship Reconsidered: Priorities of the Professoriate.* Menlo Park, CA, Carnegie Foundation for the Advancement of Teaching.

Brady, Mary Pat. 2002. *Extinct Lands, Temporal Geographies: Chicana Literature and the Urgency of Space.* Durham, NC: Duke University Press.

Cabán, Pedro A. 2001. *Constructing a Colonial People: Puerto Rico and the United States, 1898–1932.* Boulder, CO: Westview Press.

Cabán, Pedro. 2003. "Moving from the Margins, to Where? Three Decades of Latino Studies," *Latino Studies* 1 (1): 5–35.

Calderón, José Zapata. 2015. *Lessons from an Activist Intellectual: Teaching, Research, and Organizing for Social Change.* Lanham, MD: University Press of America.

Camarillo, Albert. 1979. *Chicanos in a Changing Society: From Mexican Pueblos to American Barrios in Santa Barbara and Southern California, 1848–1930.* Cambridge, MA: Harvard University Press.

Caminero-Santangelo, Marta. 2009. *On Latinidad: U.S. Latino Literature and the Construction of Ethnicity.* Gainesville: University of Florida Press.

Candelario, Ginetta E. B. 2007a. *Black Behind the Ears: Dominican Racial Identity from Museums to Beauty Shops.* Durham, NC: Duke University Press.

Candelario, Ginetta E. B. 2007b. "Color Matters: Latina/o Racial Identities and Life Chances," pp. 337–50 in *A Companion to Latina/o Studies,* edited by Juan Flores and Renato Rosaldo. Malden, MA: Blackwell.

Candelario, Ginetta E. B., Elizabeth S. Manley, and April J. Mayes, eds. 2016. *Cien Años de Feminismos Dominicanos. Tomo I: El Fuego Tras Las Ruines, 1865–1931.* Santo Domingo: Editora Centenario, Archivo General de la Nación.

Cantú, Norma E., and María E. Fránquiz, eds. 2010. *Inside the Latin@ Experience: A Latin@Studies Reader.* Boulder, CO: Palgrave Macmillan.

Carrasco, Enrique R. 1996. "Opposition, Justice, Structuralism, and Particularity: Intersections between Latcrit Theory and Law and Development Studies," *University of Miami Inter-American Law Review* 28: 313–37.

CCCHE (Chicano Coordinating Council on Higher Education). 1969. *El Plan de Santa Barbara.* Oakland: La Causa.

Cepeda, María Elena. 2010. *Musical ImagiNation: U.S. Colombian Identity and the Latin Music Boom.* New York: New York University Press.

Cervantes, Fred A. 2003. "Chicanos as a Postcolonial Minority: Some Questions Concerning the Adequacy of the Paradigm of Internal Colonialism," pp. 331–42 in *Latino/a Thought: Culture, Politics, and Society,* edited by Francisco H. Vázquez and Rodolfo D. Torres. Lanham, MD: Rowman and Littlefield.

Chabram, Angie, and Rosa Linda Fregoso. 1990. "Chicana/o Cultural Representations: Reframing Alternative Critical Discourses," *Cultural Studies* 4: 203–16.

Chavez, Cesar. 2008. *An Organizer's Tale: Speeches*, edited by Ilan Stavans. New York, NY: Penguin.

Chávez, Karma R. 2013. *Queer Migration Politics: Activist Rhetoric and Coalitional Possibilities*. Urbana: University of Illinois Press.

Chavez, Leo R. 1997. "Immigration Reform and Nativism: The Nationalist Response to the Transnationalist Challenge," pp. 61–77 in *Immigrants Out! The New Nativism and the Anti-Immigrant Impulse in the United States*, edited by Juan Perea. New York: New York University Press.

Chavez, Leo R. 2001. *Covering Immigration: Popular Images and the Politics of the Nation*. Berkeley: University of California Press.

Chavez, Leo R. 2008. *The Latino Threat: Constructing Immigrants, Citizens, and the Nation*. Palo Alto, CA: Stanford University Press.

Chavez, Leo R. 2012. *Shadowed Lives: Undocumented Immigrants in American Society*. New York, NY: Wadsworth.

Cho, Sumi, and Robert Westley. 2002. "Historicizing Critical Race Theory's Cutting Edge: Key Movements that Performed the Theory," pp. 32–70 in *Crossroads, Directions, and a New Critical Race Theory*, edited by Francisco Valdes, Jerome McCristal Culp, and Angela P. Harris. Philadelphia, PA: Temple University Press.

Chomsky, Aviva. 2007. *They Take Our Jobs! And 20 Other Myths about Immigration*. Boston, MA: Beacon Press.

Cisneros, Sandra. 2003. *Caramelo*. New York, NY: Vintage.

Cobas, J. A., J. Duany, and J. R. Feagin, eds. 2009. *How the United States Racializes Latinos: White Hegemony and its Consequences*. Boulder, CO: Paradigm.

Córdova, Teresa. 2016. "The Neoliberal Policy Regime and Implications for Latino Studies Scholarship," *Aztlán: A Journal of Chicano Studies* 41 (1): 55–83.

Cotera, Marta. 1997. "Our Feminist Heritage," pp. 41–3 in *Chicana Feminist Thought: The Basic Historical Writings*, edited by Alma Garcia. New York, NY: Routledge.

Crenshaw, Kimberlé Williams. 2002. "The First Decade: Critical Reflections, or a 'Foot in the Closing Door'," pp. 9–31 in *Crossroads, Directions, and a New Critical Race Theory*, edited by Francisco Valdes, Jerome McCristal Culp, and Angela P. Harris. Philadelphia, PA: Temple University Press.

Cruz, Cindy. 2001. "Toward an Epistemology of a Brown Body," *Qualitative Studies in Education* 14 (5): 657–69.

Cruz, José E. 1998. "Pushing Left to Get to the Center: Puerto Rican Radicalism in Hartford, Connecticut," pp. 69–87 in *The Puerto Rican Movement: Voices from the Diaspora*, edited by Andrés Torres and José E. Velázquez. Philadelphia, PA: Temple University Press.

Cuadraz Holguin, Gloria, and Yolanda Flores. 2017. *Coming Home: Testimonios de Los Valles*. Tucson: University of Arizona Press.

Dávila, Arlene. 1997. *Sponsored Identities: Cultural Politics in Puerto Rico*. Philadelphia, PA: Temple University Press.

Dávila, Arlene. 2001. *Latinos, Inc.: The Marketing and Making of a People*. Berkeley: University of California Press.

Dávila, Arlene. 2004. *Barrio Dreams: Puerto Ricans, Latinos, and the Neoliberal City*. Berkeley: University of California Press.

Dávila, Arlene. 2008. *Latino Spin: Public Image and the Whitewashing of Race*. New York: New York University Press.

De Genova, Nicholas. 2002. "Migrant 'Illegality' and Deportability in Everyday Life," *Annual Review of Anthropology* 31: 419–47.

De Genova, Nicholas. 2005. *Working the Boundaries: Race, Space, and "Illegality" in Mexican Chicago*. Durham, NC: Duke University Press.

De Genova, Nicholas, and Ana Ramos-Zayas. 2003. *Latino Crossings: Mexicans, Puerto Ricans, and the Politics of Race and Citizenship*. New York, NY: Routledge.

De León, Arnoldo. 1983. *They Called Them Greasers: Anglo Attitudes toward Mexicans in Texas, 1821–1900*. Austin: University of Texas Press.

de los Angeles Torres, María. 2001. *In the Land of Mirrors: Cuban Exile Politics in the United States*. Ann Arbor: University of Michigan Press.

de los Angeles Torres, María. 2004. *The Lost Apple: Operation Pedro Pan, Cuban Children in the U.S., and the Promise of a Better Future*. Boston, MA: Beacon Press.

de Onís, Catalina (Kathleen) M. 2017. "What's in an 'x'? An Exchange about the Politics of 'Latinx'," *Chiricú Journal* 1 (2): 78–91.

Delgado, Grace Peña. 2013. *Making the Chinese Mexican: Global Migration, Localism, and Exclusion in the U.S.–Mexico Borderlands*. Palo Alto, CA: Stanford University Press.

Delgado, Richard. 1989. "Storytelling for Oppositionalists and Others: A Plea for Narrative," *Michigan Law Review* 87 (8): 2411–41.

Delgado, Richard. 1995. *The Rodrigo Chronicles: Conversations About America and Race*. New York: New York University Press.

Delgado, Richard. 1996. *The Coming Race War: And Other Apocalyptic Tales of America after Affirmative Action and Welfare*. New York: New York University Press.

Delgado, Richard. 2013. "Precious Knowledge, State Bans on Ethnic Studies, Book Traffickers (Librotraficantes) and a New Type of Race Trial," *North Carolina Law Review* 91: 1513–24.

Delgado, Richard, and Jean Stefancic. 2004. *Understanding Words that Wound*. Boulder, CO: Westview Press.

Delgado, Richard, and Jean Stefancic. 2010. *The Latina/o Condition: A Critical Reader*, 2nd edn. New York: New York University Press.

Demby, Gene. 2013. "'Latin@' Offers A Gender-Neutral Choice; But How To Pronounce It?" National Public Radio, January 7. http://www.npr.org/sections/thetwo-way/2013/01/07/168818064/latin-offers-a-gender-neutral-choice-but-how-to-pronounce-it

Denis, Nelson A. 2016. *War Against All Puerto Ricans: Revolution and Terror in America's Colony*. New York, NY: Nation Books.

Denning, Michael. 1998. *The Cultural Front: The Laboring of American Culture in the Twentieth Century*. New York, NY: Verso Books.

Deutsch, Sarah. 1989. *No Separate Refuge: Culture, Class, and Gender on an Anglo-Hispanic Frontier in the American Southwest, 1880–1940*. New York, NY: Oxford University Press.

Diaz, Ella Maria. 2017. *Flying Under the Radar with the Royal Chicano Air Force: Mapping a Chicano/a Art History*. Austin: University of Texas Press.

Duany, Jorge. 2002. *The Puerto Rican Nation on the Move: Identities on the Island and in the United States*. Chapel Hill: University of North Carolina Press.

Duany, Jorge. 2008 [1994]. *Quisqueya on the Hudson: The Transnational Identity of Dominicans in Washington Heights*. CUNY Dominican Studies Institute. http://academicworks.cuny.edu/dsi_pubs/1

Eckstein, Susan, and Giovanni Peri. 2018. "Immigrant Niches and Immigrant Networks in the US Labor Market," *RSF: The Russell Sage Foundation Journal of Social Sciences* 4 (1): 1–17.

Enck-Wanzer, Darrel, ed. 2010. *The Young Lords: A Reader*. New York: New York University Press.

Espitia, Marilyn. 2004. "The Other 'Other' Hispanics: South American-Origin Latinos in the United States," pp. 257–80 in *The Columbia History of Latinos in the United States Since 1960*, edited by David G. Gutiérrez. New York, NY: Columbia University Press.

Falconi, José Luis, and José Antonio Mazzotti, eds. 2007. *The Other Latinos: Central and South Americans in the United States*. Cambridge, MA: David Rockefeller Center for Latin American Studies, Harvard University Press.

Feagin, Joe R. 2006. *Systemic Racism: A Theory of Oppression*. New York, NY: Routledge.

Ferriss, Susan, and Ricardo Sandoval. 1998. *The Fight in the Fields: César Chávez and the Farmworkers Movement*. San Diego, CA: Mariner Books.

Fink, Leon. 2003. *The Maya of Morganton: Work and Community in the Nuevo New South*. Chapel Hill: University of North Carolina Press.

Flores, Juan. 2000. *From Bomba to Hip-Hop: Puerto Rican Culture and Latino Identity*. New York, NY: Columbia University Press.

Flores, Juan. 2009. *The Diaspora Strikes Back: Caribeño Tales of Learning and Turning*. New York, NY: Routledge.

Flores, Juan, and Renato Rosaldo, eds. 2007. *A Companion to Latina/o Studies*. Malden, MA: Blackwell.

Flores, Richard R. 1995. *Los Pastores: History and Performance in the Mexican Shepherd's Play of South Texas*. Washington, DC: Smithsonian Press.

Flores, Richard R. 2002. *Remembering the Alamo: Memory, Modernity, and the Master Symbol*. Austin: University of Texas Press.

Foley, Douglas E., Clarice Mota, Donald E. Post, and Ignacio Lozano. 1988. *From Peones to Politicos: Class and Ethnicity in a South Texas Town, 1900–1987*. Austin: University of Texas Press.

Foley, Neil. 1999. *The White Scourge: Mexicans, Blacks, and Poor Whites in Texas Cotton Culture*. Berkeley: University of California Press.

Fox, Jonathan, and Gaspar Rivera-Salgado, eds. 2004. *Indigenous Mexican Migrants in the United States*. La Jolla, CA: Center for US-Mexican Studies, UCSD, and Center for Comparative Immigration Studies, UCSD.

Fraga, Luis R., John A. Garcia, Michael Jones-Correa, Valerie Martinez-Ebers, and Gary M. Segura. 2012. *Latinos in the New Millennium: An Almanac of Opinion, Behavior, and Policy Preferences*. New York, NY: Cambridge University Press.

Galarza, Ernesto. 1956. *Strangers in Our Fields: Based on a Report Regarding Compliance with the Contractual, Legal, and Civil Rights of Mexican Agricultural Contract Labor in the United States*, 2nd edn. Washington, DC: United States Section, Joint United States–Mexico Trade Union Committee.

Galarza, Ernesto. 1964. *Merchants of Labor: The Mexican Bracero History*. Santa Barbara, CA: McNally and Loftin.

Galarza, Ernesto. 1970. *Spiders in the House, Workers in the Field*. Notre Dame, IN: University of Notre Dame Press.

Galarza, Ernesto. 2013. *Man of Fire: Selected Writings of Ernesto Galarza*, edited by Armando Ibarra and Rodolfo Torres. Urbana-Champaign: University of Illinois Press.

Gándara, Patricia. 2016. "Policy Report/*Informe*, The Students We Share/*Los estudiantes que compartimos*," *Mexican Studies/Estudios Mexicanos* 32 (2): 357–78.

Garbow, Diane Goode. 2016. *Crafting Colombianidad: The Politics of Race, Citizenship and the Localization of Policy in Philadelphia*. Unpublished doctoral dissertation, Temple University.

Garcia, John A. 2016. *Latino Politics in America: Community, Culture, and Interests*, 3rd edn. Lanham, MD: Rowman and Littlefield.

García, Maria Cristina. 1996. *Havana USA: Cuban Exiles and Cuban Americans in South Florida, 1959–1994*. Berkeley: University of California Press.

García, Mario T. 1981. *Desert Immigrants: The Mexicans of El Paso 1880–1920*. New Haven, CT: Yale University Press.

García, Mario T. 1989. *Mexican Americans: Leadership, Ideology, and Identity, 1930–1960*. New Haven, CT: Yale University Press.

García, Mario T. 1995. *Memories of Chicano History: The Life and Narrative of Bert Corona*. Berkeley: University of California Press.

García, Mario T., ed. 2008. *A Dolores Huerta Reader*. Albuquerque: University of New Mexico Press.

Garcia, Matt. 2014. *From the Jaws of Victory: The Triumph and Tragedy of César Chávez and the Farm Worker Movement*. Berkeley: University of California Press.

García Bedolla, Lisa. 2005. *Fluid Borders: Latino Power, Identity, and Politics in Los Angeles*. Berkeley: University of California Press.

García Bedolla, Lisa. 2014. *Latino Politics*, 2nd edn. Cambridge: Polity.

García Canclini, Néstor. 1995. *Hybrid Cultures*. Minneapolis: University of Minnesota Press.

García Márquez, Gabriel. 1990. *The General in His Labyrinth*. New York, NY: Vintage.

Gilmore Wilson, Ruth. 2005. "Pierce the Future for Hope: Mothers and Prisoners in the Post-Keynesian California Landscape," pp. 231–53 in *Global Lockdown: Race, Gender, and the Prison-Industrial Complex*, edited by Julia Sudbury. New York, NY: Routledge.

Gonzales, Roberto G. 2015. *Lives in Limbo: Undocumented and Coming of Age in America.* Oakland: University of California Press, 2015.

Gonzales, Rodolfo. 2003. "I Am Joaquín: An Epic Poem," pp. 75–87 in *Latino/a Thought: Culture, Politics, and Society,* edited by Francisco H. Vázquez and Rodolfo D. Torres. Lanham, MD: Rowman and Littlefield.

Gonzalez, Juan. 2011. *Harvest of Empire: A History of Latinos in America.* New York, NY: Penguin.

Grasmuck, Sherri, and Patricia R. Pessar. 1991. *Between Two Islands: Dominican International Migration.* Berkeley: University of California Press.

Griswold del Castillo, Richard. 1980. *The Los Angeles Barrio, 1850–1890: A Social History.* Berkeley: University of California Press.

Grosfoguel, Ramon. 2008. "World-System Analysis and Postcolonial Studies: A Call for a Dialogue from the 'Coloniality of Power' Approach," pp. 94–104 in *The Postcolonial and the Global,* edited by Revathi Krishnaswamy and John C. Hawley. Minneapolis: University of Minnesota Press.

Grosfoguel, Ramón, Nelson Maldonado-Torres, and Jose David Salvídar. 2006. *Latin@s in the World-System: Decolonization Struggles in the 21st Century U.S. Empire.* New York, NY: Routledge.

Grossberg, Lawrence. 1997. *Bringing It All Back Home: Essays on Cultural Studies.* Durham, NC: Duke University Press.

Guerra, Lilian. 2016. "Late Twentieth Century Immigration and US Foreign Policy," pp. 126–49 in *The New Latino Studies Reader: A Twenty-First-Century Perspective,* edited by Ramón A. Gutiérrez and Tomás Almaguer. Berkeley: University of California Press.

Guevara, Ernesto Che. 1964. "Address to United Nations General Assembly," December 11. https://www.marxists.org/archive/guevara/1964/12/11.htm

Guevara, Ernesto Che. 2003. *The Motorcycle Diaries: Notes on a Latin American Journey.* New York, NY: Ocean Press.

Guevarra Jr., Rudy P. 2012. *Becoming Mexipino: Multiethnic Identities and Communities in San Diego.* New Brunswick, NJ: Rutgers University Press.

Gutiérrez, David, ed. 2004. *The Columbia History of Latinos in the United States Since 1960.* New York, NY: Columbia University Press.

Gutiérrez, José Angel. 1999. *The Making of a Chicano Militant: Lessons from Cristal.* Madison: University of Wisconsin Press.

Gutiérrez, Ramón A. 1991. *When Jesus Came, the Corn Mothers Went Away: Marriage, Sexuality, and Power in New Mexico, 1500–1846.* Palo Alto, CA: Stanford University Press.

Gutiérrez, Ramón A. 2016. "What's in a Name?" pp. 19–53 in *The New Latino Studies Reader: A Twenty-First-Century Perspective,* edited by Ramón A. Gutiérrez and Tomás Almaguer. Berkeley: University of California Press.

Guttman, Matthew. 2006. *Meanings of Macho.* Berkeley: University of California Press.

Habell-Pallán, Michelle. 2005. *Loca Motion: The Travels of Chicana and Latina Popular Culture.* New York: New York University Press.

Hall, Stuart. 1996. "New Ethnicities," pp. 441–9 in *Stuart Hall: Critical Dialogues in Cultural Studies,* edited by David Morley and Kuan-Hsing Chen. New York, NY: Routledge.

Hallett, Miranda Cady. 2012. "'Better Than White Trash': Work Ethic, Latinidad and Whiteness in Rural Arkansas," *Latino Studies* 10 (1–2): 81–106.

Hames-García, Michael R. 2011. "Queer Theory Revisited," pp. 19–45 in *Gay Latino Studies: A Critical Reader*, edited by Michael R. Hames-Garcia and Ernesto Javier Martínez. Durham, NC: Duke University Press.

Hamilton, Nora, and Norma Stoltz Chinchilla. 1991. "Central American Migration: A Framework for Analysis," *Latin American Research Review* (Winter): 75–110.

Hamilton, Nora, and Norma Stoltz Chinchilla. 2001. *Seeking Community in a Global City: Guatemalans and Salvadorans in Los Angeles*. Philadelphia, PA: Temple University Press.

Haney López, Ian. 1997. "Race, Ethnicity, Erasure: The Salience of Race to LatCrit Theory," *La Raza Law Journal* 10: 57–125.

Haney López, Ian. 2000. "Institutional Racism: Judicial Conduct and a New Theory of Racial Discrimination," *Yale Law Journal* 109: 1717–1884.

Haney López, Ian. 2006. *White by Law: The Legal Construction of Race*. New York: New York University Press.

Haney López, Ian. 2015. *Dog Whistle Politics: How Coded Racial Appeals Have Reinvented Racism and Wrecked the Middle Class*. New York, NY: Oxford University Press.

Harris, Angela P. 1989–90. "Race and Essentialism in Feminist Legal Theory," *Stanford Law Review* 42: 581–616.

Hattam, Victoria. 2005. "Ethnicity and the Boundaries of Race," *Daedalus* 134: 61–70.

Hernández, Jose A. 1983. *Mutual Aid for Survival: The Case of the Mexican American*. Malabar, FL: Kreiger.

Hernández, Tanya. K. 2003. "Response to Silvio Torres-Saillant: 'Too Black to Be Latino/a': Blackness and Blacks as Foreigners in Latino Studies," *Latino Studies* 1: 152–9.

Hernández-Truyol, Berta E. 1996. "Building Bridges: Bringing International Human Rights Home," *La Raza Law Journal* 9: 69–81.

Hernández-Truyol, Berta E. 2008. "The Gender Bend: Culture, Sex and Sexuality – A LatCritical Human Rights Map of Latina/o Border Crossings," *Indiana Law Journal* 83: 1283–1331.

Heyman, Josiah. 2008. "Constructing a Virtual Wall: Race and Citizenship in U.S.–Mexico Border Policing," *Journal of the Southwest* 50: 305–34.

History Task Force, Center for Puerto Rican Studies. 1979. *Labor Migration under Capitalism*. New York, NY: Monthly Review Press.

Hondagneu-Sotelo, Pierrette. 1994. *Gendered Transitions: Mexican Experiences of Immigration*. Berkeley: University of California Press.

Horton, John. 1995. *The Politics of Diversity: Immigration, Resistance, and Change in Monterey Park, California*. Philadelphia, PA: Temple University Press.

Hurtado, Aída, and Mrinal Sinha. 2016. *Beyond Machismo: Intersectional Latino Masculinities*. Austin: University of Texas Press.

Inda, Jonathan Xavier. 2006. *Targeting Immigrants: Government, Technology, and Ethics*. Malden, MA: Blackwell.

Irizarry, Ylce. 2016. *Chicana/o and Latina/o Fiction: The New Memory of Lati-nidad*. Urbana: University of Illinois Press.

Jiménez Román, Miriam. 2007. "Looking at that Middle Ground: Racial Mixing as Panacea?" pp. 325–36 in *A Companion to Latina/o Studies*, edited by Juan Flores and Renato Rosaldo. Malden, MA: Blackwell.

Jiménez Román, Miriam, and Juan Flores, eds. 2010. *The Afro-Latin@ Reader: History and Culture in the United States*. Durham, NC: Duke University Press.

Johnson, Kevin R., ed. 2003a. *Mixed-Race America and the Law: A Reader*. New York: New York University Press.

Johnson, Kevin R. 2003b. *The "Huddled Masses" Myth: Immigration and Civil Rights*. Philadelphia, PA: Temple University Press.

Jones-Correa, Michael. 2007. "Swimming in the Latino Sea: The Other Latinos and Politics," pp. 21–38 in *The Other Latinos: Central and South Americans in the United States*, edited by José Luis Falconi and José Antonio Maz-zotti. Cambridge, MA: David Rockefeller Center for Latin American Studies, Harvard University Press.

Juárez, Benito. 1905 [1862, December 4]. "El cuidadano Benito Juárez, Presi-dente Constitucional de la República, a la nación," in *Discursos y manifiestos de Benito Juárez*, edited by Angel Pola. Mexico: Biblioteca Reformista.

Kandel, William, and John Cromartie. 2004. "New Patterns of Hispanic Set-tlement in Rural America," *USDA Online*, http://www.ers.usda.gov/media/561319/rdrr99_1_.pdf

Kun, Josh, and Laura Pulido, eds. 2014. *Black and Brown in Los Angeles: Beyond Conflict and Coalition*. Berkeley: University of California Press.

La Fountain-Stokes, Lawrence. 2009. *Queer Ricans: Cultures and Sexualities in the Diaspora*. Minneapolis: University of Minnesota Press.

Ladson-Billings, Gloria and William F. Tate IV. 1995. "Toward a Critical Race Theory of Education," *Teachers College Record* 97: 47–68.

Lawrence III, Charles R. 2008. "Unconscious Racism Revisited: Reflections on the Impact and Origins of 'The Id, the Ego, and Equal Protection'," *Connecti-cut Law Review* 40: 931–78.

León-Portilla, Miguel. 2006. *The Broken Spears: The Aztec Account of the Conquest of Mexico*. Boston, MA: Beacon Press.

Levitt, Peggy. 2001. *The Transnational Villagers*. Berkeley: University of Cali-fornia Press.

Lewis, Oscar. 1959. *Five Families: Mexican Case Studies in the Culture of Poverty*. New York, NY: Basic Books.

Lewis, Oscar. 1968. *La Vida: A Puerto Rican Family in the Culture of Poverty – San Juan and New York*. New York, NY: Vintage.

LFG (Latina Feminist Group). 2001. *Telling to Live: Latina Feminist Testimo-nios*. Durham, NC: Duke University Press.

Limón, José E. 1994. *Dancing with the Devil: Society and Cultural Poetics in Mexican-American South Texas*. Madison: University of Wisconsin Press.

Limón, José E. 1999. *American Encounters: Greater Mexico, the United States, and the Erotics of Culture*. Boston, MA: Beacon Press.

Limón, José E. 2003. "El Primer Congreso Mexicanista de 1911: A Precursor to Contemporary Chicanismo," pp. 220–39 in *Latino/a Thought: Culture,*

Politics, and Society, edited by Francisco H. Vázquez and Rodolfo D. Torres. Lanham, MD: Rowman and Littlefield.

Lipsitz, George. 1998. *The Possessive Investment in Whiteness: How White People Profit from Identity Politics*. Philadelphia, PA: Temple University Press.

Lomas, Laura. 2008. *Translating Empire: José Martí, Latino Subjects, and American Modernities*. Durham, NC: Duke University Press.

López, Gustavo, and Kristen Bialik. 2017. "Key Findings about U.S. Immigrants." *FactTank*, May 3. Pew Research Center. http://www.pewresearch.org/fact-tank/2017/05/03/key-findings-about-u-s-immigrants

Lopez, Mark Hugo. 2013. "Hispanic or Latino? Many Don't Care, Except in Texas." http://www.pewresearch.org/fact-tank/2013/10/28/in-texas-its-hispanic-por-favor

López-Garza, Marta, and David R. Diaz, eds. 2001. *Asian and Latino Immigrants in the Restructuring Economy: The Metamorphosis of Southern California*. Palo Alto, CA: Stanford University Press.

Lugones, María. 2007. "Heterosexualism and the Colonial/Modern Gender System," *Hypatia* 22 (1): 186–219.

Lytle Hernández, Kelly. 2010. *Migra! A History of the U.S. Border Patrol*. Berkeley: University of California Press.

Malagon, Maria C., Lindsay Perez Huber, and Veronica N. Velez. 2009. "Our Experiences, Our Methods: Using Grounded Theory to Inform a Critical Race Theory Methodology," *Seattle Journal for Social Justice* 8: 253–70.

Malavé, Idelisse, and Esti Giordani. 2015. *Latino Stats: American Hispanics by the Numbers*. New York, NY: New Press.

Manrique, Jaime. 2007. *Our Lives Are the Rivers*. New York, NY: HarperCollins.

Marchi, Regina M. 2009. *Day of the Dead in the USA: The Migration and Transformation of a Cultural Phenomenon*. New Brunswick, NJ: Rutgers University Press.

Mariscal, George. 1999. *Aztlán and Viet Nam: Chicano and Chicana Experiences of the War*. Berkeley: University of California Press.

Marrow, Helen. 2011. *New Destination Dreaming: Immigration, Race, and Legal Status in the Rural American South*. Palo Alto, CA: Stanford University Press.

Martí, José. 2002. *Selected Writings*. New York, NY: Penguin.

Martinez, Elizabeth. 1998. *De Colores Means All of Us: Latina Views for a Multi-Colored Century*. Boston, MA: South End Press.

Martinez, Ernesto. 2008. *Border Chinese: Making Space and Forging Identity in Mexicali, Mexico*. Unpublished doctoral dissertation, Harvard University.

Martinez, George A. 1997. "The Legal Construction of Race: Mexican-Americans and Whiteness," *Harvard Latino Law Review* 2: 321–47.

Martínez, Oscar J. 2006. *Troublesome Border*. Tucson: University of Arizona Press.

Marx, Karl. 1858. "Bolivar y Ponte, Simon," *The New American Cyclopaedia, vol. III*. https://www.marxists.org/archive/marx/works/1858/01/Bolívar.htm

Massey, Douglas, ed. 2008. *New Faces in New Places: The Changing Geography of American Immigration*. New York, NY: Russell Sage Foundation.

Massie, Chris. 2017. "Steve King: Blacks and Hispanics 'Will Be Fighting Each Other' Before Overtaking Whites in Population," *CNN*, March 14. http://www.cnn.com/2017/03/14/politics/kfile-steve-king-prediction/index.html

Matsuda, Mari J. 1987. "Looking to the Bottom: Critical Legal Studies and Reparations," *Harvard Civil Rights-Civil Liberties Law Review* 22: 323–400.

Matsuda, Mari J., Charles R. Lawrence III, Richard Delgado, and Kimberlé Williams Crenshaw. 1993. *Words That Wound: Critical Race Theory, Assaultive Speech, and the First Amendment*. Boulder, CO: Westview Press.

McDowell, Meghan G., and Nancy A. Wonders. 2009. "Keeping Migrants in Place: Technologies of Control and Racialized Public Space in Arizona," *Social Justice* 36: 54–62.

Meléndez, Edgardo. 2017. *Sponsored Migration: The State and Puerto Rican Postwar Migration to the United States*. Columbus: Ohio State University.

Melendez, Miguel "Mickey." 2005. *We Took the Streets: Fighting for Latino Rights with the Young Lords*. New Brunswick, NJ: Rutgers University Press.

Menjívar, Cecilia. 2000. *Fragmented Ties: Salvadoran Immigrant Networks in America*. Berkeley: University of California Press.

Menjívar, Cecilia. 2017. "Studying Central Americans in Latino Studies," *Latino Studies* 15 (1): 91–4.

Meyer, Michael C., and William H. Beezley. 2000. *The Oxford History of Mexico*. New York, NY: Oxford University Press.

Millard, Ann V., and Jorge Chapa. 2004. *Apple Pie and Enchiladas: Latino Newcomers in the Rural Midwest*. Austin: University of Texas Press.

Minh-Ha, Trinh T. 1989. *Woman, Native, Other: Writing Postcoloniality and Feminism*. Bloomington: Indiana University Press.

Mize, Ronald L. 2008. "Interrogating Race, Class, Gender and Capitalism Along the U.S.–Mexico Border: Neoliberal Nativism and *Maquila* Modes of Production," *Race, Gender and Class* 15 (1/2): 134–55.

Mize, Ronald L. 2014. "The Contemporary Assault on Ethnic Studies," *John Marshall Law Review* 47 (4): 1189–1210.

Mize, Ronald L. 2016a. "Oregon Latino Agenda for Action (OLAA) Full Report," presented to OLAA Summit 2016: Stronger Together/*Fuerza Unida*. Portland State University, September 24. http://www.olaaction.org.

Mize, Ronald L. 2016b. *The Invisible Workers of the U.S.–Mexico Bracero Program: Obreros Olvidados*. Lanham, MD: Lexington Books.

Mize, Ronald L., and Grace Peña Delgado. 2012. *Latino Immigrants in the United States*. Cambridge: Polity.

Mize, Ronald L., and Alicia C. S. Swords. 2010. *Consuming Mexican Labor: From the Bracero Program to NAFTA*. Toronto: University of Toronto Press.

Molina-Guzmán, Isabel. 2010. *Dangerous Curves: Latina Bodies in the Media*. New York: New York University Press.

Montejano, David. 1987. *Anglos and Mexicans in the Making of Texas, 1836–1986*. Austin: University of Texas Press.

Montejano, David. 2010. *Quixote's Soldiers: A Local History of the Chicano Movement, 1966–1981*. Austin: University of Texas Press.

Montoya, Margaret E. 1994. "*Mascaras, Trenzas, y Grenas*: Un/Masking the Self While Un/Braiding Latina Stories and Legal Discourse," *Harvard Women's Law Journal* 17: 185–220.

Mora, G. Cristina. 2014. *Making Hispanics: How Activists, Bureaucrats, and Media Constructed a New American*. Chicago, IL: University of Chicago Press.

Moraga, Cherríe, and Gloria Anzaldúa, eds. 1981. *This Bridge Called My Back: Writings by Radical Women of Color*. San Francisco, CA: Kitchen Table/ Women of Color Press.

Morales, Iris. 2016. *Through the Eyes of Rebel Women: The Young Lords 1969–1976*. New York, NY: Red Sugarcane Press.

Morales, Rebecca, and Frank Bonilla, eds. 1993. *Latinos in a Changing U.S. Economy: Comparative Perspectives on Growing Inequality*. Newbury Park, CA: Sage.

Morgan, Shanté. 2015. "CSUN Establishes Nation's First Department of Central American Studies," *CSUN Today*. https://csunshinetoday.csun.edu/university-news/csun-establishes-nations-first-department-of-central-american-studies

Moynihan, Daniel Patrick. 1965. *The Negro Family: The Case for National Action*. Washington, DC: U.S. Department of Labor, Office of Policy Planning and Research.

Muñoz Jr., Carlos. 2007. *Youth, Identity, Power: The Chicano Movement*. New York, NY: Verso Books.

Muñoz, José Esteban. 1999. *Disidentifications: Queers of Color and the Performance of Politics*. Minneapolis: University of Minnesota Press.

Muñoz, José Esteban. 2009. *Cruising Utopia: The Then and There of Queer Futurity*. New York: New York University Press.

Nakano Glenn, Evelyn. 2015. "Settler Colonialism as Structure: A Framework for Comparative Studies of U.S. Race and Gender Formation," *Sociology of Race and Ethnicity* 1: 52–72.

NACCS (National Association for Chicana and Chicano Studies). n.d. "History of NACCS." https://www.naccs.org/naccs/History.asp

Negrón-Muntaner, Frances. 2004. *Boricua Pop: Puerto Ricans and the Latinization of American Culture*. New York: New York University Press.

Negrón-Muntaner, Frances. 2015. "The Look of Sovereignty: Style and Politics in the Young Lords," *Centro Journal* 27 (1): 4–33.

Nowrasteh, Alex. 2017. "Immigration Myths: Crime and the Number of Illegal Immigrants," *Cato at Liberty*, March 20. https://www.cato.org/blog/immigration-myths-crime-number-illegal-immigrants

O'Brien, Eileen. 2008. *The Racial Middle: Latinos and Asian Americans Living Beyond the Racial Divide*. New York: New York University Press.

Oboler, Suzanne. 1995. *Ethnic Labels, Latino Lives: Identity and the Politics of (Re)Presentation in the United States*. Minneapolis: University of Minnesota Press.

Oboler, Suzanne, and Deena J. González, eds. 2005. *The Oxford Encyclopedia of Latinos and Latinas in the United States*, 4 vols. New York, NY: Oxford University Press.

Oboler, Suzanne, and Deena J. González, eds. 2015. *The Oxford Encyclopedia of Latinos and Latinas in Contemporary Politics, Law, and Social Movements.* New York, NY: Oxford University Press.

Obregón Pagán, Eduardo. 2003. *Murder at the Sleepy Lagoon: Zoot Suits, Race, and Riot in Wartime L.A.* Chapel Hill: University of North Carolina Press.

Ocampo, Anthony C. 2016. *The Latinos of Asia: How Filipino Americans Break the Rules of Race.* Palo Alto, CA: Stanford University Press.

Omi, Michael, and Howard Winant. 1993. "On the Theoretical Concept of Race," pp. 3–10 in *Race, Identity, and Representation in Education,* edited by Cameron McCarthy and Warren Crichlow. New York, NY: Routledge.

Omi, Michael, and Howard Winant. 1994. *Racial Formation in the United States: From the 1960s to the 1990s,* 2nd edn. New York, NY: Routledge.

Oropeza, Lorena. 2005. *¡Raza Sí! ¡Guerra No!: Chicano Protest and Patriotism during the Viet Nam War Era.* Berkeley: University of California Press.

Orozco, Cynthia. 1997. "Sexism in Chicano Studies and the Community," pp. 265–9 in *Chicana Feminist Thought: The Basic Historical Writings,* edited by Alma M. García. New York, NY: Routledge.

Pacheco, Denise, and Veronica N. Velez. 2009. "Maps, Mapmaking, and Critical Pedagogy: Exploring GIS and Maps as a Teaching Tool for Social Change," *Seattle Journal for Social Justice* 8: 273–99.

Padilla, Elena. 1958. *Up from Puerto Rico.* New York, NY: Columbia University Press.

Padilla, Elena. 2011. *Latino Urban Ethnography and the Work of Elena Padilla,* edited by Mérida Rúa. Urbana: University of Illinois Press.

Padilla, Felix M. 1985. *Latino Ethnic Consciousness: The Case of Mexican Americans and Puerto Ricans in Chicago.* Notre Dame, IN: University of Notre Dame Press.

Padilla, Felix M. 1987. *Puerto Rican Chicago.* Notre Dame, IN: University of Notre Dame Press.

Pardo, Mary. 1998. *Mexican American Women Activists.* Philadelphia, PA: Temple University Press.

Paredes, Americo. 1996 [1958]. *With His Pistol in His Hand: A Border Ballad and its Hero.* Austin, TX: University of Texas Press.

Paredez, Deborah. 2009. *Selenidad: Selena, Latinos, and the Performance of Memory.* Durham, NC: Duke University Press.

Peña, Devon. 1997. *The Terror of the Machine: Technology, Work, Gender, and Ecology on the U.S.–Mexico Border.* Austin: University of Texas Press.

Perales, Monica. 2010. *Smeltertown: Making and Remembering a Southwest Border Community.* Chapel Hill: University of North Carolina Press.

Pérez, Emma. 1999. *The Decolonial Imaginary: Rewriting Chicanas into History.* Bloomington: Indiana University Press.

Pérez, Gina M. 2004. *The Near Northwest Side Story: Migration, Displacement, and Puerto Rican Families.* Berkeley: University of California Press.

Pérez, Laura. 2007. *Chicana Art: The Politics of Spiritual and Aesthetic Altarities.* Durham, NC: Duke University Press.

Perez, William. 2009. *We Are Americans: Undocumented Students Pursuing the American Dream.* New York, NY: Stylus.

Perez, William. 2011. *Americans by Heart: Undocumented Latino Students and the Promise of Higher Education*. New York, NY: Teachers College Press.

Pérez-Torres, Rafael. 2006. *Mestizaje: Critical Uses of Race in Chicano Culture*. Minneapolis: University of Minnesota Press.

Pesquera, Beatriz, and Denise Segura. 1997. "There Is No Going Back: Chicanas and Feminism," pp. 294–309 in *Chicana Feminist Thought: The Basic Historical Writings*, edited by Alma M. García. New York, NY: Routledge.

Pessar, Patricia R. 1996. *A Visa for a Dream: Dominicans in the United States*. New York, NY: Pearson.

Poniatowska, Elena. 1979. *Hasta no verte Jesús mío*. Mexico City: Ediciones Era.

Poniatowska, Elena. 1998. *La noche de Tlatelolco: Testimonios de historia oral*, 2nd edn. México, D.F. Mexico City: Ediciones Era.

Potowski, Kim. 2015. "Ethnolinguistic Identities and Ideologies among Mexicans, Puerto Ricans, and 'MexiRicans' in Chicago," pp. 13–30 in *A Sociolinguistics of Diaspora: Latino Practices, Identities, and Ideologies*, edited by Rosina Márquez Reiter and Luisa Martín Rojo. New York, NY: Routledge.

Prewitt, Kenneth. 2005 "Racial Classification in America: Where Do We Go from Here?" *Daedalus* 134 (1): 5–18.

Pulido, Laura. 2006. *Black, Brown, Yellow and Left: Radical Activism in Los Angeles*. Berkeley: University of California Press.

Quijano, Anibal. 2000. "Coloniality of Power, Eurocentrism, and Latin America," *Nepantla: Views from South* 1 (3): 533–80.

Quiroz, Pamela A. 2006. "Book Review, *Education in the New Latino Diaspora: Policy and the Politics of Identity*," *Latino Studies* 4: 340–1.

Ramírez, Catherine S. 2009. *The Woman in the Zoot Suit: Gender, Nationalism, and the Cultural Politics of Memory*. Durham, NC: Duke University Press.

Ramos Zayas, Ana. 2003. *National Performances: The Politics of Class, Race, and Space in Puerto Rican Chicago*. Chicago, IL: University of Chicago Press.

Ricourt, Milagros, and Ruby Danta. 2002. *Hispanas de Queens: Latino Panethnicity in a New York City Neighborhood*. Ithaca, NY: Cornell University Press.

Rios, Victor M. 2011. *Punished: Policing the Lives of Black and Latino Boys*. New York: New York University Press.

Rios, Victor M. 2017. *Human Targets: Schools, Police, and the Criminalization of Latino Youth*. Chicago, IL: University of Chicago Press.

Rivera, Christopher. 2014. "The Brown Threat: Post-9/11 Conflations of Latina/os and Middle Eastern Muslims in the US American Imagination," *Latino Studies* 12 (10): 44–64.

Rivera-Servera, Ramon H. 2012. *Performing Queer Latinidad: Dance, Sexuality, Politics*. Ann Arbor: University of Michigan Press.

Rocco, Raymond. 2004. "Transforming Citizenship: Membership, Strategies of Containment, and the Public Sphere in Latino Communities," *Latino Studies* 2: 4–25.

Rodríguez, Clara E. 2000. *Changing Race: Latinos, the Census, and the History of Ethnicity in the United States*. New York: New York University Press.

Rodríguez, Clara E., Irma M. Olmedo, and Mariolga Reyes-Cruz. 2003. "Deconstructing and Contextualizing the Historical and Social Science Literature on Puerto Ricans," pp. 288–314 in *Handbook of Research on Multicultural*

Education, 2nd edn, edited by James Banks and Cherry McGee Banks. New York, NY: Jossey-Bass.

Rodríguez, Havidán, Rogelio Sáenz, and Celia Menjívar, eds. 2007. *Latinas/os in the United States: Changing the Face of América*. New York, NY: Springer.

Rodríguez, Juana María. 2003. *Queer Latinidad: Identity Practices, Discursive Spaces*. New York: New York University Press.

Rodríguez, Juana María. 2014. *Sexual Futures, Queer Gestures, and Other Latina Longings*. New York: New York University Press.

Rodríguez, Luis J. 2005. *Always Running, La Vida Loca: Gang Days in L.A.* New York, NY: Touchstone.

Román, Ediberto, and Christopher B. Carbot. 2008. "Freeriders and Diversity in the Legal Academy: A New Dirty Dozen List?" *Indiana Law Journal* 83 (4): 1235–66.

Romero, Frances. 2010. "A Brief History of Martin Luther King Day," *Time Magazine*, January 18. http://www.time.com/time/nation/article/0,8599,1872501,00.html#ixzz0qIuNByN3

Romero, Mary. 1992. *Maid in the U.S.A.* New York, NY: Routledge.

Romero, Mary, and Marwah Serag. 2005. "Violation of Latino Civil Rights Resulting from INS and Local Police's Use of Race, Culture and Class Profiling: The Case of the Chandler Roundup in Arizona," *Cleveland State Law Review* 52: 75–86.

Romero, Mary, Pierrette Hondagneu-Sotelo, and Vilma Ortiz, eds. 1997. *Challenging Fronteras: Structuring Latina and Latino Lives in the U.S.* New York, NY: Routledge.

Romero, Robert Chao. 2012. *The Chinese in Mexico, 1882–1940*. Tucson: University of Arizona Press.

Romo, Ricardo. 1983. *East Los Angeles: History of a Barrio*. Austin: University of Texas Press.

Rondilla, Joanne L., Rudy P. Guevarra Jr., and Paul Spickard, eds. 2017. *Red and Yellow, Black and Brown: Decentering Whiteness in Mixed Race Studies*. New Brunswick, NJ: Rutgers University Press.

Rosa, Jonathan. 2015. "Nuevo Chicago? Language, Diaspora, and Latina/o Panethnic Formations," pp. 31–47 in *A Sociolinguistics of Diaspora: Latino Practices, Identities, and Ideologies*, edited by Rosina Márquez Reiter and Luisa Martín Rojo. New York, NY: Routledge.

Ruiz, Vicki. 1987. *Cannery Women, Cannery Lives: Mexican Women, Unionization, and the California Food Processing Industry, 1930–1950*. Albuquerque: University of New Mexico Press.

Ruiz, Vicki, and Ellen Carol DuBois, eds. 2007. *Unequal Sisters: An Inclusive Reader in U.S. Women's History*, 4th edn. New York, NY: Routledge.

Ruiz, Vicki, and Virginia Sánchez Korrol, eds. 2006. *Latinas in the United States: A Historical Encyclopedia*. Bloomington: Indiana University Press.

Rumbaut, Rubén. 2008. "Undocumented Immigration and Rates of Crime and Imprisonment: Popular Myths and Empirical Realities," Invited Address to the Immigration Enforcement and Civil Liberties: The Role of Local Police National Conference, Police Foundation, Washington, DC. https://ssrn.com/abstract=1877365

Rumbaut, Rubén. 2009. "Pigments of Our Imagination: On the Racialization and Racial Identities of Hispanics and Latinos," pp. 15–36 in *How the United States Racializes Latinos: White Hegemony and its Consequences*, edited by José A. Cobas, Jorge Duany, and Joe R. Feagin. Boulder, CO: Paradigm.

Sáenz, Rogelio, and Maria Cristina Morales. 2015. *Latinos in the United States: Diversity and Change*. Cambridge: Polity.

Saito, Leland. 1998. *Race and Politics: Asian Americans, Latinos, and Whites in a Los Angeles Suburb*. Urbana: University of Illinois Press.

Salazar, Ruben. 1995. *Border Correspondent: Selected Writings, 1955–1970*, edited by Mario T. García. Berkeley: University of California Press.

Salazar-Porzio, Margaret. 2014. "Latina/o Intersections: Renegotiating Race and Multiculturalism at the Smithsonian National Museum of American History." Presented at Latino Studies Association Conference: Chicago, IL.

Saldaña-Portillo, Maria Josefina. 2007. "From the Borderlands to the Transnational? Critiquing Empire in the Twenty-First Century," pp. 502–12 in *A Companion to Latina/o Studies*, edited by Juan Flores and Renato Rosaldo. Malden, MA: Blackwell.

Salvídar, Ramón. 2006. *Borderlands of Culture: Américo Paredes and the Transnational Imaginary*. Durham, NC: Duke University Press.

Sampson, Robert J. 2008. "Rethinking Crime and Immigration," *Contexts* 7: 28–33.

Sanchez, George I. 1940. *The Forgotten People: A Study of New Mexicans*. Albuquerque: University of New Mexico Press.

Sánchez, George J. 1995. *Becoming Mexican American: Ethnicity, Culture, and Identity in Chicano Los Angeles, 1900–1945*. New York, NY: Oxford University Press.

Sanchez-Jankowski, Martin. 1991. *Islands in the Street: Gangs and American Urban Society*. Berkeley: University of California Press.

Sánchez Korrol, Virginia. 1983. *From Colonia to Community: The History of Puerto Ricans in New York City*. Berkeley: University of California Press.

Sandoval, Chela. 2000. *Methodology of the Oppressed*. Minneapolis: University of Minnesota Press.

Santa Ana, Otto. 2002. *Brown Tide Rising: Metaphors of Latinos in Contemporary American Public Discourse*. Austin: University of Texas Press.

Sassen, Saskia. 2005. "Global Cities and Processes," in *The Oxford Encyclopedia of Latinos and Latinas in the United States*, edited by Suzanne Oboler and Deena Gonzalez. New York, NY: Oxford University Press.

Saucedo, Leticia M., and Mootz, Francis Joseph. 2012. "The 'Ethical' Surplus of the War on Illegal Immigration," *Iowa Journal on Gender, Race and Justice*. https://ssrn.com/abstract=2042688

Segura, Denise A. 1993. "Inside the Work Worlds of Chicana and Mexican Immigrant Women," pp. 95–112 in *Women of Color in U.S. Society*, edited by Maxine Baca Zinn and Bonnie Thornton Dill. Philadelphia, PA: Temple University Press.

Segura, Denise, and Patricia Zavella, eds. 2007. *Women and Migration in the U.S.–Mexico Borderlands: A Reader*. Durham, NC: Duke University Press.

Silva, Kumarini. 2016. *Brown Threat: Identification in the Security State.* Minneapolis: University of Minnesota Press.

Singer, Audrey, Susan W. Hardwick, and Caroline B. Brettell, eds. 2008. *Twenty-First Century Gateways: Immigrant Incorporation in Suburban America.* Washington, DC: Brookings Institution Press.

Smith, Andrea. 2010. "Indigeneity, Settler Colonialism, White Supremacy," *Global Dialogue* 12 (2). http://www.worlddialogue.org/content.php?id=488

Smith, Robert C. 2006. *Mexican New York: Transnational Lives of New Immigrants.* Berkeley: University of California Press.

Smith, Stacy L., Marc Choueiti, and Katherine Pieper. 2016. *Inclusion or Invisibility? Comprehensive Annenberg Report on Diversity in Entertainment.* http://annenberg.usc.edu/pages/~/media/MDSCI/CARDReport%20FINAL%202022216.ashx

Soja, Edward. 1996. *Thirdspace: Journeys to Los Angeles and Other Real-and-Imagined Places.* Malden, MA: Blackwell.

Soldatenko, Michael. 2009. *Chicano Studies: The Genesis of a Discipline.* Tucson: University of Arizona Press.

Solorzano, Daniel, Miguel Ceja, and Tara Yosso. 2000. "Critical Race Theory, Racial Microaggressions, and Campus Racial Climate: The Experiences of African American College Students," *The Journal of Negro Education* 69 (1/2): 60–73.

Stefancic, Jean. 2014. "Reflections on Reform Litigation: Strategic Intervention in Arizona's Ethnic Studies Ban," *John Marshall Law Review* 47 (4): 1181–8.

Stephen, Lynn. 2007. *Transborder Lives: Indigenous Oaxacans in Mexico, California, and Oregon.* Durham, NC: Duke University Press.

Telles, Edward E., and Vilma Ortiz. 2009. *Generations of Exclusion: Mexican-Americans, Assimilation, and Race.* New York, NY: Russell Sage Foundation.

Thomas, Piri. 1997 [1967]. *Down These Mean Streets.* New York, NY: Vintage.

Tijerina, Reies López. 2000. *They Called Me "King Tiger": My Struggle for the Land and Our Rights.* Houston, TX: Arte Publico Press.

Torres, Lourdes, and Kim Potowski. 2008. "A Comparative Study of Bilingual Discourse Markers in Chicago Mexican, Puerto Rican, and MexiRican Spanish," *International Journal of Bilingualism* 12 (4): 263–79.

Torres-Saillant, Silvio. 2003. "Inventing the Race: Latinos and the Ethnoracial Pentagon," *Latino Studies* 1: 123–51.

Truett, Samuel, and Elliott Young, eds. 2004. *Continental Crossroads: Remapping U.S.–Mexico Borderlands History.* Durham, NC: Duke University Press.

Vaca, Nick C. 1970a. "The Mexican American in the Social Sciences, 1912–1970. Part I: 1912–1935," *El Grito* 3 (3): 3–24.

Vaca, Nick C. 1970b. "The Mexican American in the Social Sciences, 1912–1970. Part II: 1936–1970," *El Grito* 4 (1): 17–51.

Valdés, Francisco. 1995. "Queers, Sissies, Dykes, and Tomboys: Deconstructing the Conflation of 'Sex,' 'Gender,' and 'Sexual Orientation' in Euro-American Law and Society," *California Law Review* 83 (1): 3–377.

Valdés, Francisco. 1996. "Foreword – Latina/o Ethnicities, Critical Race Theory, and Post-Identity Politics in Postmodern Legal Culture: From Practices to

Possibilities," *La Raza Law Journal* 1, reprinted in *LatCrit Primer* 1. http://www.latcrit.org/media/medialibrary/2014/01/lcprimeri.pdf

Vargas, Zaragosa. 1999. *Proletarians of the North: Mexican Industrial Workers in Detroit and the Midwest, 1917–1933.* Berkeley, University of California Press.

Vargas, Zaragosa. 2010. *Crucible of Struggle: A History of Mexican Americans from Colonial Times to the Present Era.* New York, NY: Oxford University Press.

Vasconcelos, Jose. 1997 [1948]. *The Cosmic Race/La Raza Cosmica: A Bilingual Edition,* 2nd edn. Baltimore, MD: Johns Hopkins University Press.

Vázquez, Francisco H., and Rodolfo D. Torres, eds. 2003. *Latino/a Thought: Culture, Politics, and Society.* Lanham, MD: Rowman and Littlefield.

Velasco Ortiz, Laura. 2005. *Mixtec Transnational Identity.* Tucson: University of Arizona Press.

Venator Santiago, Charles. 2005. "Countering Kulturkampf Politics through Critique and Justice Pedagogy: Race, Kulturkampf, and Immigration," *Seton Hall Law Review* 35 (4): 1155–89.

Viego, Antonio. 2007. *Dead Subjects: Toward a Politics of Loss in Latino Studies.* Durham, NC: Duke University Press.

Vigil, Ernesto B. 1999. *The Crusade for Justice: Chicano Militancy and the Government's War on Dissent.* Madison: University of Wisconsin Press.

Vigil, James Diego. 1994. *Barrio Gangs: Street Life and Identity in Southern California.* Austin: University of Texas Press.

Vila, Pablo. 2000. *Crossing Borders, Reinforcing Borders: Social Categories, Metaphors, and Narrative Identities on the U.S.–Mexico Frontier.* Austin: University of Texas Press.

Vila, Pablo, ed. 2003. *Ethnography at the Border.* Minneapolis: University of Minnesota Press.

Vila, Pablo. 2005. *Border Identifications: Narratives of Religion, Gender, and Class on the U.S.–Mexico Border.* Austin: University of Texas Press.

Villanueva, Nicholas. 2017. *The Lynching of Mexicans in the Texas Borderlands.* Albuquerque: University of New Mexico Press.

Villaseñor, Arturo González, Indira Cato Guión, and Juan Antonio Mecalco Cruz. 2014. *Llévate Mis Amores.* Film. México, 90 mins.

Walker, Hunter. 2015. "Donald Trump Just Released an Epic Statement Raging Against Mexican Immigrants and 'Disease'," *Business Insider.* http://www.businessinsider.com/donald-trumps-epic-statement-on-mexico-2015-7

Whalen, Carmen. 2001. *From Puerto Rico to Philadelphia: Puerto Rican Workers and Postwar Economies.* Philadelphia, PA: Temple University Press.

Wilson, Christopher E., and Erik Lee, eds. 2013. *The State of the Border Report: A Comprehensive Analysis of the U.S.–Mexico Border.* Border Research Partnership. https://www.wilsoncenter.org/sites/default/files/mexico_state_of_border_0.pdf

Wolfe, Patrick. 2006. "Settler Colonialism and the Elimination of the Native," *Journal of Genocide Research* 8 (4): 387–409. http://www.kooriweb.org/foley/resources/pdfs/89.pdf

Wortham, Stanton, Enrique G. Murillo, and Edmund T. Hamann, eds. 2002. *Education in the New Latino Diaspora: Policy and the Politics of Identity.* Westport, CT: Ablex.

Yosso, Tara. 2005. *Critical Race Counterstories along the Chicana/Chicano Educational Pipeline.* New York, NY: Routledge.

Young Lords Party and Michael Abramson. 2011. *Palante: Voices and Photographs of the Young Lords, 1969–1971.* Chicago, IL: Haymarket Books.

Zavella, Patricia. 1987. *Women's Work and Chicano Families: Cannery Workers of the Santa Clara Valley.* Ithaca, NY: Cornell University Press.

Zúñiga, Víctor, and Rubén Hernández-León, eds. 2005. *New Destinations: Mexican Immigration in the United States.* New York, NY: Russell Sage Foundation.

Index